MW01489048

China's Assimilationist Language Policy

This interesting and coherent volume is an important instalment in the small field of English material devoted to understanding the complex and critical world of China's minority language policies ... it is vital that more is understood of the vast and longstanding Chinese experience of managing ethnic and linguistic differences.

Joseph Lo Bianco, Professor of Language and Literacy Education,
University of Melbourne, Australia

Working from historical, legal, theoretical and richly empirical perspectives, the authors and editors leave no stone unturned in exploring and documenting language education policies and practices for China's vast numbers of Indigenous and minority [... it] makes a clear and convincing call for a steadfast multilingual education policy for China.

Nancy H. Hornberger, Professor of Educational Linguistics and Sociolinguistics,
University of Pennsylvania, USA

China has a huge number of ethnic minorities – over 40 different groups with a total population of over 100 million. Over time China's policies towards minority languages have varied, changing from policies which have accommodated minority languages to policies which have encouraged integration. At present, integrationist policies predominate, notably in the education system, where instruction in minority languages is being edged out in favor of instruction in Mandarin Chinese. *China's Assimilationist Language Policy* assesses the current state of indigenous and minority language policy in China. It considers especially language policy in the education system, including in higher education, and provides detailed case studies of how particular ethnic minorities are being affected by the integrationist approach.

Gulbahar H. Beckett is Associate Professor of Sociolinguistics at the University of Cincinnati, USA.

Gerard A. Postiglione is Professor and Head, Division of Policy, Administration and Social Sciences, and Director of the Wah Ching Center of Research on Education in China of the University of Hong Kong.

Comparative development and policy in Asia series
Series Editors
Ka Ho Mok, *Faculty of Social Sciences, The University of Hong Kong, China*
Rachel Murphy, *Oxford University, UK*
Yongjin Zhang, *Centre for East Asian Studies, University of Bristol, UK*

1. **Cultural Exclusion in China**
   State education, social mobility and
   cultural difference
   Lin Yi

2. **Labour Migration and Social Development in Contemporary China**
   Edited by Rachel Murphy

3. **Changing Governance and Public Policy in East Asia**
   Edited by Ka Ho Mok and Ray Forrest

4. **Ageing in East Asia**
   Challenges and policies for the
   twenty-first century
   Edited by Tsung-hsi Fu and Rhidian Hughes

5. **Towards Responsible Government in East Asia**
   Trajectories, intentions and
   meanings
   Edited by Linda Chelan Li

6. **Government and Policy-Making Reform in China**
   The implications of governing
   capacity
   Bill K.P. Chou

7. **Governance for Harmony in Asia and Beyond**
   Edited by Julia Tao, Anthony Cheung, Martin Painter and Chenyang Li

8. **Welfare Reform in East Asia**
   Towards workfare?
   Edited by Chak Kwan Chan and Kinglun Ngok

9. **China's Assimilationist Language Policy**
   The impact on indigenous/minority
   literacy and social harmony
   Edited by Gulbahar H. Beckett and Gerard A. Postiglione

China's Assimilationist Language Policy

The impact on indigenous/minority literacy and social harmony

Edited by
Gulbahar H. Beckett and
Gerard A. Postiglione

LONDON AND NEW YORK

First published in 2012
by Routledge
2 Park Square, Milton Park, Abingdon, Oxon, OX14 4RN

Simultaneously published in the USA and Canada
by Routledge
711 Third Avenue, New York, NY 10017

Routledge is an imprint of the Taylor & Francis Group, an informa business

British Library Cataloguing in Publication Data
A catalogue record for this book is available from the British Library

Library of Congress Cataloging in Publication Data
China's assimilationist language policy: impact on indigenous/minority literacy
  and social harmony / edited by Gulbahar H. Beckett and Gerard A. Postiglione.
    p. cm.
Includes bibliographical references and index.
1. Language policy—China. 2. Linguistic minorities—China.
3. Language and education—China. I. Beckett, Gulbahar H., 1959–
II. Postiglione, Gerard A., 1951–
P119.32.C6.C55 2011
306.44′951—dc22
2011010380

ISBN13: 978-0-415-59605-3 (hbk)
ISBN13: 978-0-203-80407-0 (ebk)

Typeset in Times New Roman
by Book Now Ltd, London

MIX
Paper from
responsible sources
FSC
www.fsc.org FSC® C004839

Printed and bound in Great Britain by the MPG Books Group

Contents

List of illustrations   vii
Notes on contributors   ix
Acknowledgments   xiii

PART I
Background and historical review   1

1 **China's language policy for indigenous and
minority education**   3
GULBAHAR H. BECKETT AND GERARD A. POSTIGLIONE

2 **Historical review of the PRC's minority/indigenous
language policy and practice: nation-state building
and identity construction**   18
MINGLANG ZHOU

PART II
Empirical research studies   31

3 **The development of minority education and the practice
of bilingual education in Xinjiang Uyghur Autonomous Region**   33
RONG MA

4 **A brief report on bilingual education for the Dongxiangs:
a new initiative**   75
YISU ZHOU

5 **China's minorities without written scripts: the case of
education access among the Dongxiang**   84
JIAYI WANG AND GERARD A. POSTIGLIONE

6 **Bilingual education in China: the case of Yunnan**   105
LINDA TSUNG, GE WANG, AND QUNYING ZHANG

7 Language hegemony in its relation to Chinese marriage migrants' mothers' adaptations to and educational involvements in Taiwan 121

YI-HSUAN CHELSEA KUO

8 The influence of cultural and linguistic backgrounds on the social and academic adjustment of students at an ethnic minority university in China 136

MEI WU, JERRY TUCHSCHERER, AND FORREST W. PARKAY

9 Language issues in Chinese higher education: the case of Korean and Mongol minority groups 156

W. JAMES JACOB AND HEEJIN PARK

PART III
Theoretical, ideological, and legal issues 173

10 Chinese–English bilingual education in the PRC: implications for language education for autochthonous ethnic minorities 175

GUANGWEI HU

11 From neo-liberal ideology to critical sustainability theory for language policy studies in the PRC 190

SEONAIGH MACPHERSON

12 Minority language rights and education in China: the relevance of human rights law and substantive equality 207

KELLEY LOPER

Index 225

Illustrations

Figures

5.1   Factors that affect the dropout rate   97
6.1   Naxi–Han bilingual program in School 1   111
6.2   The Yi–Han bilingual program in School 2   112
6.3   The Tibetan–Han bilingual program in School 3   112
6.4   The Dai–Han bilingual program in School 4   113
8.1   Conceptual framework of the study   140
8.2   The language abilities of four types of students   147
8.3   Collective self-esteem and the four student types   150
8.4   Interrelationships among four factors and language abilities   152

Tables

3.1   Statistics as to teachers and students at different schools in Xinjiang (December, 2004)   36
3.2   The enrollment number of schools at different levels in Xinjiang in 2004   37
3.3   Statistics of *Putonghua* and Uyghur language student performance on high school entrance exam throughout Xinjiang (2002)   41
3.4   Statistics of student performance in the high school entrance exam in Urumqi (2003–2005)   42
3.5   Statistics of the development of bilingual experimental classes in Xinjiang (September 2005)   45
3.6   Bilingual classes and students in different areas of Xinjiang (October 2005)   48
3.7   The situation of enrollment in institutions of higher education for students from Xinjiang (1977–1997)   50
3.8   Proportion of *Min kao Han* students in Han schools   52
3.9   The development of bilingual education in the Kashgar Prefecture   53

4.1	Adult illiteracy among the Dongxiang	76
5.1	Basic information about the sample schools	88
5.2	Distribution of subjects	89
5.3	Factor analysis of the student questionnaires	92
5.4	Alpha coefficient for the questionnaire and factors	93
5.5	Analysis of variance for the Chinese proficiency level	93
5.6	Step-wise regression	93
5.7	Results of enter regression	94
5.8	Regressional analysis of the shaping factors of the Chinese proficiency	95
5.9	Analysis of variance for the impact of background factors on students' academic performance	95
5.10	Correlation between the background factors and students' academic performance	96
6.1	Fifteen distinctive ethnic minority groups and their language use in Yunnan	106
8.1	Demographic information for respondents	144
8.2	Number of students according to the four types	145
8.3	Language abilities of the four types of students	146
8.4	Reliability of the instruments	148
8.5	Correlations among language abilities and the four factors	151
9.1	Proportion of ethnic minority student enrollments at Chinese universities	159
9.2	Proportion of ethnic minority faculty members in Chinese higher education institutions	160
9.3	CAEs by ethnic origin	164

Contributors

Gulbahar H. Beckett is Associate Professor of Sociolinguistics at the University of Cincinnati. She has published books, chapters, and numerous articles on language policies and literacy in such major international journals as *TESOL Quarterly, Modern Language Journal, Canadian Modern Language Review, TESL Canada Journal, English Language Teaching (ELT) Journal, Bilingual Journal of Research and Practice, Journal of Asian Pacific Communication*, and *Distance Education*. She serves on three journal editorial boards, including that of *Diaspora, Indigenous, and Minority Education: An International Journal*.

Guangwei Hu is an Associate Professor at the National Institute of Education, Nanyang Technological University, Singapore. His research interests include academic discourse, bilingual education, language policy, second language acquisition, and second language writing. He has published extensively on these topics.

W. James Jacob is Director of the Institute for International Studies in Education at the University of Pittsburgh. He has written extensively on comparative, international, and development education topics with an emphasis on higher education, indigenous education, and HIV prevention and capacity building initiatives.

Yi-Hsuan Chelsea Kuo is an Assistant Professor of Sociology at Mercy College, New York. Her scholarly interests include international migration, social stratification, and minority education. She holds a master's degree from Harvard in Regional Studies: East Asia, and a doctorate from Teachers College, Columbia University in International and Transcultural Studies.

Kelley Loper is Director of the Masters of Law in Human Rights Programme, Deputy Director of the Centre for Comparative and Public Law, and Assistant Professor in the Faculty of Law at the University of Hong Kong.

Rong Ma is Professor of Sociology and Chair of the Department of Sociology and Institute of Sociology and Anthropology at Peking University. He has conducted numerous research studies and published widely on China's various minority population in numerous books and journals such as *Asian Ethnicity, Policy and Society,* and *Development and Society.* He is also an editorial member of several journals including *Front of Social Sciences, Hong Kong Journal of Social Sciences,* and *Journal of Beijing University.*

Seonaigh MacPherson of ELSA-Net in British Columbia, is co-editor of the journal *Diaspora, Indigenous, and Minority Education.* She has published widely on indigenous and minority issues. Her book, *Education and Sustainability* will be released in January 2011 as part of the Research in Education series by Routledge.

Heejin Park is a project associate at the Institute of the International Studies in Education at the University of Pittsburgh where she also recently completed her degree in Education Policy and Administration. Her research focuses on education issues related to cultural, linguistic, and ethnic minorities in Asia.

Forrest W. Parkay is Professor of Educational Leadership and Higher Education, at Washington State University. His research areas include international education and cross-national partnerships. He was Visiting Professor at Beijing Normal University's College of Education Administration during Spring 2010.

Gerard A. Postiglione is Professor and Head, Division of Policy, Administration and Social Sciences, and Director of the Wah Ching Center of Research on Education in China of the University of Hong Kong. He has published over 100 journal articles and book chapters, and 10 books. He is editor of the journal, *Chinese Education and Society,* and a four book series. His books include: *Asian Higher Education, East Asia at School, Education and Social Change in China, China's National Minority Education,* and *Crossing Borders in East Asian Higher Education.*

Linda Tsung is Senior Lecturer in the Faculty of Arts at the University of Sydney, Australia. She specializes in teaching Chinese as a second language and Chinese teacher education. She has a track record in research into bilingualism and bilingual education for ethnic minority students, and their educational experiences and outcomes in China. She is author or editor of many publications including *Minority Languages, Education and Communities in China,* published by Palgrave Macmillan in 2009; *Teaching and Learning Chinese in Global Contexts,* published by Continuum in 2010.

Jerry Tuchscherer is an Associate Professor in the College of Education at the University of Idaho. His research interests are international education, communications, human development, and administration in higher education.

Ge Wang is Professor of the School of Foreign Languages, Yunnan University, China. He is currently a PhD candidate at the University of Hong Kong. His research interest is in applied linguistics, bi/trilingual education and identity study.

Jiayi Wang is Professor and Vice-president of Northwest Normal University. He has advised the Ministry of Education on educational policy and played a key role in the development of rural education in western China. He has participated in many international development projects in ethnic minority regions of China and had major roles in several World Bank projects to improve access to quality education.

Mei Wu received a Ph.D. in higher education from the University of Idaho. Her research interests include diversity and minority education, trans-cultural communication, international education, and higher education administration. She is an Instructor at the Research Institute of Higher Education (RIHE), Yunnan University, in Kunming, China.

Qunying Zhang is Post-Doctoral Fellow in the Faculty of Education at the University of Hong Kong. Her research interests include educational provision for language minority students, second language education, and cross-cultural studies of teaching conceptions and practices.

Minglang Zhou is Associate Professor and Director, the Chinese program and Center for East Asian Studies at the University of Maryland, College Park. His research focuses on the sociology of language and ethnic relations in China. He has published extensively on these topics.

Yisu Zhou is a Ph.D. candidate in Educational Policy Program, College of Education, Michigan State University. His current focus of research is on the teacher labor market and economics of education. He interests also cover a variety of issues in education reform and social development in China. Yisu's work in this book is supported by the Summer Research Development Fellowship from the College of Education, Michigan State University.

Acknowledgments

We would like to thank our colleagues who contributed to this volume. Thank you all for your cooperation and great work. We would also like to thank Adam Cooper, University of Cincinnati doctoral candidate, for his timely and thorough proof-reading of nine of the chapters. Thank you, Adam. You did a superb job.

The Editors would like to thank the following for permission to reprint material in this book:

Journal of Asia Pacific Communications for kind permission to reprint China's Minorities without Written Scripts: The Case of Education Access among the Dongxiang, by Jiayi Wang and Gerard A. Postiglione. First published in *Journal of Asia Pacific Communications*, 18 (2) 2008, 166–189; reprinted here as Chapter 5.

Springer Science + Business Media and *Frontiers of Education in China* journal for kind permission to reprint The Development of Minority Education and the Practice of Bilingual Education in Xinjiang Uyghur Autonomous Region by Rong Ma. Originally printed in *Frontiers of Education in China*, 2008, 4(2): 188–252. Reprinted here as Chapter 3, with kind permission of Higher Education Press and Springer Science + Business Media.

Part I

Background and historical review

1 China's language policy for indigenous and minority education

Gulbahar H. Beckett and Gerard A. Postiglione

Worrying trends

China has experienced rapid changes in political, economic, educational, and language policies and practices. These changes not only impact society in general, but especially its 110 million-strong indigenous and minority population, most notably in the areas of language of instruction and cultural identity (Beckett & Postiglione, 2010). Language policies have alternated between what Zhou (2003) calls pluralistic and integrationist approaches, emphasizing accommodation and assimilation, respectively (also see Zhou & Sun, 2004). During pluralistic periods of accommodation, additive, and even elite bilingual policies, initiatives, and programs are welcomed, while during integrationist periods of assimilation, subtractive, folk bilingual, and monolingual *Hanyu* (aka Mandarin Chinese or *Putonghua*) as the language-of-instruction programs predominate (also see Lam, 2005). We choose to use the term *Hanyu* because it is a more accurate representation and it allows for inclusion of literacy *Hanzi* in the discussion. Other authors in the volume use various other terms such as Mandarin, *Putonghua*, and Chinese, which we respect because they represent their unique perspectives.

The twenty-first century has already seen an evolution of language policies to sustain an assimilationist trend through schooling. The national language, *Hanyu*, as the medium of instruction within a discourse of progress, opportunity, national unity, and harmonious society, continues to marginalize indigenous and minority languages. The increasing number of boarding schools for Tibetan and Uyghur children (see Chen, 2010) and the "bilingual" education policy being implemented in Xinjiang (see Ma, 2009) are two of the most notable evidences of this policy. While some applaud these policies and practices as enhancing educational and economic opportunities for indigenous and minority people (see Ma, Chapter 3 in this volume), others express concern that such policies and practices only accelerate cultural assimilation, language loss, identity disarray, and social displacement, and could disrupt harmonious inter-ethnic co-existence (see Dwyer, 2005; MacPherson & Beckett, 2008), as evidenced by a series of language right protests in 2010.

On October 19, 2010, hundreds of Tibetan students from Rebkong County in Qinghai Province took to the streets in protest against a new educational policy that stipulated all school subjects be taught in *Hanyu* and all textbooks be written in

Hanzi, except for Tibetan language and English classes and the textbooks used in them. Later that month, Uyghur middle school students in Xinjiang joined the protest in support of the Tibetan students in their fight for language rights. One month earlier, Han Chinese youth took to the streets in Guangzhou to protest the government's decision to ban television stations that use the local Cantonese Chinese dialect instead of the national dialect (*Hanyu*). As the world's number-two economy, China is finding that globalization also means an intensification of multiculturalism with direct implications for local cultures and indigenous languages. Yet, China's policies concerning language and education continue to oscillate.

Since the last decade, there has been a historic shift from pluralist to assimilationist policies for minority languages in education (Zhou & Sun, 2004). Even today, tension surrounds the state's effort to define itself as a multiethnic nation with ethnic autonomous regions that limits the promotion of multiculturalism and use of indigenous languages. The implications of state multiculturalism for minority languages in schools are far-reaching, contradictory, beneficial, and damaging all at the same time. Indigenous and minority languages, especially the ones with scripts, are promoted as a medium of instruction in order to increase school access rates; but they are also gradually marginalized at each higher grade level in the education system. The often-cited rationale for this policy and practice is that indigenous and minority languages have little economic value and limit students' opportunities because *Hanyu* has been made the language of "opportunities" especially as the advance of the market economy has brought the relentless migration of the majority Han Chinese to ethnic autonomous regions. The resulting transformation of the language landscape in ethnic autonomous territories has both intensified and obscured ethnic unity as "most ethnic groups, albeit with some regret, are resigned to being a minority population in their own ethnic autonomous regions" (Jankowiak, 2008, p. 102).

The uniqueness of China's situation can be seen in the state's hesitation to characterize its ethnic minorities as indigenous, despite the fact that they have no tradition of immigration and many have occupied the same lands for hundreds of years. Now called ethnic autonomous regions, these territories cover about half of the country. Historically, the central government's narrative is that autonomous regions are an inalienable part of China because the majority Han Chinese have always lived in these lands. This narrative is also used to nullify any claim of indigenous status on the part of ethnic minority communities. Language plays a key role in the absorption of indigenous and ethnic minorities into the national fabric. How that happens is part of what this book is about, expanding the discussion about language policy and practice by providing historical perspectives, empirically based fieldwork, theoretical analysis and legal interpretation of selected aspects of this increasingly complex issue facing China's developmental model.

The 18 scholars in this volume from different parts of China, different countries in Asia, from Australia, and from North America, have contributed chapters about the challenges facing indigenous and minority languages, including their possible replacement due to a loss of ethnic identity and decline in minority language literacy, with each chapter contributing a unique and fresh perspective. Specific topics discussed include historical and sociopolitical influences on language policies; language and access to schooling; minority language in higher education and employment; language factors in raising academic achievement; implications of a globalizing English language among China's minorities; and contemporary theoretical and constitutional discourses that inform language policies and practices.

Overview of the book

Changing policies and consequences

Language policy in multiethnic nations is often controversial and vulnerable to changing socio-political environments. Language policy has been transformed by authoritarian regime change as in the ex-Soviet Republics, co-opted by political parties to win democratic elections as was the case with bilingual education policy in California, and modified when empirical research points to inadequacies, as in Hong Kong when research results prompted the government to promote a mother-tongue medium of instruction in schools. Over a period of 60 years, language policies have been at the mercy of the winds of political change in China. In Chapter 2, Minglang Zhou follows the evolution of language ideology and language order as between superstructure and reality. Since the founding of the People's Republic of China, policies and practices have followed two models of nation-state building, namely the Soviet model and the Chinese model. The Soviet model of the 1950s represented a satellite-and-center-of-gravity relationship between *Hanyu* and minority languages. It supported a multilingual ideology and language order in which indigenous languages were the primary *lingua franca* in ethnic autonomous areas and *Hanyu* was spoken as a supplementary language (Stites, 1999). However, *Hanyu* exerted a centripetal pull on indigenous languages. This led to linguistic integration in which the structure of indigenous languages eventually became aligned with, read and spelled like, *Hanyu* and *Hanzi* (Han script). This was a state-building model in which speaking *Hanyu* was not essential for becoming a citizen.

The Cultural Revolution with its monolingual policy devastated ethnic cultures and after its culmination, a return to the parallel language order was no longer viable. The new era of reform ushered in a national language program, even while there was a resurgence of ethnicity in minority regions following the Cultural Revolution. The linguistic landscape was transformed as national language usage became mainstreamed in education. An amendment to the Constitution in 1982 (Article 19) made *Hanyu* the official common spoken language for all indigenous and nationality people (later referred to as ethnic groups). These changes invalidated language indigeneity and placed pressure on the expression of ethnic identities in cultural life.

According to Zhou (2003), school access rates in ethnic autonomous regions remained low until pluralistic language policies retuned in the 1980s as part of a multilingual ideology that encouraged the use of indigenous languages. The

State Council Document 32 (1991) re-evaluated the language writing systems created in the 1950s to supplement *Hanzi*. However, in 2001, the revised *Ethnic Region Autonomy Law* and the 2001 *National Commonly-Used Language and Script Law* fostered a return to accelerated assimilation, which required an earlier transition to *Hanyu* medium instruction. Minority officials in autonomous governments were discouraged from speaking their native languages and were encouraged to learn and use both *Hanyu* and *Hanzi*, proficiency being a prerequisite for promotion.

Empirically based research

While China in the twenty-first century has taken a generally assimilationist road, empirical research in schools and communities reveals a more complex picture. The chapters in Part II provide field-based evidence of language education in practice. These include studies in three provinces of western China, including Xinjiang, Yunnan, and Gansu. These studies provide a view of how language practices affect the education and lives of several indigenous and minority groups, including the Uyghur, Yi, Dai, Tibetans, Jingpo, and Dongxiang. The case of Taiwan also provides an interesting contrast.

In Chapter 3, Rong Ma discusses bilingual policies and practices in the Xinjiang Uyghur Autonomous Region—China's largest province by area. In a case study of the city of Kashkar, where Uyghurs account for more than 90 percent of the population, Ma identifies the fundamental mode of ethnic language education and elaborates on the development of and problems related to bilingual education policies and practices. His findings show, among other things, that after a half century of development, all ethnic groups in Xinjiang have achieved some level of progress in student enrolment and teacher employment. Ma details the substantial changes in Xinjiang language policies and practices that have both encouraged and discouraged interest in indigenous language medium instruction, as noted by Zhou above. According to Ma, the range of language approaches runs from offering *Putonghua* as a second language in Uyghur, Kazak, and Mongol schools, to providing *Hanyu* medium schools for all minorities, and even to providing boarding schools for both minority and Han students. Ma concludes that many parents, local school authorities, and government officials enthusiastically support *Hanyu* medium instruction and even send their children to boarding schools in other parts of the country to receive *Hanyu* medium education in the belief that it will make their children more employable. Some parents also point out that bilingual classes are more costly because they require extra fees for learning resources in two languages.

Ma's findings also reveal why the language of instruction plays a crucial role in school achievement (Ma, 2007). Han students achieve at significantly higher levels than Uyghur students in various examinations, most of which are administered in Hangyu and Hanzi. Although government policy does provide for college entrance examinations to be taken in Uyghur, Kazak and Mongol languages, it is seldom done in practice, a phenomenon that seldom seems to be discussed in the literature as a possible contributor to indigenous and minority students' low test scores. Ma attributes low test scores to the lack of qualified teachers, poor learning environments, and inadequate learning materials. Indeed, many schools attended by Uyghurs lack libraries, science laboratories, standard classrooms, and sufficient operating budgets. Additionally, many students come from low income families who cannot afford to supplement their education by paying for after-school tutorials. The role of language in instruction and test-taking must also be added as important contributory factors to low test scores and they should be addressed by developing strategies to help students do better.

Ma's chapter also reveals that few teachers in Kashkar are qualified to teach in both Uyghur and Chinese languages. Even those qualified to teach in Uyghur often prefer to teach in *Hanyu* because their teacher training was conducted in *Hanyu* and their own content area learning in science subjects was through textbooks written in *Hanzi*. Ma contends that the teacher shortage is too often addressed through unrealistically short-term training programs. Teachers are sent on *Hanyu* training courses for a year, which often carries a heavy financial burden for the trainee. Moreover, the language standard of trainers is often inadequate and the quality of their pedagogy is unremarkable. Ma's study points out the inefficiency of offering bilingual classes to students who had no prior *Hanyu* proficiency. It is not surprising that teachers generally say that while *Hanyu* is beneficial for finding employment after graduation, content knowledge acquisition occurs more efficiently in their native language, a sentiment expressed by Han university students who believed that while English is a useful tool for gaining employment, subject matter content courses taught to them in English had no depth and therefore they should be taught in students' native languages (Beckett & Li, forthcoming).

In Chapters 4 and 5, Yisu Zhou, Jiayi Wang and Gerard Postiglione report on education initiatives for the Dongxiang, who have the lowest level of literacy and school access of any indigenous/minority group in China. According to a 2001 survey, the adult illiteracy rate was over 80 percent among people over age 15; the enrolment rate of school-aged children was 81 percent (61 percent for school-aged girls); and the dropout rate for primary school students was 10 percent. According to these authors, the land occupied by the Dongxiang is surrounded by mountains with poor transportation and communication facilities. Droughts are common, leaving it with a low agricultural yield and lack of industrial production. The Dongxiang minority has a strong belief in Islam as well as a native language, but is without a commonly used written script. The prefecture they occupy is commonly referred to as China's Mecca because it has long been the area with the highest concentration of Mosques and devout Muslims in China. Local intellectuals and some officials have attributed many of the educational difficulties they face to language-related factors.

The authors point out that the Dongxiangs live in a harsh natural environment, where they have historically been engaged in subsidized agriculture for survival (Zhang, 2007). In recent years, however, substantial numbers of Dongxiang have migrated to metropolitan areas such as Lanzhou, Jiuquan, and Baiyin for better employment opportunities, but with a still-high illiteracy rate of 63 percent (76 percent female and 50 percent male) among the population aged 15 and over, their work opportunities are limited to the so-called "3D" (Dangerous, Difficult, Dirty) low-end jobs (Ma, 2004).

In Chapter 4, Zhou finds that Dongxiang students had very limited exposure to *Hanyu* prior to entering the first grade since only Dongxiang language was spoken at home (Qin & Ma, 2004). There is little opportunity to learn *Hanyu* in preschools because, as is the case in most poor rural areas, preschool is not part of the free compulsory education system and most families cannot afford preschool education for their children. As a result, the transition from home language to *Hanzi* literacy is a major challenge. Zhou discusses a new bilingual education initiative designed to help address this issue by providing Dongxiang people with a written form of their language to facilitate their learning of *Hanzi*. The initiative adopts the mono-literacy model by using a transcript system to annotate *Hanzi*-based textbooks for primary school with the aim of promoting *Hanzi* literacy.

Zhou's findings suggest that the new bilingual program has promoted student learning, increased achievement, and reduced dropout rates. For example, he reports that Dongxiang students who received bilingual education (the experimental group) did not drop out of school while 4–5 percent of the students in the control group (students who did not receive bilingual education) did drop out. The test results also show that the average pass rate for the experimental class was 10 percent higher than those of the control groups in the Chinese Language Arts class (*Yuwen ke*). This is equivalent to a five-point average difference on a 100-point scale. For Mathematics, the experimental class had a 2 percent higher pass rate than the control group. Zhou's reaction to this initiative for the Dongxiang is generally optimistic. However, he also points out a problem of several misalignments. The Chinese textbooks for teaching and learning are beyond the proficiency levels of most students. Moreover, the content of the textbooks is irrelevant to students' daily lives. Some parents responded to the situation by sending their children to local mosques for education and to acquire knowledge about their history and religion. Zhou's findings reveal an urgent need for qualified teachers exemplified by the fact that teachers involved in the bilingual initiative had only two months of training on the Dongxiang transcript system prior to their using the materials. Many teachers were still uncertified and not properly qualified to teach, while many qualified teachers have relocated to urban areas for better benefits.

In Chapter 5, Wang and Postiglione identify the major difficulties in school-based learning for Dongxiang-speaking children. Specifically, they explore local perspectives on how language and other factors affect school enrolment and achievement. The research includes survey questionnaires, open-ended and in-depth interviews, field visits, observations, and case studies. They analyze the difficulties of language transition and their results reveal that although native language does not directly cause schoolchildren to discontinue their studies, native language does have an important indirect influence, especially on the education of girls. Their findings indicate that especially in the early years of schooling, students struggle to learn through the medium of *Hanyu*, resulting in poor performance, a decline of interest in learning, a sense of frustrated achievement, and a decline in self-respect. Many students drop out as part of a vicious cycle that sees a reproduction of poor conditions for learning.

In Chapter 6, Tsung, Wang, and Zhang describe changes over ten years of bilingual education policies and practices in Yunnan through two empirical studies conducted in 1999 and 2008. They examine why Naxi-Han, Yi–Han, Tibetan–Han, and Dai–Han bilingual and bi-literacy programs are still fraught with discrepancies. Their research demonstrates how stakeholders approach minority student education with two detrimental mentalities: the "great Han mentality" and the "pragmatism mentality," both of which espouse mono-literacy through *Hanyu* medium instruction. *Hanyu* and *Hanzi* literacy are developed by using native language in early grades but only as a transitional tool. The educational discourse imposed on these ethnic communities is that *Hanyu* is more beneficial than their native language for their children's academic success and future job prospects. Tsung, Wang, and Zhang argue that bilingual education policies are poorly planned and executed, as well as being fragmented and lacking continuity. Indigenous and minority students are forced to function in *Hanyu* before they attain basic literacy in their native language. Not unlike Ma's observation in his study of the Uyghurs in Kashkar (Chapter 3), Tsung, Wang, and Zhang find a severe shortage of teaching/learning resources, with the little material that is available being of poor quality, out-dated, irrelevant, and taught by lowly-paid, over-worked, monolingual, unqualified, and ineffective teachers. Furthermore, the context of much of what is learned in school is far removed from the realities of daily life, and from local values and customs. The localization of school curriculum, though permitted in policy, is hampered by a lack of qualified teachers and financial support. Even for parents, most of whom are poor, the additional expense of bilingual learning materials is a burden they cannot support. Therefore, it is no surprise that students' interest in school is moderate at best, that student drop-out rates are unacceptably high, and that religious institutions compete for students. For example, classes taught by Burmese monks are popular among students for offering free instruction in the Dai script. It is understandable that students who find themselves marginalized in the state schools will opt for attending temple or church schools instead. Moreover, some parents prefer donating to temple or church schools rather than to public schools. Tsung and her colleagues call for improved bilingual and bi-literacy programs, policies for protecting the indigenous languages and identities of individual minorities, as well as a commitment to humanitarian concerns and social justice (see Loper's Chapter 12).

In Chapter 7, Yi-Hsuan Chelsea Kuo examines linguistic issues in Taiwan for female marriage migrants from the Chinese Mainland. Kuo argues that the "great Han" mentality extends across the Taiwan Straits. Female marriage migrants from the mainland display a sense of entitlement and superiority to other marriage migrants and working-class Taiwanese who do not speak *Hanyu*.

At the same time, female marriage migrants also encounter linguistic discrimination by Taiwan citizens that claim *Guoyu*, not Mainland *Hanyu* or *Putonghua*, is the proper version of Mandarin. Interviews suggest that Taiwanese feelings of superiority stem from their financial position and "classier" speech. Kuo finds that the linguistic status of these women (native speaker or non-native speaker) and their locality (urban or rural) are not immediate determinants of their involvement in their children's education. Adaption strategies vary and the agency these women demonstrate betrays a simple belief in assimilation. These female migrants play more of an active role in the complex linguistic landscape of old Mainland *Guoyu*, new Mainland *Hanyu*, and native Taiwanese *Minnanhua*.

As opportunities to attend university in China increase, language proficiency becomes a salient issue for ethnic minorities in higher education as well. In Chapter 8, Wu, Tuchscherer, and Parkay discuss the results of their empirical study of linguistic proficiency in relation to self-esteem and academic and social adjustment. Based on their findings, they argue that those who speak better *Hanyu* tend to have higher personal self-esteem and that personal self-esteem has no direct significant relationship with social and academic adjustment.

Wu, Tuchscherer, and Parkay's analysis of collective self-esteem from a religious perspective did not provide any evidence suggesting that students' religious affiliation causes significant differentiation among them. Another key finding of the study is that a psychological collegiate sense of community is highly correlated with social and academic adjustment, suggesting that a collegiate environment characterized by a sense of belonging, togetherness, and a feeling of respect for one another is important for ethnic minority students if they are to adjust socially and academically while attending university in China. This raises the issue of whether meaningful access to higher learning for ethnic minority students is partially determined by how much their ethic and cultural heritage receives recognition on campus. Nevertheless, the authors call for universities to enhance students' sense of belonging to a community, thereby improving their prospects of academic success.

In Chapter 9, Jacob and Park examine native language preservation and learning experiences in higher education of ethnic Koreans and Mongols. These groups are among China's largest minorities and are unique in several respects. They are cross-national groups whose ethnic cousins have their own country, one developed and one developing, with written scripts in common use. Due to years of separation from their ethnic cousins, the way that China's Mongols and Koreans speak their native language differs somewhat from the way it is commonly spoken in the Republic of Mongolia and the two Koreas. Moreover, the Republic of Mongolia continues to use Cyrillic script, adopted during the Soviet era, while still teaching basic aspects of traditional Mongolian script in school. Chinese Mongols have education levels nearly equal to the national average while Koreans have the highest levels of educational attainment of any ethnic group in China, including Han Chinese. Both groups occupy areas of northeast China, though the Mongols can be found across northern China and some also reside in the southwest. Jacob and Park interviewed a number of university professors, doctoral students and government officials with expertise in ethnic affairs. All recognized the need for China to adopt *Hanyu* to unify the Chinese national identity and that *Hanyu* proficiency opens up opportunities in society and the economy (Yu, 2010). Yet, some respondents advocated the maintenance of first languages and cultures through school education. In this sense, the one-language-for-all policy leads to a neglect and potential loss of ethnic languages in China, though not in the adjoining countries where national languages are sustained. Economic incentives for *Hanyu* will continue to compete with those for Korean and Mongolian, even while the former has been growing in popularity due to Korean TV dramas and soap operas. Nevertheless, there is a growing trend of Trilingualism (*Putonghua*, Native language, and English) among ethnic minority university students. The authors argue that even in ethnic autonomous regions of China, minority students must begin the study of English in the third grade of primary school as they continue to struggle with issues related to stereotypes and their small numbers at university and less attractive economic and employment prospects after graduation.

Theoretical, ideological, and legal issues

In Chapter 10, Hu draws upon scholarship that adopts a public policy perspective on language policy. In doing so, he takes a critical view of the current English-medium instruction initiative (EMI) (aka English-Chinese bilingual education) because it works more for the benefit of the ethnic majority Han than for indigenous/minority students in China. Due to the popular belief that English provides access to knowledge, development, power and well-being, and with China's growing economic integration and deepening political engagement with the rest of the world, the acceleration of English acquisition has been mostly directed toward the Han majority. In fact, the use of English as a medium of instruction has garnered popularity and momentum, and made significant inroads into the school system (Beckett & Li, forthcoming; Feng, 2005; Hu, 2007). Hu eschews EMI because most students lack the sociolinguistic environment to succeed in learning it and never attain the threshold level of understanding the content transmitted to them. Furthermore, the great majority of Chinese will not use English for sociocultural purposes (Yang, 2006; W. J. Zhang, 2002). Hu argues that EMI is a wrongheaded policy option for both majority and minority groups. He points to evidence suggesting that promoting EMI constitutes a misallocation of precious resources that could otherwise be spent on more encompassing and worthwhile educational policy options. From a rights-based perspective, everyone should be entitled to learn English. In fact, Tibetans and some other ethnic minorities seem to learn English more easily than Chinese, perhaps due to similarities with their native languages (Upton, 1999). In his plenary talk at the conference on minority language education in China held at the University of Hong Kong (2008), Ma recalled being surprised to find out that Uyghur university students do much better in courses taught in English than in *Hanyu*. However, Hu argues that an EMI option for indigenous minority peoples is impractical and that

English is only one of many requirements necessary for access to educational, social, and economic opportunities. He advocates a bilingual education in which minority children in their early education achieve full literacy, first in their native language and second in *Putonghua*, arguing that it would be a better use of resources in empowering indigenous/minority students with the economic and cultural capital necessary for social advancement. The theoretical discussions that justify his argument are informative and refreshing.

In Chapter 11, MacPherson identifies shortcomings in the dominant neo-liberal ideology in language and language education policy in China with its focus on national integration and economic globalization. Despite the fact that the Chinese government eschews modernization with Western characteristics as well as cultural globalization for its negative consequences, MacPherson contends that the dominant ideology driving Chinese language policy decisions and discourse involves the appropriation of modernization and globalization. These two are appropriated and reinterpreted well beyond their critical, social scientific roots to refer to the unquestioned virtues of a cohesive nation-state competing in a global marketplace. This neo-liberal ideology, MacPherson argues, re-directs development of domestic policies towards a citizenry reduced to a workforce and a nation-state reduced to a competitive marketplace. Such an ideology has little regard for linguistic, cultural, and biological diversity and places indigenous and minority languages at risk of extinction by positioning them as having no value in a competitive economic marketplace (Beckett & MacPherson, 2005; MacPherson & Ghoso, 2008). In particular, MacPherson critiques two prominent language policy theories: critical theory and language ecology/eco-linguistics theory as failing to adequately unpack inherent conceptual conflicts. She points to a disjuncture between critical and sustainability theories as they idealize and overlook key contradictions. Instead, MacPherson argues in favor of a hybrid critical sustainability theory for China because it offers a robust theoretical lens with which to critique and develop language and language education policies capable of meeting a sustainable development standard. She believes that a hybrid critical sustainability theory offers a way to ground a more authentic use of the phrase ethnic harmony in China within the broader objectives of ecological harmony, thereby holding out the promise of a reoriented policy for peaceful co-existence beyond a particular ethnic group, nation-state, or species. Such a renewed critical sustainability theory can come closer to the intention of sustainable development as outlined in the UN vision that is articulated in *Our Common Future* (United Nations, 1987).

The UN outline for indigenous language rights in education is the subject of Loper's analysis in Chapter 12. She discusses the complex legal dynamics as well as constitutional and human rights issues that multicultural and multilingual societies face in their language policy. This is couched in a discussion that views language participation in terms of access to opportunities and as part of exercising a right to identity. Loper analyzes various perspectives on minority claims and human rights. Theories of formal and substantive equality promote varying objectives which lead to divergent outcomes and conflicting implications. Loper notes China's involvement in various international civil, humanitarian, educational, and political rights treaties (the right of minority groups to enjoy their culture, the right to equality, and participation rights are of particular significance). She also places emphasis on the Convention on the Rights of the Child, which states in Article 29(1)(c):

> the education of the child shall be directed to ... [t]he development of respect for ... his or her own cultural identity, language and values, for the national values of the country in which the child is living, the country from which he or she may originate, and for civilizations different from his or her own.

Language and education are important vehicles for ensuring the survival of minority cultures as well as means for promoting the national language to meet state-building objectives. To this effect, she reviews the Constitution of the People's Republic of China, the Law on Ethnic Regional Autonomy and policy documents that contain protections for indigenous language rights. In fact, the Constitution guarantees the right of minorities "to use and develop their own spoken and written languages and [the] right to use the spoken and written languages of one's own nationality in court proceedings (Constitution, 1984). Yet, as is clear from various chapters in this book, full realization of these rights in practice is often limited. To fulfill its international obligations, authorities must not only abide by the Constitution but also remedy past discrimination to attain substantive equality. As Loper points out, substantive equality can act as a balancing principle and is measured by the capacity to ensure dignity, identity, and participation. The principle of substantive equality acts as a check to counter isolation and exclusion. If an ethnic culture is being assimilated and identity rights are at stake, substantive equality becomes a basis to restore equilibrium. The precise manner of applying the principle of substantive equality will depend on each specific situation because substantive equality recognizes the importance of context. In short, substantive equality is empirical, practical, and recognizes the rights of minority communities as well as the rights of individuals within those communities. We agree with Loper that more research is required on the impact of policies on ethnic minority identity and on the nature of the disadvantages they encounter. Only then can China's implementation of its legal obligations to ensure substantive equality be adequately assessed.

Conclusion

This volume raises a number of issues about China's language-in-education policies and practices regarding its indigenous and minority peoples. Regions of the country are designated as ethnically autonomous on the basis of the cultural characteristics, including language, of local inhabitants. Shortly after the founding of the People's Republic of China, the government commissioned several study delegations to identify and recognize ethnic minority groups. The method of identification relied on Joseph Stalin's four criteria: "common language, common territory, common economic life and common psychological make-up" (cited in Gladney, 1998, p. 65; Ma, 2004, p. 45). Thus, language is a critical feature of the reproduction and sustainability of ethnic autonomous regions. The empirical research in this volume points to the possibility that over time, minority languages may become unsustainable as literacy rates among indigenous and minority people continue to suffer, especially if historically chaotic and irresponsible policies and practices continue. The increased Han migration to ethnic autonomous areas, a neo-liberal ideology found in assimilationist policies and practices, as well as loose implementation of the Constitution with respect to laws protecting indigenous languages, will hasten that demise. In response, this volume calls for a more responsible and balanced language in education policy that does not shift depending on the political mood of the country. It is important to understand that constant changes in language policies and practices are extremely detrimental and disruptive to literacy development. They create generational gaps that put parents, sometimes even siblings, in helpless situations when it comes to children's school work, to say the least, not to mention additional gaps in historical knowledge. It sends a message that indigenous and minority languages are unimportant, which can lead to low self-esteem, poor academic achievement, depression, and anger. Moreover, this can jeopardize the economic advancement which current language policies and practices claim to support.

More adequate learning resources and teacher support that can help reduce drop-out rates and increase retention rates through education in first languages especially in the formative years are also called for. This is crucial because it is language, particularly academic language, that students need most for learning school subjects. Decades of research have shown that those who happened to be born in households where there is exposure to such language make the transition from home to school and then to society much easier. Those who are not, but speak the everyday version of the language, must work harder to make those transitions. Most indigenous and minority students in China do not have either. Therefore, they need to work three, four, or even five times harder to do what their Han peers do, mostly with little help at home and with far fewer or no other resources because their parents do not speak *Hanyu*, are possibly illiterate in *Hanzi*, and/or have no financial means to give them necessary assistance such as private tutoring and after-school programs that most of their Han peers take for granted. Many indigenous and minority students' families have limited financial means to help their children because they have lost their jobs and are unemployed due to the fact that they do not speak enough *Hanyu*. It must be understood that this is a serious matter that affects students' understanding of what is being taught at school. If people do not understand what they are presented with, they cannot learn, and they will feel useless and drop out of school, undermining any progress that has been made and jeopardizing goals for future. For more discussion about the importance of language in learning, see Cazden (1988), Gee (2007), Heath (1983); Michaels and Cazden (1986), Mohan (1986), and Ochs (1989).

The argument for the promotion of *Hanyu* is always that it improves employment opportunities and the insufficient number of qualified teachers, up-to-date textbooks, and other sources in indigenous/minority languages. While it is true that *Hanyu*, like any other language or any other skill, can be useful for seeking more opportunities and that study after study, including the ones in this volume, do show that there is severe resource shortage in indigenous and minority regions, we must make it clear that language alone is not the answer to getting jobs. Otherwise, China would not have the millions of unemployed *Hanyu*-speaking Han Chinese university graduates. If language is the only answer to employment, millions of native English-speaking Americans would not have lost their jobs over the past few years. Jobs do not magically appear just because someone speaks a certain language. They have to be created and made available for citizens by their governments. Likewise, qualified teachers and up-to-date texts do not just appear because someone needs them. They have to be trained, written, and made available for citizens who need them in citizens' native languages and scripts in which learning can take place. That is, policy-makers need to go beyond superficial arguments and address the roots of the issues that indigenous and minority people face, which of course are also issues that the country faces. Left unaddressed, the problems could escalate and disrupt China's ethnic harmony, something which the country is experiencing already. The language rights protests discussed earlier are a case in point.

It is important to note that the argument for education in indigenous and minority languages does not mean that indigenous and minority populations in China should not learn *Hanyu* or work towards the same or higher levels of academic achievement as their Han peers do. *Hanyu* is the national language and should be learned by all citizens, including the indigenous and minority citizens of the nation. All citizens, however, should also have opportunity to achieve their highest potential in every aspect of their lives, including first, second, and third language literacies as well as perform well in school and society with dignity and confidence, which can benefit from a strong first language literacy foundation. There is plenty of research in North America that suggests exactly this and indicates that first language literacy skills transfer to second language literacy (Cummins, 1979, 1981; Sparks, Patton, Ganschow, & Humbach, 2009; Tong, Lara-Alecio, Irby, Mathes, & Kwok, 2008). This body of work also shows that students with a strong first language literacy foundation are much more likely to succeed in second and subsequent languages. Additionally, indigenous and minority students should be provided with as many opportunities and resources to learn English as their Han peers and to have access to all linguistic, cultural, and economic capital afforded to their Han peers in order to compete for opportunities on an equal footing without the "attitudes which cause or perpetuate substantive or de facto discrimination" (CESCR, 2009). Only such a language policy and practice can create a collegial environment characterized by a sense of belonging, togetherness, and a feeling of respect which is essential for harmonious co-existence and social stability.

Recommendations for how this can be accomplished are beyond the scope of this chapter, but a steady, thoughtful, and responsible trilingual language (first language, *Hanyu*, and English) policy and research-based pedagogy that affirms and incorporates indigenous and minority students' first languages and cultures are crucial. Students are less likely to fail in schools where they feel positive about both their own languages/cultures and a majority culture that does not alienate them (Au & Jordan, 1981; Cummins, 1986; Ladson-Billings, 2009). There are numerous successful bilingual and second language policy instruction strategies that can be "borrowed" from other countries such as Australia and Canada.

References

Au, K., & Jordan, C. (1981). Teaching reading to Hawaiian children: Finding a culturally appropriate solution. In H. Trueba, G.Guthrie, & K. Au (Eds.), *Culture and bilingual classrooms: Studies in classroom ethnography* (pp. 139–152). Rowledy, MA: New Bury House.

Beckett, G. H. & Li, F. (In Review). Content-Based English education in China: Students' experiences and perspectives. *The Journal of Contemporary Issues in Education.*

Beckett, G., & MacPherson, S. (2005). Researching the impact of English on minority and indigenous languages in non-"Western" contexts. *TESOL Quarterly*, 38(2), 299–308.

Beckett, G. H., & Postiglione, G. (2010). Introduction. In G. H. Beckett & G. Postiglione (Guest Eds.), *Ethnic minority education in China: Language policies and practices. Special issue of Diaspora, Indigenous, and Minority Education: An International Journal*, 4(1), 1–3.

Cazden, C. B. (1988). *Classroom discourse: The language of teaching and learning.* Portsmouth, NH: Heinemann.

CESCR (Committee on Economic, Social and Cultural Rights) (2009). General Comment No. 20, E/C.12/GC/20. Available at: http://www2.ohchr.org/english/bodies/cescr/docs/gc/E.C.12.GC.20.doc (accessed August 25, 2010).

Chen, Y. (2010). Boarding school for Uyghur students: Speaking Uyghur as bonding social capital. *Diaspora, Indigenous, and Minority Education: An International Journal*, 4(1), 4–16.

Cummins, J. (1979). Linguistic interdependence and the educational development of bilingual children. *Review of Educational Research*, 49, 222–251.

Cummins, J. (1981). The role of primary language development in promoting educational success for language minority students. In California State Department of Education (Ed.), *Schooling and language minority students: A theoretical framework* (pp. 3–49). Los Angeles: National Dissemination and Assessment Center.

Cummins, J. (1986). Empowering minority students. *Harvard Education Review*, 17(4), 18–36.

Dwyer, A. M. (2005). *The Xinjiang conflict: Uyghur identity, language policy, and political discourse.* Washington, DC: East-West Center.

Feng, A. W. (2005). Introduction. In A. W. Feng (Ed.), *Bilingual education in China: Practices, policies, and concepts* (pp. 1–10). Clevedon, UK: Multilingual Matters.

Gee, J. P. (2007). *What video games have to teach us about learning and literacy* (2nd ed.). New York: Palgrave Macmillan.

Gladney, D. (Ed.) (1998). *Making majorities: Composing the nation in Japan, China, Korea, Malaysia, Fiji, Turkey, and the United States.* Stanford, CA: Stanford University Press.

Heath, S. B. (1983). *Ways with words: Language, life, and work in communities and classrooms.* Cambridge, UK: Cambridge University Press.

Hu, G. W. (2007). The juggernaut of Chinese–English bilingual education. In A. W. Feng (Ed.), *Bilingual education in China: Practices, policies and concepts* (pp. 94–126). Clevedon, UK: Multilingual Matters.

Jankowiak, W. R. (2008). Ethnicity and Chinese identity. In K. Louie (Ed.), *China Handbook* (pp. 83–102). Cambridge, UK: Cambridge University Press.

Ladson-Billings, G. (2009). Dreamkeepers: Successful teachers of African American children (2nd ed.). San Francisco, CA: Jossey-Bass.

Lam, A. (2005). *Language education in China: Policy and experience from 1949.* Hong Kong: Hong Kong University Press.

Ma, R. (2007). Bilingual education for China's ethnic minorities. *Chinese Education and Society*, 40(2), 9–25.

Ma, R. (2008). Education of ethnic minorities in contemporary China. *Plenary delivered at the Conference on Minority Language Education in China: Issues and Perspectives.* Hong Kong: University of Hong Kong, April.

Ma, R. (2009). Development of minority education and practice of bilingual education in Xinjiang. *Front Education China*, 4, 188–251.

Ma, T. (2004). Dongxiang nongcun laodongli zhuanyi tedian jiqi sikao [Characteristics of rural Dongxiang migrating labor]. *Journal of Northwest University for Nationalities*, 1, 92–94.

MacPherson, S., & Beckett, G. H.. (2008). The hidden curriculum of assimilation in modern Chinese education: Fuelling indigenous Tibetan and Uygur cessation movements. In Z. Bekerman & E. Kopelowitz (Eds.), *Cultural education/Cultural sustainability: Identity, tolerance, and multicultural issues in minority, diaspora, and indigenous education* (pp. 103–122). Mahwah, NJ: Lawrence Erlbaum.

MacPherson, S. A., & Ghoso, D. B. (2008). Multilingual practices in emerging diasporas: A Tibetan case study. *Diaspora, Indigenous & Minority Education: An International Journal*, 2(3), 188–216.

Michaels, S., & Cazden, C. B. (1986). Teacher-child collaboration on oral presentation for literacy. In. B. B. Schieffelin & P.Gilmore (Eds.), *Acquisition of literacy: Ethnographic perspectives* (pp. 132–154). Norwood, NJ: Ablex.

Mohan, B. (1986). *Language and content*. Reading, MA: Addison-Wesley.

Ochs, E. (1989). *Culture and language development: Language acquisition and language socialization in a Samoan village*. Cambridge: Cambridge University Press.

Qin , Z., & Ma, G. (2004). *Dongxiang: A survey in Hanzeling village, Dongxiang county, Gansu province (Dongxiang Zu: Gansu Dongxiang Hanzeling Cun Diaocha)* (p. 320). Kunming: Yunnan University Press.

Sparks, R., Patton, J., Ganschow, L., & Humbach, N. (2009). Long-term crosslinguistic transfer of skills from L1 to L2. *Language Learning*, 59(1), 203–243. Retrieved from ERIC database. http://www.eric.ed.gov/.

Stites, R. (1999). Writing cultural boundaries: National minority language policy, literacy planning, and bilingual education. In G. Postiglione (Ed.), *China's national minority education: Culture, schooling and development* (pp. 95–130). New York: Falmer Press.

Tong, F., Lara-Alecio, R., Irby, B., Mathes, P., & Kwok, O. (2008). Accelerating early academic oral English development in transitional bilingual and structured English immersion programs. *American Educational Research*, 45, 1011–1044. doi: 10.3102/0002831208320790.

United Nations. (1987). United Nations Report: Our Common Future. Available at: http://sustainablecommunityinitiative.com/index.php?option=com_content&view=article&id=66:united-nations-report-our-common-future-1987&catid=40:policy-innovations&Itemid=68 (accessed August 30, 2011).

Upton, J. (1999). The development of modern school based language education in the PRC. In G. Postiglione (Ed.), *China's national minority education: Culture, schooling, and development* (pp. 281–342). New York: Falmer Press.

William, J. (2008), Ethnicity and Chinese identity: Ethnographic insight and political positioning, in K. Louie (Ed.), *Modern Chinese culture*. Cambridge, UK: Cambridge University Press.

Yang, J. (2006). Learners and users of English in China. *English Today*, 22(2), 3–10.

Yu, H. B. (2010). *Identity and schooling among the Naxi: Becoming Chinese with Naxi identity*. New York: Rowman and Littlefield.

Zhang, W. J. (2002). Shuangyu jiaoxue de xingzhi tiaojian ji xiangguan wenti [The nature and conditions of bilingual education and some related problems]. *Yuyan Jiaoxue yu Yanjiu*, 4, 20–26.

Zhou, M. (2003). *Multilingualism in China: The politics of writing reforms for minority languages, 1949–2002*. New York: Mouton de Gruyter.

Zhou, M. L., & Sun, H. K. (Eds.) (2004). *Language policy in the People's Republic of China: Theory and practice since 1949*. Norwell, MA: Kluwer Academic Press.

2 Historical review of the PRC's minority/indigenous language policy and practice

Nation-state building and identity construction

Minglang Zhou

Background

The PRC has a minority population of over 106 million, most of whom are indigenous. How have the PRC's language policy and practice for this minority population evolved in the past six decades? This question essentially concerns what minority communities have experienced in their language use in school, at work, and even at home in a multilingual China, where over 129 languages are spoken (Sun, Hu, & Huang, 2007). Further, the answer to this question involves the relationship between the PRC's language policy and identity construction, that is, the role the PRC has expected language to play in the state's efforts at shaping linguistic and ethnic minorities' awareness of who they are in this multicultural and multilingual land. To answer this question critically and meaningfully, the chapter examines how the PRC's adoption of the Soviet model of multinational state building and its home-grown model of an inclusive Chinese nation with diversity (*zhonghua minzu duoyuan yiti*) have supported certain language ideologies and orders in identity construction.

In this chapter, I first briefly review current scholarship on the PRC's language policy and practice, and then present a conceptual framework for my analysis of its policy development, implementation, and change over the past 60 years. With this conceptual framework, the study first focuses on language policy and practice within the Soviet model during the first four decades of the PRC, and then examines the transition to the Chinese model since the mid-1990s as a response to the collapse of the Soviet Union and to the needs of a changing China. I demonstrate that a model of nation-state building has a parameter within which a certain language ideology is endorsed and a language order is established as the state engages linguistic citizenship in identity construction. When one model replaces another, the paradigm changes and thus the parameters are changed. Therefore, the evolution of the PRC's minority language policy and practice has been subjected to the dynamics within each model as well as to the transition from one model to the other model. Within a model, language policy and practice are developed and implemented in the scope of that model's parameters. During the transition, language policy and practice are maintained in paradigmatically different ways across models of nation-state building to serve their respective goals in identity construction.

Literature review

Existing scholarship takes three general conceptual approaches to the PRC's language policy and practice: (1) the descriptive; (2) the civilizing; and (3) the political. The first is a descriptive approach taken by most scholars within China. In this approach, scholars (see Sun 1989; Zhou & Sun, 2004; Yan, 1983) review the PRC's policies and their implementation in various minority communities over the years. These scholars assess what has been achieved and what is still desired, usually without critically questioning the state's motivation in policy-making, and with or without criticism of the state's strategies in policy implementation. Practitioners of this approach generally believe that the state is well motivated in this regard, but the Cultural Revolution and other political turmoil are blamed for problems in policy implementation.

In the second conceptual approach, scholars (see Harrell, 1993; Hill, 2010) regard PRC language policy and practice in minority communities essentially as a continuation of imperial China's civilizing project. Imperial China considered the Han civilization to be superior and attempted to civilize or sinicize the frontier peoples by means of education in Confucian values and in the Han language.[1] The goal was to assimilate these peoples into the empire culturally, linguistically, and politically. To embrace minorities as equal citizens of a multinational state, the PRC has attempted to educate them in Marxist doctrines and in Han and/or minority languages. However, ideologically, the PRC cannot avoid the drawbacks that confronted imperial China, since the Marxist social evolution theory, based on Morgan's work, tends to categorize minority cultures as backward and the Han culture as advanced (Blum, 2001, p. 47). Fueled by such an ideology, and coupled with the traditional Han chauvinism, the state may be readily influenced by any factor to sideline minority language use in education and government in the name of cultural advancement. Generally speaking, scholars in this approach are critical of Han chauvinism and Han chauvinistic practices, and recognize the PRC's attempts to maintain minority languages and its embroilment in the conflict between accommodation and assimilation of linguistic and ethnic minorities (see Dwyer, 2005).

Other scholars take what I call the "political" approach to the PRC's language policy and practice in minority communities. In this approach, some scholars (e.g., Zhou, 2001, 2003) believe that the policy evolution has been extensively shaped by the politics within the Chinese Communist Party (CCP). The conflict between accommodation and assimilation is a struggle between two opposing views regarding the pace of the evolution from socialism to communism. The long-term view holds that the evolution toward communism is a long process where diverse linguistic and ethnic groups must coexist before integrating into one people speaking one language. The short-term view considers the evolution to communism and to one people as a rapid process. Thus, the long-term view supports linguistic accommodation for minorities, but the short-term view promotes the use of Han as a shortcut. Without exploring the motivations, some scholars (e.g., Stites, 1999) see China's development of language policy as a conflict in itself. Minority language policy has been developed to maintain boundaries between the minority and majority, and among the minorities themselves, whereas the Han language policy that promotes *Putonghua* (Mandarin) is intended to reach across those boundaries. Other scholars (e.g., Lin, 1997; Schwarz, 1962) examine PRC language policy and practice in light of the tension between regional autonomy and CCP control. The scope of minority language use is in essence associated with the scope of autonomy: More minority language use equals more autonomy and more CCP control means less minority language use.

Regardless of the conceptual approaches taken, case studies of specific minority communities often find local practices that support different points of view. For example, Bradley (2001) found many positive practices in Yi communities in southwestern China, though there is plenty of room for improvement. However, Xiao (1998) discovered that Dai and Jingpo were barely used in public domains, including education, in Dehong, which is a Dai and Jingpo autonomous prefecture. Similar problems, particularly in education, are found in Tibetan communities (Postiglione, 2008). In fact, in some cases, the situation is more complicated than simply the positive or negative evidence of practice, as in the case of the Mongolian community (see Bilik, 1998). Obviously, many factors, such as local economic development, local leaders' attitudes, and local mother-tongue awareness, influence the PRC's language policy implementation and actual local language use in minority communities. In fact, these factors are closely interrelated at both the local and national levels.

Current conceptual framework

To provide a bird's eye view, I examine the evolution of the PRC's language policy and practice in relation to its models of nation-state building. I consider a model of nation-state building as the ideological parameters within which a state makes laws and develops policies to consolidate its citizens' national identity for territorial and national integrity. Within these parameters, the state engages dimensions of citizenship according to its priority, resulting in what I call "prioritized" or "ordered dimensions of" citizenship (see Zhou, 2008a). These dimensions include civil, political, social, territorial, racial, social, economic and even cultural citizenship (Brubaker, 1992; Eley & Palmowski, 2008; Marshall, 1964; Shih, 2002). The state may engage them as a matter of priority, or more pragmatically only engage some of them at a certain period of time to achieve its goals. For example, the Chinese state actively deployed social and cultural citizenship in the schooling of minority youth (Yi, 2006) while minority college students are negotiating with the state for more citizenship rights (Zhao, 2010).

One of the most important dimensions is linguistic citizenship, which is not fully considered by scholars of citizenship. Linguistic citizenship is engaged within the parameter of nation-state building that is underpinned by language ideology and language order (Zhou, 2008a, 2009). Following the Marxist tradition (Marx & Engels, [1846] 1947), language ideology may be considered a system of ideas, assumptions, beliefs, and values related to the question of whether and to what degree a state practices monolingualism or multilingualism. These two polarizing ideologies become the extremes of an ideological continuum. Monolingualism, as an ideology or linguistic nationalism, is based on the belief that a nation should be founded on one common language (see Galindo, 1997; Gonzalez & Melis, 2001; Hornberger, 2007). Multilingualism, as an ideology, considers languages as rights of their speakers and resources for both the speakers and the community (Cummins, 2000; Hornberger, 1988).

Language order is an institutionalized, hierarchical relationship between two or more languages spoken in a community or nation. A language order is theoretically underpinned by the state's language ideology, and politically and legislatively established by the state within its ideological parameter. The state decides which language is adopted for its official business and for the creation, transmission, and deposit of knowledge. The chosen language is given full access to or monopoly power over political, legal, institutional, human, financial, and discourse resources, while other languages are only given partial access to these resources. In this order, the most resourceful and powerful language is the superior language; other languages are subordinate and may be further ranked according to their access to these resources, with less access resulting in a lower rank. In a national or international community, there are usually three strata of languages: the super, some regional, and some local (Fishman, 1998), suggesting that language order can be a powerful linguistic and social reality.

The relationship between language ideology and order is that which is between a superstructure and reality in the Marxist tradition. Language ideology not only represents the reality of language order, but acts upon it as well. Depending on how the state engages linguistic citizenship, a language ideology may be realized as a language law, policy, or regulation, though it actually is none of these (Spolsky, 2004). Even when it is not realized as such, language ideology functions as the parameter within which people perceive, understand, and manage individual and societal multilingualism or monolingualism in China, the US, or elsewhere. Thus, it is apparent that linguistic citizenship is a powerful tool of nation-state building. In the following two sections, I demonstrate how the PRC engages, in its two different models, linguistic citizenship in language use and identity construction for its minority communities.

The Soviet model

When the PRC was founded in 1949, it adopted the Soviet model of multinational state building with some modification, an adoption that was to bring about serious reconsiderations 50 years later in the 1990s (Dreyer, 1976; Zhou, 2010a). Essentially it replaced a union of republics with a central government consisting of both directly-ruled local governments and autonomous local governments. This model was constitutionally institutionalized, recognizing the equality of all nationalities, giving regional autonomy to the officially identified 55 minority nationalities, and guaranteeing them the freedom to use and develop their languages and writing systems (Macherras, 1994). Thus, endorsing multilingualism, this model accommodated a language order of two parallel language-policy developments, one for the Han and one for minority languages, with the former as the center of gravity and the latter as satellites (for details and conceptual illustration, see Zhou, 2010b).

On the Han track, the Han linguistic nationalism to promote a standard spoken Han and reform the Han script for a strong and unified China was vigorously revitalized in the early 1950s (Chen, 1999). Consensus was reached on two goals at the PRC's first national conference on language reform in October 1955. Motivated by the belief that ideographic and logographic scripts were barriers to mass literacy and modernization, the first goal was to simplify the traditional Han script for the promotion of mass literacy and to prepare a Roman-script phonetic writing system for modernization. This phonetic system, known as *Pinyin* and formally proclaimed in 1957, was supposed to function first as a pronunciation assistant system and eventually as a writing system to replace the Han script. Inspired by the belief in the principle of one language for one nation, the second goal was to promote a standard spoken Han, known as *Putonghua* (Mandarin). *Putonghua* was then intended to unify numerous Han dialects or Sinitic languages, whether or not they were mutually intelligible, and to consolidate various local identities of the Han Chinese into a single Han national identity.

On the minority track, the PRC provisional Constitution—the *Common Program* of 1949—and the subsequent formal Constitution passed in 1954, had already established a constitutional principle for the coexistence of the Han and minority languages. What was needed was a practical model that could accommodate the coexistence constitutionally. Having already adopted the Soviet model of multinational state building, the PRC again turned to the Soviet Union for advice and received "the Soviet experience." G. B. Serdyuchenko (1955, 1956), a Soviet linguistic advisor who worked extensively on minority languages in China from 1954 to 1957, systematically introduced the Soviet linguistic model for the maintenance and development of minority languages within a multinational state (for a summary, see Zhou, 2003, pp. 169–208, and for the primary sources of all of Serdyuchenko's speeches, see Zhou, 2003, pp. 432–433). Based on Stalin's (1975) concept of a nation "formed on the basis of a common language, territory, economic life, and psychological make-up manifested in a common culture" (p. 22), this Soviet linguistic model has five essential aspects.

First, a standard language should be developed for a nationality. It is different from local dialects in that it is planned and codified. The standardization of pronunciation, vocabulary, grammar and orthography of a language can lead that language to become the common language for a nationality. It is much richer and more commonly used than any local dialect, so that it can serve all social, political, administrative, scientific and cultural needs of the people and unify the nationality.

Second, a standard language facilitates national and linguistic convergence. For example, many minority languages in the Soviet Union developed from clan languages into tribal languages, and then into ethno-national languages.

Third, in the process of creating a unified writing system, the base dialect for the standard language must be selected first, so that its grammar and vocabulary can become the basis for the development of the standard ethno-national language. Then the standard pronunciation must be selected, usually based on the most prestigious dialect used in the political, economic and cultural center of the concerned minority nationality.

Fourth, the standardization of terminology is an essential component of the development of a standard language for a minority nationality. For example, the vocabulary of Soviet minority languages developed in three ways: (1) semantic change in old terms; (2) loss of some outdated terms; and (3) enrichment with new terms from Russian and the native language.

Fifth and finally, loanwords from the majority language could contribute to the development of minority national languages. In the Soviet case, for example, Russian loanwords developed in two different stages in minority languages. During the first stage, Russian loanwords underwent phonological changes in accordance with the phonology of the borrowing languages. In the second stage, Russian loanwords kept their original phonology and grammar so that they enriched the phonology and grammar of the borrowing minority languages, making them ready for future linguistic convergence into Russian.

This Soviet model is based on three essential assumptions: (1) each minority nationality, with its own political, economic, and cultural center, and each minority language, with its own standard dialect and written language based on that center, are initially satellites of the majority nationality and the majority language; (2) standardization of a minority language first consolidates various dialects within the language and then facilitates that language's eventual convergence with the majority language; and (3) linguistic convergence of dialects and languages leads to consolidation and convergence of different ethnic identities into a single (ethno)national identity, and finally various (ethno)national identities into a unified national identity.

China implemented this model in the 1950s, standardizing the languages of 16 minority nationalities, and reforming or creating writing systems for them (for a complete account, see Zhou, 2003). China generally followed the Soviet model's three theoretical assumptions. For example, the dialect of a political and economic center was usually selected as the standard, regardless of its popularity among a minority nationality, because the center was expected to unify the given nationality politically, economically, culturally, and linguistically in the future. In standardization, the writing systems were made to conform to *Pinyin* in script and spelling rules, and Han loans were generously introduced with the expectation that, in the future, minority languages and Han would be read and spelled very similarly.

With regard to the third assumption about identity, China made two exceptions to the Soviet practice. The first was an "alliance of writing systems" between the Zhuang and Bouyei nationalities, which are neighbors in southern China and speak languages of the same group. In this alliance, two writing systems were created to be as similar as possible so that the two groups could converge into a single nationality and speak and write in one language, though it was theoretically not expected until communism. The second exception, however, was the creation of more than one standard dialect and writing system for a single nationality, as in the case of the Miao. Several million Miaos are distributed throughout six provinces in southern China and speak dialects/languages that are mostly mutually intelligible. Though technically it was possible to select one standard dialect and create one writing system for the scattered Miao nationality, the state selected four standard dialects and created four writing systems for the Miao. It is obvious that, even when the Soviet model was fully implemented, the state took local situations into consideration and adapted the process to its advantage. When deemed necessary, the state sped up the consolidation of various ethnic identities, but it stopped or delayed such a consolidation when it might cause political problems.

The politics within the CCP was the most significant factor affecting how the model should be implemented, as it swayed between multilingual and monolingual ideologies. As the Great Leap Forward emerged in the late 1950s, the view of a rapid evolution to communism began to dominate the CCP. Originally, with the exception of the satellite relationship that sets the trajectory of remote future convergence, the standardized minority languages were supposed to develop into the ethno-national languages of the respective minority nationalities, while *Putonghua* was to become the ethno-national language for the Han majority only. Now, the Han language was promoted to replace minority languages as a shortcut for rapid linguistic convergence. This process was greatly accelerated during the Cultural Revolution (1966–1976) when the dominant ideology became monolingual: one people speaking one language.

When the Cultural Revolution ended, the parallel language order with the satellite- and center-of-gravity relationship could no longer be restored for both political and linguistic reasons. First, the supposed political, economic, and cultural centers of minority communities never materialized when their autonomous government seats became a link in the administrative chain under Beijing. Second, the landscape of language use in China changed, where Han had already spread to government, education, and other public domains in minority communities. Very soon this new linguistic landscape was constitutionally legitimized, when the PRC Constitution was amended in 1982 (Article 19) and *Putonghua* was officially made the common speech for all nationalities in China. Given this reality in the 1980s, minority communities tried to find a lesser role for their languages, a role to supplement Han in government and education so that their native languages could facilitate the maintenance of their national identities and their cultural needs. With the return to a multilingual ideology, some progress was made along this line in the 1980s as autonomous laws and pluralistic language policies were passed to encourage the use of minority languages in government and education. The most progressive policy during this period was the State Council Document #32 (1991, see China, 1996, pp. 707–711), which was to revaluate the writing systems created in the 1950s for supplementary use along with the Han script.

In summary, the PRC's Soviet model set the parametric scope for language policy evolution. In theory, as described above, all the changes in language policy-making and implementation were dynamically driven by the CCP's views on the pace of the evolution from socialism to communism. In practice, it was the push-and-pull of the center of gravity that determined how minority languages were actually used publicly as satellites of the Han language. When evolving at a slow pace to communism, multiple steps were allowed to reach the goal of a unified national identity while speaking Han was not considered essential to be a Chinese citizen. However, at a fast pace, multiple steps were reduced to a singe step transition to a Chinese identity that was expected to be symbolized by the use of Han.

The Chinese model

However, two events fundamentally changed the relationship among language, ethnicity, and the state in China in the 1990s. The first was the economic reform breakthrough that has successfully introduced a market-oriented economy in China, and the second was the collapse of the Soviet Union at the end of 1991, an event that has resulted in the PRC's eventual abandonment of the failed Soviet model in favor of a Chinese model of nation-state building (e.g., Zhou, 2010a). This change of nation-state building models resembles China's replacement of its Soviet economic model with a Chinese-style market economy in that the CCP retains the terminology that legitimize its rule. In the economic reform, China maintains terms such as "socialist" and "communist," while in the model change China keeps terms such as "*minzu*" and "autonomous region."[2] The essences of laws, policies, and practices, however, have been fundamentally changed, and even official discourses on the topic are usually conducted in different terms, such as *zhonghua minzu ningjuli* (cohesiveness of the Chinese nation) and *sange libukai* (three cannots) (for a detailed discussion, see Zhou 2010a).

In the early 1990s, after over a decade of economic reform, a market-oriented economy finally began to replace the Soviet-style planned economy in China. The market-oriented economy has basically freed people from the state-controlled job market, and subsequently from the household registration system that pinned a person in one job in one place for his/her whole life. People, particularly farmers (including minorities), moved to coastal and eastern China for better-paying jobs and a better life. Having increased to 100 million in the late 1990s and then to about 200 million currently, the population movement has created a strong demand for a lingua franca to serve communication needs. *Putonghua* has been there ready for this role of lingua franca for years (see Zhou, 2006). When, in 2000, the PRC launched its "Open Up the West Campaign" (*xibu da kaifei*), which aims at economically integrating western and coastal China, capital and labor migration rushed toward western China, creating an ever-increasing demand for *Putonghua*. Now *Putonghua* has experienced a revolution, developing from a state-endorsed language to one that is endorsed by the state and empowered by the market.

Within a few years after the collapse of the Soviet Union in 1991, the PRC has gradually replaced the Soviet model of multinational state building with a Chinese model of "one nation with diversity" (*zhonghua minzu duoyuan yiti*) (Zhou, 2010a). Developed from Fei Xiaotong's (1999) ideas, the Chinese model consists of three concepts: (1) the inclusive Chinese nation (*zhonghua minzu*); (2) the process of the formation of this Chinese nation; and (3) diversity in unity of this Chinese nation. The inclusive Chinese nation includes the 56 ethnic groups (55 minority groups plus the Han majority) as its basis, but it is not just a collection of those ethnic groups; it is a national entity that has developed from a common desire by all the 56 ethnic groups for a shared fate and destiny with respect to opportunities and successes. This concept entails two levels of identity representation: a lower level of ethnic identities for each of the 56 ethnic groups, of which the Han majority is one; and a higher level of an inclusive Chinese national identity for all Chinese citizens, effectively downgrading "ethno national identity" to "ethnic identity" by eliminating the former category. In the process of forming the Chinese nation, it is believed that the Han Chinese played the core role of integrating various national elements into the inclusive Chinese nation—a nation that has since surpassed the Han to embrace ethnic, cultural and linguistic diversity. The concept of "the diversity in unity of the Chinese nation" assumes that the two levels of identities do not replace each other nor contradict each other, but coexist and co-develop with linguistic and cultural diversity.

This Chinese model completely abandoned the language order in the Soviet model when the State Council withdrew the implementation of its Document #32 (1991) in the mid-1990s. The Chinese model endorses a weak bilingual ideology that promotes *Putonghua* as the national common language for all Chinese citizens, while allowing minority languages as symbols of linguistic diversity. Thus, this model constructs a strictly-structured order of functions and resources for languages, replacing the satellite relationship in the Soviet model, where each minority language has its own perimeter of functions and resources while all are being drawn to the Han language. This order treats *Putonghua* as the superlanguage and reserves for it most public functions and political, legal, financial, and human resources while politically and functionally marginalizing minority languages.

This order is legislatively represented in the 2001 revised *PRC Minority Regional Autonomous Law* and the 2001 new *PRC National Commonly-Used Language and Script Law*. For example, the new autonomous law requires that the teaching of *Putonghua* start either in the early or late years in primary schools in minority communities, instead of just the late years in primary schools, or in middle schools, as in the old version of the law. This revised law stipulates that minority officials in autonomous governments learn to use both *Putonghua* and standard written Han. Moreover, the language law designates domains for *Putonghua* use and specifies ways to measure an individual's *Putonghua* proficiency for jobs related to those domains. These laws completely legitimize the role of Han as the national common language in government and education in minority communities, where some native languages used to serve such functions. With this language ideology and order, the state aims at educating minority students as *Putonghua* users while allowing the transitional and/or supplementary use of minority languages.

In short, the PRC's Chinese model endorses an unbalanced bilingual ideology and a structured language order where minorities are supposed to use *Putonghua* as the primary language and their native languages as the supplementary or transitional in public domains. This approach takes a single step to construct the inclusive Chinese national identity when speaking Chinese is essential for a PRC citizen.

Conclusion

A model of nation-state building determines how the state engages linguistic citizenship by endorsing a certain language ideology and establishing a certain language order for its citizens. This language ideology underpins the state's language policy and this language order frames language practice. Thus different models of nation-state building have different paradigms of language policy and practice that facilitate the state's respective goals in national identity construction. The change of models of nation-state building is a change of paradigms regarding linguistic citizenship in identity construction. Thus, *Putonghua* or Han is promoted across the Soviet model and the Chinese model in completely different ways and with completely different motivations, and thus multilingualism has been maintained or denied differently across these models in the PRC in the past six decades.

Models are ideals since their implementations may be influenced by political, economic, local, and geopolitical factors. The Soviet model, the Chinese model, and their transition have completely different implications for minority communities in China. The Soviet model developed for minority communities an expectation of two connecting linguistic worlds, where these communities could maintain their ways of sociolinguistic life while venturing into the world of Han sociolinguistic life or vice versa for the Han people. Even today that expectation persists and many minorities still view it as a gold standard of true autonomy, although the implementation of the Soviet model was frequently superseded by the politics within the CCP in the 1950s, 1960s, and 1970s (Stites, 1999; Zhou, 2003).

It is clear now that minority languages play a much less prominent role in the Chinese model than was expected in the Soviet model. At this moment it is still too early to evaluate the implications of the Chinese model for minority communities. I have argued elsewhere that the success of the Chinese model depends on the creation of a vehicle, or at least the perception of one, that helps in reaching freedom and equal opportunity, for all Chinese citizens, regardless of their ethnicity, in their pursuit of "the Chinese dream" (Zhou, 2010a). It could be envisioned that minorities would use Han extensively, instead of their native languages, in pursuing this dream, though they have the constitutional guarantee of their linguistic rights.

However, the transition from the Soviet model to the Chinese model has resulted in some serious implications in the past decade. First, there was an uncertainty of the future for the role of minority languages. When China abandoned its State Council's Document #32 (1991) in the mid-1990s, neither the state nor the minority communities was certain about the role of minority languages in a changing and globalizing China. In the following few years, it became clear to the state that it would promote *Putonghua* extensively as it passed the *National Common Language Law* in 2000, but minority communities still lived in linguistic uncertainty. Second, there was an overwhelming and rapid spread of *Putonghua* brought about by the state's promotion of bilingual education and the market economy. The state's bilingual education programs are transitional, aiming at facilitating minority students' shift from their native languages to Han. The expansion of these programs caught many schools, teachers, students and parents unprepared, resulting in higher drop-out rates from schools and other difficulties in minority communities (Gelek, 2009; Guljennet, 2009). On the other hand, the increasingly competitive job market is linguistically discriminative. Businesses, whether private or public, tend to hire good *Putonghua* speakers or Han-minority bilingual speakers while rejecting minority applicants who do not speak fluent *Putonghua* (see Ma 2010, for further discussion). Such drop-out rates, failing education, and decreasing social mobility that resulted from the implementation of this new language policy may cause serious social problems in minority communities in the larger Chinese society. I suspect that linguistic and cultural uncertainty might have contributed to recent unrest in Tibetan communities and Xinjiang, though socio-economic disparity and pressure from rapid modernization may be the direct causes. This situation leaves a lot of doubts about the Chinese model, though these problems might be transitional. After all, China's current situation shows a closer relation among socio-economic development, language use, and identity construction, which the state and minority communities expect to (re)align in different ways.

Notes

1 I use "the Han Language" or "Han" instead of "Chinese" and "Mandarin" in this chapter because I have taken into consideration minority scholars' preference. A dozen minority scholars, whose articles I have edited in English, communicated to me that they prefer to use "the Han language," "Han" or "*Hanyu*" in their English publications when they discuss the relationship between their native languages and the Han majority's language. They would use "Chinese" when they discuss it in relation to foreign languages, such as English and Japanese. They would say "Do you speak Chinese or English?" but "Do you speak Yi or *Hanyu*?" However, they use "*Putonghua*" when specifically referring to the standard oral language. The use of these terms represents the politics of ethnic relations in China.
2 For example, China changed the English name of its "State Commission on Minority Nationalities Affairs" to "State Commission on Ethnic Affairs" in the late 1990s. The Central University for Minority Nationalities changed its English name to "Central Minzu University" in the past two years. All these efforts indicate that China is reinterpreting the meaning of "*minzu,*" steering away from the Stalinist notion of nation and nationality—the foundation of the Soviet model.

References

Bilik, N. (1998). Language education, intellectuals and symbolic representation: Being an urban Mongolian in a new configuration of social evolution. In W. Safran (Ed.), *Nationalism and ethnoregional identities in China* (pp. 47–67). London: Frank Cass.

Blum, S. D. (2001). Portraits of "primitives": Ordering human kinds in the Chinese nation. Lanham, MD: Rowman & Littlefield Publishers.

Bradley, D. (2001). Language policy for the Yi. In Stevan S. Harrell (Ed.), *Perspectives on the Yi of southwest China* (pp. 195–213). Berkeley: University of California Press.

Brubaker, R. (1992). *Citizenship and nationhood in France and Germany.* Cambridge, MA: Harvard University Press.

Chen, P. (1999). *Modern Chinese: History and sociolinguistics.* Oxford: Oxford University Press.

China (1996). *Guojia Minwei Wenjian Xuanbian* [Selected Documents of the State Commission on Nationalities Affairs]. Beijing: Hong Kong Press.

Cummins, J. (2000). Foreword. In R. D. Gonzalez and I. Melis (Eds.), *Language ideologies: Critical perspectives on the official English movement* (vol. 1, pp. ix–xx). Mahwah, NJ: Lawrence Erlbaum.

Dreyer, J. T. (1976). *China's forty million: Minority nationalities and national integration in the People's Republic of China.* Boston: Harvard University Press.

Dwyer, A. M. (2005). *The Xinjiang conflict: Uyhur identity, language policy, and political discourse.* Washington, DC: The East-West Center.

Eley, G., & Palmowski, J. (Eds.) (2008). *Citizenship and national identity in twentieth-century Germany.* Stanford, CA: Stanford University Press.

Fei, X. T. (Ed.) (1999). *The pattern of diversity in unity of the Chinese nation* [Zhonghua minzu duoyuan yiti geju]. Revised ed. Beijing: Central University for Nationalities Press.

Fishman, J.A. (1998). The new linguistic order. *Foreign Policy*, 113(Winter), 26–40.

Galindo, R. (1997). Language wars: The ideological dimensions of the debates on bilingual education. *Bilingual Research Journal*, 21(2&3), 163–201.

Gelek, L. (2009). Anthropological field survey on basic education development among Machu Tibetan nomads. In M. Zhou, & A. M. Hill (Eds.), *Affirmative action in China and the U. S.: A dialogue on inequality and minority education* (pp. 119–126). New York: Palgrave Macmillan.

Gonzalez, R. D. & Melis, I. (Eds.) (2001). *Language ideologies: Critical perspectives on the official English movement* (vol. 2). Mahwah, NJ: Lawrence Erlbaum.

Guljennet, A. (2009). Present state and prospects of bilingual education in Xinjiang. *Chinese Education & Society*, 41(6), 37–49.

Harrell, S. (1993). Linguistics and hegemony in China. *International Journal of the Sociology of Language*, 103, 97–114.

Hill, A. M.. (2010). Native and nation: Assimilation and the state in China and the U. S. In M. Zhou, & A. M. Hill (Eds.), *Affirmative action in China and the U. S.: A dialogue on inequality and minority education* (pp. 247–260). New York: Palgrave Macmillan.

Hornberger, N. H. (1988). Language planning orientations and bilingual education in Peru. *Language Problems and Language Planning*, 12(1), 14–29.

Hornberger, N. H. (2007). Multilingual language policies and the continua of biliteracy: An ecological approach. In O. Garcia, & C. Baker (Eds.), *Bilingual education: An introductory reader* (pp. 177–194). Buffalo, NY: Multilingual Matters.

Lin, J. (1997). Policies and practices of bilingual education for the minorities in China. *Journal of Multilingual and Multicultural Development*, 18, 193–205.

Ma, R. (2010). Issues of minority education in Xinjiang, China. In M. Zhou, & A. M. Hill (Eds.), *Affirmative action in China and the U. S.: A dialogue on inequality and minority education* (pp. 179–198). New York: Palgrave Macmillan.

Macherras, C. (1994). *China's minorities: Integration and modernization in the twentieth century.* Hong Kong: Oxford University Press.

Marshall, T. H. (1964). *Class, citizenship, and social development.* New York: Doubleday.

Marx, K., & Engels, F. ([1846] 1947). *The German ideology.* New York: International Press.

Postiglione, G. A. (2008). Making Tibetans in China: The educational challenges of harmonious multiculturalism. *Educational Review*, 60(1), 1–20.

Schwarz, H. G. (1962). Communist language policies for China's ethnic minorities: The first decade. *The China Quarterly*, 12, 170–182.

Serdyuchenko, G. P. (1955). *Guanyu zhongguo gezu renmin de yuyan wenzi* [On minority languages and scripts in China]. Beijing: Chinese Academy of Social Sciences.

Serdyuchenko, G. P. (1956). Sulian chuangli wenzi he jianli biaozhun yu de jingnian [The Soviet experience in creating writing systems and establishing standard languages]. *Yuyan Yanjiu* [Language Research], 1, 129–167.

Shih, C. Y. (2002). Negotiating ethnicity in China: Citizenship as a response to the state. New York: Routledge.

Spolsky, B. (2004). *Language policy: Key topics in sociolinguistics*. Cambridge: Cambridge University Press.

Stalin, J. (1975). *Marxism and the national-colonial question*. San Francisco, CA: Proletarian Publishers.

Stites, R. (1999). Writing cultural boundaries: National minority language policy, literacy planning, and bilingual education. In G. A. Postiglione (Ed.), *China's national minority education: Culture, schooling, and development* (pp. 95–130). New York: Falmer Press.

Sun, H. K. (1989). Sketch of China's developing language planning. *Journal of Chinese Linguistics*, 17(1), 1–49.

Sun, H. K., Hu, Z. Y., & Huang, X. (Eds.). (2007). *Zhongguo de yuyan* [Languages of China]. Beijing: Shangwu Yinshuguan.

Xiao, H. (1998). Minority languages in Dehong, China: Policy and reality. *Journal of Multilingual and Multicultural Development*, 19(3), 221–235.

Yan, X. J. (1983). Chinese policy on the language and education of national minorities. *Language Learning and Communication*, 2(2), 133–179.

Yi, L. (2006). Choosing between ethnic and Chinese citizenship: The educational trajectories of Tibetan minority children in northwestern China. In V. L. Fong, & R. Murphy (Eds.), *Chinese citizenship: Views from the margins* (pp. 41–67). New York: Routledge.

Zhao, Z. Z. (2010). Practice of citizenship rights among minority students at Chinese universities. *Cambridge Journal of Education*, 40(2), 131–144.

Zhou, M. (2001). The politics of bilingual education in the People's Republic of China since 1949. *Bilingual Research Journal*, 25(1 & 2), 147–171.

Zhou, M. (2003). *Multilingualism in China: The politics of writing reforms for minority languages 1949–2002*. New York: Mouton de Gruyter.

Zhou, M. (Ed.) (2006). *Language planning and varieties of (modern standard) Chinese: Special issue of Journal of Asian Pacific Communication* 16(2). Philadelphia: John Benjamins.

Zhou, M. (2008a). Models of (multi)nation-state building and the meaning of being Chinese in contemporary *China. Paper presented at the Critical Han Studies Conference*, Stanford University, CA.

Zhou, M. (2008b). Linguistic diversity and language harmony in contemporary China: Guest editor's Introduction. *Chinese Education and Society*, 41(6), 3–9.

Zhou, M. (2009). Yuyan yishi xingtai he yuyan zhixu: Quanqiuhua yu zhong mei liang-guo de duoyu jiaoyu zhanlue [Language ideology and order: Multilingual education in the US and China during globalization]. *Journal of Jinan University* (Philosophy and Social Science Edition), 138(1), 1–12.

Zhou, M. (2010a). The fate of the Soviet model of multinational state building in China. In T. Bernstein, & H. Y. Li (Eds.), *China learns from the Soviet Union, 1949–present* (pp. 477–503). Lanham, MD: Rowman & Littlefield Publishers.

Zhou, M. (2010b). China: The Mainland, Hong Kong and Taiwan. In J. A. Fishman, & O. Garci¨a (Eds.), *Handbook of language and ethnic identity: Disciplinary and regional perspectives* (vol. I, pp. 470–484). Oxford: Oxford University Press.

Zhou, M., & Sun, H. K. (Eds.). (2004). *Language policy in the People's Republic of China: Theory and practice since 1949*. Boston: Kluwer.

Part II
Empirical research studies

3 The development of minority education and the practice of bilingual education in Xinjiang Uyghur Autonomous Region

Rong Ma

Introduction

Under the overarching principle of representing a unified nation-state, the political, economic, and cultural integration of diverse ethnic minority groups is a constant core concern of any multi-ethnic country. When each ethnic group has its own particular language and cultural traditions, the use and the future trend of their languages surely become sensitive societal issues. Countries in the contemporary world have been, to varying degrees, involved in the trend of globalization; therefore, the function of language as both a cultural carrier and a tool for education and communication takes on an important role in communication between countries and between ethnic groups within a country. Furthermore, in response to the need for increased inter-ethnic communication in trade and cultural interactions, "regional languages" emerge in different areas, meaning that the people of all groups in one region intend to learn and use one language for the sake of efficiency (Ma, 2008). Language learning is the necessary prerequisite for cultural exchange and integration among ethnic groups, and the development of languages' usage predicts the prospect for the progression of an inter-ethnic relationship.

In modern society, schools at different levels that offer formal education are places where people systematically acquire knowledge and skills, and also serve as important channels for learning social norms, becoming "socialized" and improving status in the system of social stratification. It can even be said that there is a close relationship between a person's development opportunities as well as social status, and his/her educational achievement in schools—defined as the grade s/he has reached, what kind of school s/he attended, what s/he majors in, and similar measures. In the same framework, in a multi-ethnic and multi-lingual country, the language adopted by students of each ethnic group is also of great importance, as is the linguistic and cultural environment in the classroom. Students acquire knowledge at school in order to apply it to future work and life and, at the same time, to foster communication with colleagues, clients, and other members of society. Therefore, the instructional language used in class and in textbooks will determine the students' ability to converse with peers as well as defining the scope of society within which they are able to communicate and work in the future.

According to the Chinese Constitution, each ethnic group has the right to "apply and develop" its own language. At the same time, the study and use of *Putonghua* as an "inter-group language in China" is advocated for the sake of communication among all ethnic groups and for the development of the country. *Putonghua* is the language commonly used by the Han, Hui, Manchu, Hezhi, and She in China. Large proportions of other minority groups (Mongol, Zhuang, Tujia, Dongxiang, etc.) also speak *Putonghua*. It was used to be called "*Mandarin*" in the West and was officially renamed "Han *Putonghua*" (abbreviated *Putonghua*) in 1955 by the Central Government of the PRC, and the regulations of its pronunciation, grammar, and simplified writing characters were issued in the following years. It is often called "Chinese language" in western literature.

In the ethnic minorities' autonomous regions, both the nationally popularized *Putonghua* and the languages of native ethnic minorities are recognized as official and legitimate languages that can be applied concurrently not only for official and social public occasions, but also as languages of instruction at local schools. Since the founding of the People's Republic of China, the government has gradually instituted a bilingual education system from kindergarten to college in each autonomous region for ethnic minorities, actively popularizing *Putonghua* and systematically teaching the local languages as well. Since the native minority language is a primary language of instruction in schools in ethnic minorities' areas, bilingual education is a crucial subject when it comes to the issue of education of Chinese ethnic minorities. Xinjiang is one of the five major autonomous regions in China. In the region, minorities account for 60 percent of the total population. As a result, many scholars in the field of minority education have focused on the development of bilingual education in Xinjiang.

From 2000 to 2007, I traveled to Xinjiang on many occasions, and I have cooperated with local scholars on field research concerning bilingual education and employment situation of minority students in certain areas. In August 2007, we conducted an ad hoc survey on bilingual education in the Kashgar Prefecture of southern Xinjiang (Dr. Abduqadir Semet, Dr. Zuliyati Simayi , and Zhao Rui participated in this field survey). Namely, we attended three colloquia of principals and teachers of local primary and middle schools organized by regional education bureaus; we also visited the Kashgar Education College (the normal school to train teachers), seven middle and high schools, and one kindergarten; and we had informal discussions with teachers and students, and paid home visits to a dozen students enrolled in middle schools or preschool classes. Based on the field survey data and supplementary research, this chapter aims to shed light on the developing condition of bilingual education in Xinjiang Uyghur Autonomous Region and discuss some key issues presently at stake.

The minority education system in Xinjiang

In Xinjiang, the autonomous region in which minorities account for over 60 percent of the population, various languages are adopted as teaching-languages and for the production of teaching materials. There are 56 ethnic groups in Xinjiang, some of them (e.g., Hui, Manchu, etc.) use *Putonghua* as mother tongue, while many do not have their own native-language education programs because of their small populations. The autonomous government thus makes clear policies for the teaching-language of schools based on the realities of the region: (1) Uyghur language is adopted by the three groups of Uzbek, Tartar, and Tajik in school in addition to Uyghur; (2) the seven languages of *Putonghua*, Uyghur, Kazak, Kirgiz, Mongolia, Xibe, and Russian are applied to school teaching. Since the 1950s, the government has begun to organize professionals to compile textbooks and teaching materials for primary and middle schools in the six languages of *Putonghua*, Uyghur, Kazak, Kirgiz, Mongolian, and Xibe. Then, 1998 saw the beginning of self-compilation of Russian textbooks for primary schools; (3) the four languages of *Putonghua*, Uyghur, Kazak, and Mongolian are applied to teaching in universities and colleges in Xinjiang. The college curriculum comprises the basic frame of reference for teaching-languages applied in schools at different levels in Xinjiang. To support the application of minority languages in teaching, Xinjiang Education Press published 1,550 different textbooks and teaching materials in minority languages in 2005.

After half a century of development, the scale of minority students and teachers at different levels in Xinjiang has reached a certain level. According to the statistics recorded in December, 2004, there were a total of 5,451 primary schools in the whole region, wherein 1436,257 minority students made up 64.8 percent of the total population of enrolled students, and 86,315 minority teachers 64 percent of the total population of teachers. 1,467 middle schools consisted of 742,084 minority students and 41,823 minority teachers. In the 498 high schools, there were 148,398 minority students and 9,293 minority teachers. In accordance with the statistics of the primary, middle and high schools, there are altogether 7,416 schools at which there are a total of 2,326,739 minority students (62.3 percent of the total number) and 137,431 minority teachers (59.9 percent) (Table 3.1), which corresponds with the proportion of the minority population to the total population in Xinjiang. These data show that all minority groups have achieved corresponding progress in student enrollment and teaching staff employment. The policy of equality of different ethnic groups and vigorous development of minority education enacted by the central government has been implemented and carried out.

In accordance with these language policies and development of textbooks, schools in Xinjiang follow two parallel systems based on the language of instruction: The first system is called "school of minority language system" (minority school), mainly teaching in the local language. This system may be further divided into schools taught in the Uyghur language, the Kazak language, and the Mongolian language. The second system is called the "school of *Putonghua* system" (Han school), in which teaching and learning activities are carried out in *Putonghua*. Geographical differences in ethnic composition of local populations lead to the phenomenon of Han students attending minority schools, minority students attending Han schools, and portions of minority students attending schools of other ethnic groups (for example, Kazak students attending Uyghur

Table 3.1 Statistics as to teachers and students at different schools in Xinjiang (December, 2004)

	Number of schools	Teaching and adnministrative staff		Professional teachers		Students	
		Total number	Minority	Total number	Minority	Total number	Minority
Kindergarten	977	17,767	—	9,612	2,178	262,624	77,811
%	—	—	—	100.0	22.7	100.0	29.6
Primary school	5,451	150,308	86,315	134,915	86,315	2,218,109	1,436,257
%	—	100.0	574	100.0	640	100.0	64.8
Secondary school*	1,965	113,047	59,028	94,381	51,116	1,517,948	890,482
%	—	100.0	52.2	100.0	54.2	100.0	58.7
Vocational school	84	4,732	—	3,079	—	61,502	—
%	—	—	—	—	—	—	—
Special education	8	356	—	257	—	2,549	350
%	—	—	—	—	—	100.0	13.7

schools or vice versa). Meanwhile, there are Han teachers in minority schools and a few minority teachers in Han schools. As a result of these phenomena, the number of minority students in schools at different levels does not equal that of students attending minority schools, and the number of minority teachers does not equal that of teachers working in minority schools. When reading these statistical data, attention should be paid to the different statistical perspectives as well as methods. In Table 3.2, I attempt to analyze the structure of schools in Xinjiang as a whole by comparing the various teaching-languages. There are essentially three types of schools in Xinjiang: minority schools, Han schools, and minority-Han joint schools. It has been impossible to attain a clear figure for the number of students enrolled in minority-Han joint schools because these schools have been changing continuously. The Autonomous Region began experimentally setting up a few minority-Han joint schools in 1960. Xinjiang once carried out the separation of minority and Han schools after the Cultural Revolution, but the number of such schools nevertheless increased to 165 by 1981. That number then decreased to 44 in 1984. Nonetheless, minority-Han joint schools were again encouraged in the late 1990s. In 2000, there were 461 minority-Han joint schools in total; in 2004, the number was 656; in 2005, it increased to 707. Due to the lack of statistical figures of students in minority-Han joint schools and Han schools, their respective proportion is incalculable.

From the statistics in Table 3.2, we can see that of the minority schools, Uyghur language primary schools make up 87.3 percent, Uyghur language middle schools make up 74.8 percent. These are followed by Kazak language in

Table 3.2 The enrollment number of schools at different levels in Xinjiang in 2004

	Kindergarten				Primary school				Secondary school			
	Number	%	Students in attendance	%	Number	%	Students in attendance	%	Number	%	Students in attendance	%
Ethnic minority language schools*	—	—	77,811	29.6	3,777	70.3	1,226,678	55.3	971	49.4	787,689	51.9
Uyghur	—	—	—	—	3,297	60.5	—	—	726	36.9	—	—
Kazak	—	—	—	—	375	6.9	—	—	189	9.6	—	—
Mongol	—	—	—	—	22	0.4	—	—	23	1.2	—	—
Xibe	—	—	—	—	4	0.1	—	—	4	0.22	—	—
Kirgiz	—	—	—	—	79	1.4	—	—	29	1.5	—	—
Joint	—	—	—	—	636	11.7	—	—	20	1.0	—	—
Han	—	—	—	—	1,038	19.0	—	—	974	49.6	—	—
Total	977	—	262,624	100.0	5,451	100.0	2,218,109	100.0	1,965	100.0	1,517,948	100.0

Source: Statistics from the Xinjiang Autonomous Region Bureau of Education.

Note: * There is another primary school with Russian as its teaching language, which turned into a bilingual school in 2004.

corresponding proportion. There are only a few other minority schools such as Kirgiz, Mongolian, and Xibe. This configuration reflects, on one hand, the important status of the Uyghur as the minority group with the largest population in Xinjiang; on the other hand, it shows the governmental accommodation of groups with relatively small populations and the policy protecting their languages.

The attending mode of students of different minorities

Traditionally, minority students in Xinjiang can be roughly classified into three types according to the type of school attended and the teaching-language received: (1) *Min kao Min* (test minority students with minority languages), that is, minority students attend the appropriate minority schools and receive exams presented in the corresponding language; (2) *Min kao Han* (test minority students with *Putonghua*), that is, minority students attend Han schools and receive exams on each subject in *Putonghua*; (3) *Han kao Han* (test Han students with *Putonghua*), that is, Han students attend Han schools and receive exams in *Putonghua*. In each case, the *kao* (test) refers to the language of exams, which is usually the teaching-language throughout a course of study.

The following points are worthy of attention when discussing the three traditional modes of instruction: (1) in the sphere of *Min kao Min*, there are schools of different minority language systems (Uyghur, Kazak, Mongolian, Kizgiz, and Xibe), and this sphere includes situations in which students of a certain group study in the minority school of another minority language. For example, students of Kazak or Tajik study and get tested in Uyghur; (2) in different stages of study, a student may choose to attend different types of schools. For example, some students remain within the sphere of *Min kao Min* in primary school, but they may transfer to *Min kao Han* when they are enrolled in Han middle school, which, of course, might bring some difficulties to the transferees; (3) some minority students such as Hui and Manchu speak *Putonghua* as their native language and attend Han schools. As such, the tests they pass cannot be referred to as *Min kao Han* in the true sense of the phrase. Furthermore, they may enjoy certain policy-awarded points in the college entrance examination on account of their minority status; (4) school-age children of minorities with small populations usually choose schools according to the mainstream language of their area, as is the case for students of southern minorities (Tujia, Miao, etc.) who generally choose to attend Han schools; (5) there are only a small number of *Han kao Min* students, that is, students of Han, Hui, or Manchu background with *Putonghua* as their mother tongue, who study in minority schools and sit examinations in minority languages.

Han schools teach courses in all subjects using *Putonghua* as well as one foreign language course (generally English). They do not offer courses of minority languages so their education is not truly bilingual. Seen from the point of view of the demands for language ability in the local employment market and the future development of Xinjiang, Han schools in minority areas (such as southern Xinjiang, inhabited mostly by Uyghur, and northern Xinjiang, inhabited mostly by Kazak people) should also offer a course of the minority language. Nevertheless, performance of foreign language (English) in the college entrance examination is used as a common metric, which demands students at Han schools learn the foreign language well. Considering that English may be more useful in their future careers, these Han students therefore prefer not to spend time and energy on learning minority languages. However, considering the instrumental function of language in a multi-ethnic environment, mastering a local minority language (Uyghur language or Kazak language) might be more favorable to the employment prospects and personal career paths of the Han students who do not plan to attend college, or to those who seldom use English even after graduation from college.

The bilingual education adopted by minority schools in Xinjiang can be classified, by and large, into three specific modes:

1   Traditional bilingual teaching mode
2   Bilingual education of particular minorities
3   New bilingual teaching mode

Traditional bilingual teaching mode

In this mode, priority is given to the teaching of the minority language, and a *Putonghua* course is added for 4–5 hours per week.

When publicizing the 1977 teaching plan, the Xinjiang Uyghur Autonomous Region government began to demand that *Putonghua* courses be taught from grade 3 in primary schools. In June, 1978, the Education Bureau of the Regional government issued *Opinions on Strengthening Putonghua Teaching in Minority Schools*. In 1980, the Education Bureau organized the compilation *Teaching Syllabus of Putonghua*, and recompiled the 7 volumes of *Putonghua* textbooks used by minority schools ranging from primary school to junior middle school.

The Autonomous Region government formulated in 1982 that minority students taking the college entrance examination should attend an extra examination in *Putonghua*, and their score should be taken into consideration. On January 9, 1984, the CCP Committee of the Autonomous Region stressed that *Putonghua* teaching must be strengthened. In December 28, 1984, it was claimed in the *Several Opinions about Implementing No.84 (3) Document of Autonomous Party Committee* by the Autonomous Region Bureau of Education that "the course of *Putonghua* is set up in our region from grade 3 of primary school to the last year of senior high school (Xinjiang Uyghur Autonomous Region Bureau of Education, 2007)."

The aforementioned government implemented measures have continuously strengthened the *Putonghua* teaching in minority schools, and the mode of teaching in these schools follows the prescribed outline for minority education. 2,830 schools (making up 74.9 percent of the total number of minority schools) adopted this mode in 2005. Now 1,189,456 students, making up 97 percent of the total number of minority students, and 135,584 professional teachers, making up 98.6

percent of the total number of professional in primary and minority middle schools follow this mode for *Putonghua* education in Xinjiang.

Even with these measures in place, there is still a significant difference in performance between students at Han schools and students at minority language schools, both on the performance on entrance examinations for senior high school of each subject and on the pass rate (Tables 3.3 and 3.4). This phenomenon provides evidence not only for a difference in language ability of students and teachers, but also for a difference between the professional abilities of teachers at Han schools and minority language schools. It also points to differences in the quality of textbooks, and the teaching surroundings. With set protocol for language education, it is apparent that to a large extent the discrepancies between minority school and Han school students are due to the historical failure to develop high quality minority education in Xinjiang. At present, however, we are facing the task of changing this situation. Therefore, modification and improvement of the traditional bilingual teaching mode is really needed under new social circumstances.

College education in Xinjiang has also been implementing this traditional bilingual teaching mode for a long period, and every year the Autonomous Region formulates and issues different policies for admitting students in accordance with the varying conditions of study and examination results for examinees who study in different types of schools and attend examinations in different languages. Upon entering college, minority students who graduated from minority high schools are more adept at *Putonghua* after a year of pre-college study program in college. Nevertheless, the four years of major study are carried out completely within "branches of minority languages," so the "*Putonghua* system" and "minority language system" remain virtually isolated from each other even though they occur on the same campus (Zuliyati Simayi, 2003). Minority students in minority language departments at universities generally have only a low level of *Putonghua*, and they take their specialized courses (such as computer science, biology, etc.) using minority languages. As a result, they can hardly communicate with people who do not speak their native language in study and work, which eventually leads to difficulties in obtaining employment after graduation. The field surveys we have made on the employment of college graduates in schools and universities in Xinjiang provide support for this assertion. From 2000 on, the government of the Xinjiang Autonomous Region began to emphasize *Putonghua* teaching in schools of different levels in order to address the employment difficulties of minority graduates.

Bilingual education of particular minorities

The main object of this mode is the small group of Xibe and Mongolian students who intermingle with Han. The Xinjiang government assigned the policy for this group that "native language education is the standard in primary schools with spoken *Putonghua* added. Then, *Putonghua* becomes the only teaching language in the period of middle and high schools."

Table 3.3 Statistics of *Putonghua* and Uyghur language student performance on high school entrance exam throughout Xinjiang (2002)

	Stat. Subjects		Politics	Language	Mathematics	Physics	Chemistry	English
Test paper I*	Average score	Uyghur	30.8	54.4	24.5	34.4	34.1	34.4
		Putonghua	57.3	59.1	58.8	66.8	68.0	56.8
	Pass rate (%)	Uyghur	2.7	42.7	3.0	6.0	9.1	17.3
		Putonghua	49.5	51.5	502	65.1	63.6	47.3
	Excellent rate** (%)	Uyghur	0.04	1.7	0.13	0.26	1.4	2.9
		Putonghua	2.2	1.7	13.8	18.7	31.6	14.3
Test paper II	Average score	Uyghur	17.3	29.6	7.6	12.6	12.9	13.7
		Putonghua	22.6	36.6	23.8	25.2	24.4	23.7
	Average score of students entering high school***	Uyghur	32.7	56.8	19.9	29.8	30.0	30.9
		Putonghua	52.9	66.1	53.2	59.5	58.4	52.5

Source: Xinjiang Autonomous Region Bureau of Education, 2007.

Notes

The sample size of this survey is: Uyghur students 13,126, Han students 43,419.

*The various subject portions of test paper I are worth 100 points, and it counts as a middle school graduation score. On test paper n, language and math are worth 70 points, and other subjects are worth 50 points.

**Scores higher than 85 points count as "Excellent".

***The score for entering high school is calculated by adding half of the score on test paper I to the score on test paper n for a combined total.

Table 3.4 Statistics of student performance in the high school entrance exam in Urumqi (2003–2005)

	Mathematics		Physics		Chemistry	
	Average score	Pass rate (%)	Average score	Pass rate (%)	Average score	Pass rate (%)
2003						
Putonghua	98.7	68.5	58.4	64.4	44.7	—
Uyghur language	74.7	35.8	49.3	42.5	39.5	65.7
Kazak language	53.1	13.3	36.0	12.8	32.9	44.3

	Mathematics		Physics		Chemistry	
	Average score	Pass rate (%)	Average score	Pass rate (%)	Average score	Pass rate (%)
2004						
Putonghua	89.7	56.1	61.7	71.9	44.0	77.9
Minority language	40.3	4.6	39.1	20.1	33.3	45.6
Bilingual	66.7	26.9	53.2	52.1	39.6	67.9
2005						
Putonghua	85.1	—	60.3	—	41.4	—
Minority language	42.6	—	43.3	—	30.8	—

Source: Xinjiang Automous Region Bureau of Education, 2007.

According to government statistics, there are four schools with a total of 1,271 students and 100 professional teachers of minority languages that adhered to this mode in 2005. As is illustrated by Table 3.2, there are four Xibe primary schools and four Xibe middle schools, 22 Mongolian primary schools and 23 Mongolian middle schools in Xinjiang. It is probable that the four Xibe primary schools adhere to the bilingual mode whereas a few Mongolian schools turn to bilingual teaching in middle school.

The total number of students in minority primary and middle schools in Xinjiang was 2.014 million in 2005, and the 1,271 students comprise just a minor portion of the total. Due to their small population, these students and their parents are generally subject to the application of total *Putonghua* teaching rather than native-language education. As a result of schools adopting this transitional mode at present out of convenience, the schools may be gradually transforming into Han schools.

New bilingual teaching mode

Under the forceful promotion of the Autonomous Region government, a new bilingual teaching mode has become prominent in the past years that is specifically manifested by the establishment of "bilingual experimental classes" in Han schools and minority language schools, and by the establishment of a few "bilingual schools" in areas with appropriate conditions. The configuration of the teaching languages in this mode is as follows: some of the courses, such as mathematics, physics, chemistry, biology, and English, are taught in *Putonghua*, while the rest, such as (native) language, ideology and morality, history, and geography, are taught in the native languages. The teaching effect and prospects of this teaching mode have become an attractive subject of research for insight into the present condition of minority education in Xinjiang.

Confronted with the serious pressure that minority university graduates have faced in finding employment in recent years, the government of the Xinjiang Autonomous Region has enhanced the implementation of *Putonghua* as the teaching language for minority education according to the following measures: the Autonomous Region government instituted a course of *Putonghua* study beginning in grade three of primary school, and pilot work began at Xinjiang University in 2002 to apply *Putonghua* to all courses except such particular courses as language, literature, and history of minorities.

It is also worth noting that in order to improve their *Putonghua* level, the attached middle schools of some normal universities and colleges in Xinjiang, such as Turpan, Changji, and Kashgar, are gradually adapting the mode of teaching all their courses in *Putonghua* complemented by the teaching of minority languages. Some other schools, namely the 18 bilingual classes in Zepu County of the Kashgar Prefecture, bilingual classes of Luntai County, and the bilingual classes in Kashgar No. 3 Primary School and No. 8 Primary School, are adopting the teaching mode of *Putonghua* plus Uyghur language course. In effect, the difference between this mode and that in Han schools only lies in the addition of a native language course. One of the prospects of this new mode is that the schools may develop a new mode of "trilingual schools," wherein courses of *Putonghua*, minority language, and English are opened simultaneously while all the other courses are taught in *Putonghua*.

The progression of the new bilingual teaching mode in primary and middle schools

In accordance with the program of strengthening study of *Putonghua* put forward by the Autonomous Region government, the Education Bureau of the Region issued and distributed the *Circular of Accrediting 10 Experimental Schools of "Min Han Jian Tong"*, (mastering both *Putonghua* and minority language) *in the Autonomous Region* on July 15, 1992, launching a bilingual teaching experiment wherein part of the courses, such as mathematics, physics, chemistry, and later English, would be taught in *Putonghua* while the rest of the courses would be taught in native languages in some previously Uyghur-, Mongolian-, and Kazak-language schools. By 1996, there were 26 such bilingual classes in minority schools throughout the Region, and the figure rose to 60 in 1997.

In January, 1999, *An Experimental Scheme for Bilingual Teaching in Minority Middle Schools of Xinjiang Uyghur Autonomous Region (For Discussion)* was issued by the Education Bureau of the Xinjiang Autonomous Region. On May 28 of the same year, the regional Education Bureau issued *Evaluating the Scheme for Bilingual Experimental Classes in Minority Middle Schools of the Autonomous Region (For Trial Implementation)* and *Teaching Plan of Reference Courses for Bilingual Experimental Classes in Minority Middle Schools of the Autonomous Region*. On November 30, 2000, the *Circular of Publicizing the List of Schools Opening Bilingual Experimental Classes* was issued. It listed 28 schools, including primary and middle schools, setting up 91 bilingual experimental classes. In April, 2004, the CCP Committee of the Xinjiang Autonomous Region issued its *Decision to Vigorously Promote Bilingual Teaching*. And, in 2005, it further issued *Opinions of Strengthening the Pre-school Bilingual Education for Minorities*, advancing the opening year of *Putonghua* learning from primary school to preschool and kindergarten, and emphasizing that "learning *Putonghua* should begin at an early age."

As is shown by statistics, 943 schools (making up 20 percent of the total number of minority schools) opened bilingual experimental classes in Xinjiang in 2004. 35,948 students (making up 2.9 percent of the total of enrolled minority students) and 1,847 professional teachers (accounting for 1.3 percent of the total number of professional teachers in minority primary and middle schools) participated in the new teaching mode of bilingual experimental classes. Another report indicates that of the minority teachers in Xinjiang in 2005, 8,487 took on bilingual teaching tasks, making up about 5.1 percent of the total number of professional minority teachers in the Region. If the two sets of figures are accurate, then it can only be said that a "great leap forward" was taken toward bilingual

Table 3.5 Statistics of the development of bilingual experimental classes in Xinjiang (September 2005)

	Number of bilingual classes	Number of students in bilingual classes	Percentage in total minority students	Number of bilingual minority teachers	Percentage in total minority teachers
Kindergarten (preschool class)	1,045	30,269	11.5	1,414	—
Primary school	2,074	60,886	2.8	3,098	3.6
Middle school	1,140	43,521	5.9	2,849	6.8
High school	246	10,462	6.9	1,126	12.1
Primary and secondary school total	3,460	114,869	4.9	7,073	5.1
Grand total	4,505	145,138	—	8,487	—

Source: As to the number of minority attendees, see Xinjiang Autonomous Region Bureau of Statistics (2006, p. 524).

education that year in Xinjiang. Additionally, another program plan indicates that the government will provide intensive training for 85,524 bilingual teachers under age 35 in Xinjiang from 2005–2011. This figure far exceeds the current data, which may be due to its taking into account the multi-subject teachers who teach *Putonghua* and mathematics, physics, and chemistry in bilingual classes. The above-mentioned figures could also stem from different definitions (say, whether they are professional teachers of bilingual classes or professional teachers plus multi-subject teachers who participate in the teaching of bilingual classes). Either way, it is clear that under the powerful impetus of the government of the Xinjiang Autonomous Region, bilingual education in recent years has been developing rapidly in the whole Region.

It can be seen from Table 3.5 that although the absolute figure of minority teachers engaged in bilingual education in the stage of senior high school remains small, it makes up the highest rate (12.1 percent) among minority teachers, which indicates, from another aspect, that the total number of minority teachers of minority high schools in Xinjiang is low. This may be due to the fact that the admission rate of students from middle schools to high schools in the minority school system is far lower than that in Han schools, and therefore the number of teachers is smaller in minority high schools than in Han high schools. The admission rates from junior middle to high schools of the three prefectures of Hotan, Kashgar, and Aksu, where Uyghur people settle, are just 10.9 percent, 18.7 percent, and 22.2 percent respectively. Other causes remain to be further investigated.

In accordance with statistics from the coverage of "teaching class," up to September, 2005, there were 4,505 bilingual classes in Xinjiang with 145,138 students, which were 4 times in the respective numbers in 2004 (when there were only 35,948 students in such classes). Another piece of news claims that there were 5,000 bilingual classes in Xinjiang with at least 150,000 minority attendees, making up 6.6 percent of the total number of minority students in the Region. It should be pointed out that even with bilingual classes in every quarter of Xinjiang developing rapidly under the powerful impetus of the government, the proportion of students of bilingual classes to total minority students in Xinjiang is still small.

Preferential policies implemented by the government to promote bilingual classes

To encourage the bilingual education in kindergarten, the Xinjiang Autonomous Region government has been implementing the following subsidies for attending children and teachers: (1) the meal allowance for children attending preschool bilingual classes is RMB 330 per person per year, and the textbook subsidy is RMB 20 per person per year; (2) the salary subsidy for teachers of preschool bilingual classes ranges from RMB 400–600 per month in some areas. According to the financial program of the Xinjiang Autonomous Region Education Bureau, the subsidy should include RMB 800 of monthly salary, RMB 78 of medical insurance, and RMB 84 of accumulation funds for housing. Together, the three sums amount to RMB 962 per month and RMB 11,544 per year. However, in our field survey in Shufu County of the Kashgar Prefecture, we found that the actual salary that teachers of bilingual classes in kindergarten received was only RMB 400 per month.

We conducted interviews with students and their parents as well as interviews with principals and teachers of bilingual classes in rural schools of Shufu County of the Kashgar Prefecture in August, 2007. Through these interviews we discovered that many rural families are willing to send their children to bilingual preschool classes for the following reasons: first, the meal allowance can cover their children's lunches; second, being aware that *Putonghua* is of great use in studying and future employment, the parents are willing to send their children to learn *Putonghua*; third, parents may arrange their time freely without taking care of the children when they attend the preschool classes.

Some statistics indicate that 81,000 preschool children who attended bilingual classes enjoyed meal allowance and free textbooks, and altogether 1,296 bilingual teachers enjoyed salary subsidies in 2006 in Xinjiang. If this figure is valid, then it demonstrates that the number of preschool children who attended bilingual classes in 2006 had increased by 2.7 times since 2005 and 29.4 percent of the total number of preschool minority children attend such classes.

According to the Xinjiang Education Bureau, by 2012, they plan to have over 85 percent of minority preschool children enroll in bilingual education. Raising the proportion of minority attendees of bilingual preschool classes from 29 percent to 85 percent within 6 years is clearly an ambitious goal. The key to realizing this program is the rapid training of qualified minority teachers of bilingual preschool classes. For that reason, the Education Bureau claims that within the five years from 2007 to 2011, 37,371 qualified preschool bilingual teachers are needed in the Xinjiang Autonomous Region.

The government also offers certain subsidies to teachers who teach in primary and middle school bilingual classes. According to the Education Bureau's program, graduates recruited by the special quota for bilingual teaching will be offered a lump sum of RMB 3,000 as a settlement allowance, and the wage scale for 4-year university graduates is RMB 1,848 per month. The yearly average budget of each bilingual teacher is RMB 22,500 including the wage, social security funds (unemployment, medical care, pension), and the "13th month" bonus wage.

Due to the difficulty of implementing bilingual education in southern Xinjiang where Uyghur consisted of over 90 percent of local population, the government of the Region also decided to set up a special establishment of bilingual teachers by adding an additional 10 percent (i.e., 8,706) to the present total number of teachers there. The government will make sure that the establishment will be gradually put in place in order from 2007–2012. To further implement bilingual classes, the government of the Region must enlarge the establishment of teachers and increase the subsidies of teachers and the operational expenses. Meanwhile, a large portion of the budget has been spent on training bilingual teachers on the job.

The imbalance in developing bilingual experimental classes between different areas

Among the 15 cities and prefectures (Table 3.6) in Xinjiang, bilingual experimental classes have developed in an unbalanced pattern, which is directly correlated to the ethnic structure of population and school-age children in each area. As can be seen from the column on the right side of Table 3.6, most bilingual students are located in the prefectures of Ili, Kashgar, Aksu, and Hotan, where most of the Uyghur and Kazak population are settled. The average number of students in a bilingual class is 29 both in preschools and in primary schools, 38 in middle schools, and 42.5 in high schools.

It can roughly be seen from Table 3.6 that each area of Xinjiang has its respective population characteristics, and that differences also exist between their educational backgrounds and ranks of teachers. The subordinate county of Ili Prefecture is the most prominent regarding the vigor and performance of implementing bilingual experimental classes and, as does Kashgar Prefecture, it emphasizes the primary school stage. Aksu Prefecture, on the other hand, attaches importance to the development of bilingual education in the stages of preschool and primary school, having slowly developing bilingual classes in middle school and high school stage. Comparatively, Hotan Prefecture's bilingual education is more prominent in the number of classes and attendees in middle schools. Since the basic bilingual education in the primary school stage in Hotan Prefecture is relatively weak, it remains to be investigated how the bilingual teaching in the junior middle schools manages to address the students' problems with listening comprehension.

Table 3.6 Bilingual classes and students in different areas of Xinjiang (October 2005)

Area/prefecture/city	Preschool		Primary school		Middle school		High school		Total	
	Class	Student	Class	Student	Class	Student	Class	Student	Class	Student
Urumqi City	0	0	119	3,650	50	2,142	12	641	181	6,433
Karamay City	0	0	18	443	2	91	3	116	23	650
Shihezi City	4	71	26	386	6	163	3	95	39	715
Turpan Prefecture	22	706	38	1,338	62	2,290	19	873	141	5,207
Hami Prefecture	0	0	15	536	26	974	10	350	51	1,860
Changji Hui Autonomous Prefecture	46	499	194	4,488	127	2,472	21	753	388	S212
Ili Kazakh Subordinate County	314	10,096	451	13,422	134	5,236	63	2,733	962	31,487
Tacheng Prefecture	26	180	83	1,924	39	1,297	21	649	169	4,050
Altay Prefecture	31	801	109	2,319	95	3,107	11	455	246	6,682
Bortala Mongol Autonomous Prefecture	52	1,162	146	1,910	38	868	3	106	239	4,046
Bayin'gholin Mongol Autonomous Prefecture	107	1,886	90	1,836	46	1,793	15	702	258	6,217
Aksu Prefecture	176	6,265	376	12,312	59	2,817	18	745	629	22,139
Kizilu Kirghiz Autonomous Prefecture	0	0	7	306	14	529	2	135	23	970
Kashgar Prefecture	129	6,265	376	12,312	59	2,817	18	745	629	22,139
Hotan Prefecture	138	4,595	64	2,880	248	11,072	14	700	464	19,247
Total	1,045	30,269	2,074	60,886	1,140	43,521	246	10,462	4,505	145,138

Source: Xinjiang Uyghur Autonomous Bureau of Education (2007).

The small Han population and the lack of *Putonghua* language surroundings in southern Xinjiang make bilingual education more important in that area. Accordingly, the difficulties of bilingual education in the area are greater. The extent of the difficulties can be seen in the fact that the bilingual classes in primary and middle schools of Hotan Prefecture only account for 2 percent of the total classes of local minority schools.

About the development of *Min kao Han*

Along with the continuous progress of system reform as well as the "opening up" and rapid development of the Chinese economy, the industrial structure and personal mobility in Xinjiang also began to enter a new era. The strategy of Western Development issued by the central government in 2000 brought into force a large number of infrastructure projects in Xinjiang that further promoted the rapid development of manufacturing, transportation, communication, and service industries. As a result, *Putonghua* has become, step by step, the most important and the most universal working language for communication throughout Xinjiang, especially in urban areas. The bilingual education advanced to strengthen *Putonghua* also aims to help minority graduates enter the employment market with better prospects.

In addition to giving an advantage in the employment market, another impetus for minority students to attend Han schools is the fact that students of *Min kao Han* have a wider range of choices than those of *Min kao Min* when they apply for colleges and universities, and therefore the possibility of their being admitted increases accordingly. Table 3.7 shows the enrollment statistics of university education in Xinjiang in the period of 1977–1997, which demonstrate that the proportion of Xinjiang students admitted to universities in other provinces has increased from 25 percent in 1977 to 50.8 percent in 1997. In addition, it is clearly defined by the government of the Xinjiang Autonomous Region that of those who are admitted by universities in other provinces, minority students should make up no less than 50 percent. The superiority that students of *Min kao Han* have in college entrance examination can be seen via the connection between these two proportions.

While the cutoff for *Min kao Min* students to qualify for admission is lower than that of *Min kao Han*, students of *Min kao Min* will by no means be admitted to many ordinary universities of other provinces, which means these students face greater constraint on their application for the college entrance examination and the following admission.

The application constraints that universities outside Xinjiang put on language conditions drive more and more minority students to choose to enter Han schools directly and, in doing so, become *Min kao Han* students. As is indicated by the statistics of the Education Bureau of Xinjiang, during the period of 1998–2000, the number of students of "other ethnic groups" (that is, minority students who are not Han, Hui, or Manchu, the main body of which being Uyghur, Kazak,

Table 3.7 The situation of enrollment in institutions of higher education for students from Xinjiang (1977–1997)

Year	Enrollment of universities and colleges						Number of applicants	Percentage admitted
	Total number	%	Study in Xinjiang	%	Study in other provinces	%		
1977	3,916	100.0	2,938	75.0	978	25.0	109,577	3.6
1978	4,930	100.0	3,816	77.4	1,114	22.6	66,504	7.4
1979	4,266	100.0	3,224	75.6	1,041	24.4	54,728	7.7
1980	4,807	100.0	3,346	69.6	1,461	30.4	60,370	7.9
1981	4,409	100.0	3,063	69.5	1,346	30.5	67,114	6.6
1982	5,568	100.0	3,795	68.2	1,771	31.8	69,504	8.0

Year	Enrollment of universities and colleges						Number of applicants	Percentage admitted
	Total number	%	Study in Xinjiang	%	Study in other provinces	%		
1983	7,761	100.0	4,967	64.0	2,794	36.0	77,621	10.0
1984	10,273	100.0	5,653	55.0	3,887	45.0	77,985	13.2
1985	12,000	100.0	6,741	56.2	5,259	43.8	69,673	17.2
1986	11,785	100.0	6,458	54.8	5,327	45.2	58,585	17.5
1987	12,939	100.0	7,281	56.3	5,658	43.7	73,947	17.5
1988	14,690	100.0	9,211	62.7	5,479	37.3	85,718	17.1
1989	13,405	100.0	6,903	51.5	6,502	48.5	86,499	15.5
1990	12,965	100.0	6,577	50.7	6,388	49.3	81,062	16.0
1991	12,791	100.0	6,480	50.7	6,374	49.3	79,000	16.2
1992	17,069	100.0	9,318	54.6	7,751	45.4	84,518	20.2
1993	20,143	100.0	10,475	52.0	9,668	48.0	78,675	25.6
1994	17,839	100.0	9,000	50.5	8,839	49.5	60,119	29.6
1995	17,814	100.0	9,200	51.6	8,614	48.4	54,561	32.6
1996	17,737	100.0	9,260	52.2	8,477	47.8	55,360	32.0
1997	19,299	100.0	9,496	49.2	9,803	50.8	52,381	36.8

Source: Xinjiang Uyghur Autonomous Region Bureau of Education (1998, pp. 595–596).

Kirgiz, Mongolian, students) increases every year in Han schools of different levels. During these three years, the population of students of "other ethnic groups" (mainly Uyghur and Kazak) has increased by 19 percent in primary schools, 67.7 percent in junior middle schools, and two times in senior high schools (Table 3.8). The proportion of students of "other ethnic groups" compared to that of total minority students (excluding students of Hui and Manchu) also rises every year. Within the last two years mentioned above, the proportion of students of "other ethnic groups" compared with that of total corresponding minority students has increased from 3.5 percent to 4.2 percent in primary schools, from 3.5 percent to 4.8 percent in middle schools, and from 5.0 percent to 9.5 percent in senior high schools.

This increasing trend has been sustained since 2000. According to the statistics, 79,000 *Min kao Han* students attended Han primary and middle schools in 2000. The figure increased to 131,000 in 2005, a 66 percent rate of increase over five years. As fast as it increases, the number of *Min kao Han* students still accounts only for a small proportion of total minority students. In 2005, *Min kao Han* students only made up 5.8 percent of the total minority attendees of primary and middle schools (2.262 million).

The rate of increase of the number of *Min kao Han* students is objectively constrained by the enrollment limitations of Han schools. The main problem is that most parents who would send their children to Han schools are unable to achieve their wish. In southern Xinjiang, Han kindergartens and primary schools have a considerable number of Uyghur students enrolled. Take Moyu County in Hotan Prefecture, for example: Uyghur children there make up 75 percent of the Han kindergartens and 50 percent of primary Han schools. The dean of the Kashgar Education College explains that 70 percent of the students in local Han schools are Uyghur children. In Hotan No. 1 Primary School (a Han school), Uyghur students make up 11 percent of grade 6, whereas in grade 1, Uyghur students account for 30 percent of the class. Of the first year students in Han primary schools in the fall of 2004 in Aksu Prefecture, 25.6 percent were minority students. In Kashgar city, 30 percent of the students in Han schools are Uyghur children. In Zepu County, there were 2,200 Uyghur attendees, accounting for 6.5 percent of the total minority students. Due to the small numbers and limited capacity of Han kindergartens and Han schools in minority-inhabited areas, many school-age minority children are objectively unable to attend Han schools.

Considering the developing trend of more *Min kao Han* students, some contend that the bilingual experimental class marks a macro level transition from the present mode of "teaching in native language complemented with *Putonghua*" to that of "teaching in *Putonghua* complemented with native language." When analyzing some cases, others contest that parents send their children to bilingual experimental classes due to their failure to enter the Han schools, and that they do so with the aim of helping their children enter Han schools by means of such a "transition" as bilingual experimental classes can facilitate. When *Nei gao ban* (special classes of Xinjiang minority students in the best high schools of Han regions, sponsored by the central government) attracted the particular attention

Table 3.8 Proportion of Min kao Han students in Han schools

Year	School	Han students		Hui and Manchu students		Other minorities students		Total number of students in Han schools		Minority student	Proportion of Min kao Han students to the total number of minority students*
		Number	%	Number	%	Number	%	Number	%	Total number of minority students in minority schools	
1998	Primary school	758,792	81.4	114,850	12.3	58,580	6.3	932,222	100.0	1,611,691	3.5
	Middle school	250,696	81.4	39,840	12.9	17,584	5.7	308,120	100.0	479,906	3.5
	High school	95,904	91.0	5,153	49	4,290	4.1	105,347	100.0	80,809	5.0
1909	Primary school	764,359	81.4	111,406	11.9	63,022	6.7	938,787	100.0	1,613,756	3.8
	Middle school	271,129	80.6	42,368	12.6	23,010	6.8	336,507	100.0	554,363	4.0
	High school	99,626	88.3	6,247	5.5	6,980	6.2	112,853	100.0	81,726	7.9
2000	Primary school	762,927	81.3	105,745	11.3	69,864	7.4	938,536	100.0	1,589,239	4.2
	Middle school	301,550	80.1	42,027	11.3	29,489	7.9	373,066	100.0	584,356	4.8
	High school	106,796	88.5	5,283	4.4	8,614	7.1	120,693	100.0	81,644	9.5

Source: Calculated in accordance with Statistical Materials of Education in Xinjiang compiled by the Xinjiang Uyghur Autonomous Region Bureau of Education.

Note: * The proportion of the Min kao Han students (the minority students other than Hui and Machu, mainly Uyghur and Kazak, in Han schools) in the total of Uyghur/Kazak students in both minority schools and Han schools.

of many minority parents, a bilingual class became favored as the efficient path to *Nei gao ban*. During our interviews with Uyghur teachers of primary and middle schools, some still assert that bilingual education is an ideal local education mode for its ability to give consideration to the learning of both *Putonghua* and native languages. The prospect of bilingual experimental classes in Xinjiang still needs to be explored and investigated in terms of future teaching practices and its effect on the employment market.

The current situation of bilingual education in the Kashgar Prefecture

In a subject investigation of bilingual education in the Kashgar Prefecture of southern Xinjiang conducted in August, 2007, we found that the bilingual education there developed at a considerably high speed. Comparing our research with the statistics from October, 2005 (Table 3.9), we find that within less than two years, the number of attendees of preschool bilingual classes in the Kashgar Prefecture increased by 11.8 times from 4,008 to 47,238; the contemporary number of bilingual classes in primary and middle schools has also increased by 1.7 times from 563 to 1,031.

Preschool bilingual classes

The planned enrollment figure and number of recruited teachers of preschool bilingual classes in each county must be reported to the Region for accreditation and implementation due to the demand that the meal allowance of students and wages of teachers should be allocated by the Regional Financial Bureau. For example, 2,182 children aged 5-years-old were enrolled in preschool bilingual classes in 2006 in Shufu County (of these 2,182 children, 1,466 were enrolled in township-level kindergartens and 716 in village-level kindergartens). Each student was allocated RMB 20 for textbooks per year and RMB 1.5 for meal allowance per day (which was later increased to RMB 2 by the county via the local budget). As prescribed by the Region government, one teacher was staffed to every 40 children, and the Autonomous Region was responsible for their wages

Table 3.9 The development of bilingual education in the Kashgar Prefecture

Stat. time	Preschool		Primary school		Middle school		High school		Primary and secondary schools combined	
	Class	Student	Class	Student	Class	Student	Class	Student	Class	Student
Oct. 2005	129	4,008	338	13,136	194	8,670	31	1,409	563	23,215
May 2007	697	47,328	—	—	—	—	—	—	1,031	39,293

Source: *Educational Information of Kashgar*, No. 21 (May 9, 2007).

(at this time the actual wage was RMB 400 per month). Many counties in southern Xinjiang are officially a "state-level poverty-stricken county," in which the local government is confronted with large budget deficits, so the bilingual education at the basic level is totally unable to develop without the support of a special budget from the Autonomous Region.

The duration of a preschool bilingual class is two years: In grade one, 5-year-old children are enrolled. The teaching focuses on oral practice of *Putonghua* and learning simple *Putonghua* characters. The demands for passing grade one are as follows: "being able to recite 10–20 *Putonghua* nursery songs, introduce himself/herself to others simply, pronounce the main body parts in *Putonghua*, and recognize the Arabic for numbers 1–10." In grade two, more courses begin. Specifically: "*pinyin* (*Putonghua* alphabet), mathematics, *Putonghua* (dialogue, talking, telling tales, and reading nursery songs and children's ballads), music (learning to sing in *Putonghua*), fine arts, physical exercise, and behavioral norms." Children at this level have four classes every day with 30 minutes for each class; appropriate outdoor games are also arranged. Accordingly, students of preschool bilingual classes "should be able to understand simple *Putonghua* daily speech, speak *Putonghua* for simple daily communication, read *pinyin* and Chinese characters that have been learned, learn to add and subtract within 10, and precisely recognize Arabic numbers within 100 and pronounce them in *Putonghua*" (*Opinions of Promoting Rural Pre-school Bilingual Education of Shufu County, May, 2006*).

In the Kashgar Prefecture, the Han population only accounts for 8.5 percent of the total and mainly settles in urban areas of Kashgar. In some counties (such as Shufu, Jiashi, Yingjisha), the Han population makes up less than 2 percent of the total and mainly settles in the county town areas. In villages of Shufu and Yingjisha counties, Han population only makes up 0.3–0.5 percent of the total according to the statistics of the town/*xiang*.

Under such circumstances, where few or no Han surroundings exist, the *Putonghua* ability of teachers becomes an important factor in assuring the teaching quality. In selecting teachers for Shufu County's preschool bilingual classes, teachers are chosen primarily for their *Putonghua* abilities:

> The first choice for teachers are those who were *Min kao Han* students or Han teachers recruited in the last two years; the second choices are those at work in primary schools who have a certain *Putonghua* teaching ability and graduated from normal schools for kindergarten who are suitable for preschool bilingual teaching; the third choice goes to job-awaiting graduates who are qualified for teaching in kindergarten and have reached the standard level of *Putonghua*.
>
> (Opinions of Promoting Rural Pre-school Bilingual Education of Shufu County, May, 2006)

We visited the bilingual kindergarten in Ayagemangan Xiang, in Shufu County. The 35-year-old teacher who accompanied us on visits to students' homes was a Uyghur teacher with a *Min kao Han* background. She was recruited as a preschool teacher in 2006 after being laid off when the textile plant she worked went bankrupt. She began to work in that plant after graduating from middle school. Kindergarten teachers with a *Min kao Han* background like her are scarce even in the whole county because many ordinary bilingual kindergartens have difficulties employing qualified teachers. A tentative solution adopted by Shufu County is to arrange officials and staff of the institutions under the county government and town officials to town and village bilingual kindergartens to teach in a rotational period of 4 months. In reading the government documents of this county, we find an appendix with the list of names of the officials who will be sent to kindergartens in the next circulation: 12 from county institutions (all of them are Uyghur officials of *Min kao Han*) and 13 from town/*xiang* governments (10 Han, 1 Hui, 1 Xibe, and 1 Uyghur).

Up to July, 2007, there were 73 bilingual kindergartens with 4,395 attendees and 56 bilingual teachers in this county, but "most teachers fail to reach the required standard *Putonghua* level, have poor oral ability in *Putonghua*, and can only organize teaching by means of teaching CDs" (according to summaries of the Bureau of Education of the county). As a result, it becomes a measure of great importance to send county-level and town/*xiang*-level officials to support teaching and enhance education in bilingual. There are also 56 preschool bilingual classes attached to primary schools, with 1,973 attendees in Shufu County. A generally adopted method there is to attach preschool bilingual classes to primary schools by taking advantage of existing teaching conditions and teaching staff.

In total there are 20,888 children aged from 3–6 in this county, 29.3 percent having received a bilingual preschool education. Of those, 5,048 are 6 years old and 43.1 percent of them receive a bilingual education. Some success has been obtained through this coverage of bilingual education, which can be seen in that Uyghur children in preschool classes we interviewed have been able to communicate with us in simple *Putonghua*.

Bilingual experimental classes in primary school

Since 2005, three teaching modes have been adopted by primary schools in Shufu County: (1) the *Min kao Han* mode, in which *Putonghua* is totally used in classes to teach minority pupils in the county's No. 2 Primary School (Han school); (2) in minority primary schools in county town and suburbs, *Putonghua* is used beginning in grade 1 in courses of sciences and native language is used in the rest of the courses; gradually this mode will develop into a state wherein *Putonghua* is used in all the courses but native language course; and (3) in all rural primary schools, *Putonghua* is used beginning in grade 3 in courses of sciences, and native language is used in the rest of the courses.

The county government has drawn up a program schedule for implementing bilingual teaching for each year from 2005 to 2012. The County Bureau of Education plans to completely implement bilingual teaching to pupils beginning in grade 3 in rural schools by 2011, and to implement bilingual teaching to students of middle schools beginning in grade one by 2012 (*Opinions of Bilingual Teaching in Shufu County*).

From 2007 on, the mode of *Min kao Han* in Han primary schools of Shufu has not changed, whereas the education mode of township and rural primary schools has been adjusted to a certain extent as follows:

1   In the four minority primary schools on township as well as suburbs, three courses (*Putonghua*, mathematics, and moral norms and life) are taught in *Putonghua* in grade one and two, and four courses (Uyghur language, arts, physical education, and "beautiful Xinjiang") are taught in Uyghur language. In grade three, six courses (the above-mentioned three courses plus sciences, Xinjiang comprehensive practical activities, and information technology) are taught in *Putonghua* while four courses (the same as above) are taught in Uyghur language.

2   In the bilingual classes of the nine central primary schools of township as well as the bilingual classes of all village-level primary schools of the whole county, two courses (*Putonghua*, and mathematics) are taught in *Putonghua* with the rest in Uyghur language in grade one and two. In grade three, four courses *Putonghua*, mathematics, sciences, and information technology) are taught in *Putonghua* with the rest in Uyghur language.

3   In common classes of rural minority primary schools, *Putonghua* continues to begin being used in science courses from grade three while other courses are all taught in native language.

This new adjustment further enhances *Putonghua* teaching in grades one and two of primary school. Looking at these actual trends, it is clear that developing bilingual education is the general policy advanced by the Xinjiang government. Nevertheless, each prefecture and even each county will make various specific programming choices, teaching modes, and implementation methods to take steps toward bilingual education in local schools in accordance with their practical conditions (i.e., language surroundings and conditions of teaching staff).

In 2007, among primary schools of Shufu County, there were 23 bilingual classes with 900 students in grade one, and eight bilingual classes with 262 pupils in grade two. Altogether there were 1,162 attendees of bilingual classes, making up 3.1 percent of the total primary school students in the county. Bilingual education in Xinjiang originally started in middle schools.

The original motive for beginning bilingual education at that stage was that minority graduates from colleges and universities were generally confronted with problems in employment due to their low level of *Putonghua*; it was hoped that by improving the *Putonghua* level of minority middle school students, those students would be compelled to study their specialized college courses in *Putonghua* so as to improve their employment conditions. In 1999, the Xinjiang Education Bureau planned to expand bilingual experimental classes in middle schools. In practice, it was then found that the bilingual classes in middle schools had no foundation when pupils' *Putonghua* was poor in the stage of primary school. In response, primary schools were added to "the name list of bilingual experimental schools" in 2000. Afterwards, it was found that language teaching would be more effective if bilingual education started from kindergarten; thus, from 2005 on, the Autonomous Region issued special documents for bilingual preschool education and offered special budget support accordingly.

Bilingual experimental classes in middle schools

In January, 1999, goals for the teaching of bilingual classes were issued as *Experimental Scheme of Bilingual Teaching in Minority Middle Schools of Xinjiang Uyghur Autonomous Region (For Trial Implementation)*. These goals were as follows: (1) "Graduates from senior high schools should reach a *Putonghua* level higher than level six of HSK (The *Hanyu Shuiping Kaoshi*, the official test of *Putonghua* ability)"; (2) "Strengthen the teaching of sciences, so that students' performance of mathematics, physics, and chemistry reach or approach the average performance of students in Han schools"; (3) "Ensure students' learning and mastering of their native languages such that their level of native language should not be lower than that of students in non-bilingual experimental classes of the same grade"; (4) "Students should have certain English ability so as to receive higher education more smoothly after entering university."

The *Scheme* issued specific regulations as to the enrollment methods of bilingual classes (with testing in the areas of spoken *Putonghua*, written Chinese, and mathematics), textbooks (compiled by the Autonomous Region for use in both *Putonghua* courses and native language courses, the rest adopt the teaching materials of existent compulsive education published by People's Education Press, and the English course is opened from grade one in middle school, making use of the universal textbooks in Han schools), the arrangement of periods of each subject, and testing methods. To encourage teachers to actively participate in bilingual teaching, the *Scheme* presents the favorable workload accounting method. The workload of the teachers in bilingual classes is calculated at the rate of 1.5 to 1 compared with that of the teachers in Uyghur classes. Nevertheless, during the meetings with teachers in both Kashgar City and Shufu County, teachers reported to us that due to the financial difficulty of the area, the Autonomous Region offered policy without allocating the budget, so this preferential policy failed to be effectively implemented.

2006 witnessed the commencement of establishing bilingual classes in 20 percent of rural middle schools in Shufu County. In that year, 36 bilingual classes were set up in grade one of junior middle school, 6 in grade two, and 3 in grade three for a total of 1,972 students. At the same time, three bilingual classes were set up in grade one of high school. As of 2007 in the middle schools of this county, 45 bilingual classes with a total of 1,574 students have been set up in grade one, 6 in grade two with 266 students, and 3 in grade three with 133 students. The total number of attendees of bilingual classes was 1,973, accounting for 8.7 percent of students in middle schools in the county. In addition, one bilingual class with 47 students was set up in grade one of high school and two were set up in grade two with 64 students. Hence the total number of students in bilingual classes of high schools was 111, making up 2.9 percent of current students of the county. The accelerated speed of advancing measures toward bilingual education can thus be seen in accordance with the numbers of classes and students in different grades in the middle schools.

Meanwhile, according to the advocacy of the Region, Shufu County promoted the combination of minority and Han schools, and as a result combined No. 2 Middle School (Han school) and No. 4 Middle School (Uyghur school) in 2007. By this measure, teachers in the original Han schools may teach *Putonghua* to bilingual classes, which may solve the problem of the shortage of qualified teachers in *Putonghua* in the original minority schools, and at the same time Uyghur students in bilingual classes may also have the opportunity to communicate more effectively with Han students on the same campus, which will improve their *Putonghua* level. The government of the Autonomous Region promotes the "combination of Han schools and minority language schools" in the hope of offering campus surroundings for minority students to practice *Putonghua*.

In response to the obvious differences between middle schools in towns and rural areas in terms of school conditions and quality of teaching staff, the running modes of bilingual classes in middle schools in Shufu County are classified into two types just like those in primary schools: (1) in the three middle schools in county town, the seven courses (mathematics, physics, chemistry, biology, information technology, *Putonghua*, and English) are taught in *Putonghua*; other courses are taught in Uyghur language; (2) in rural middle schools, a total of six courses (mathematics, physics, chemistry, biology, information technology and *Putonghua*) are taught in *Putonghua* while the rest are taught in Uyghur language. In theory, the only difference lies in the fact that English in rural middle schools is taught by means of students' native language. In reality, however, we discovered that due to the lack of qualified teaching staff in rural schools, the six regulated courses that should be taught in *Putonghua* are actually taught in the native language.

When we conducted interviews in Kashgar No. 1 Middle School (a Uyghur school), the Uyghur teachers presented their opinions about teaching science in *Putonghua*, based on their experiences. Take, for example, the 12 bilingual classes set up in 2007 in this school: there were three bilingual classes in each grade of the junior middle school sector and one in each grade of the senior high sector. The teachers thought that Han teachers did not understand Uyghur language and that Uyghur students generally had low *Putonghua* levels, both factors together led to the difficulties in communication between teachers and students, notably on the definitions of scientific terminology and formulas. When students have difficulty making their questions clearly understood and teachers have the same problem with explanations, the learning effect and performance of students naturally decline. It is said that only four students passed the physics exam in one class. Having recruited 10 Han teachers in succession, the school failed to keep any of them. The Uyghur teachers believe that an effective approach would be to send teachers with strong Uyghur language skills and a solid foundation of *Min kao Han* education background to receive training in *Putonghua* teaching. These teachers said that they use Chinese textbooks for the courses, teach mainly in *Putonghua* in class, and supplement explanations by means of Uyghur language. In this way, students' performance on mathematics, physics, and chemistry would be greatly improved.

Of the existing 25 teachers of bilingual classes in this school, with the exception of one Hui teacher and one Han teacher who teach *Putonghua* (both of them graduated with a major in Uyghur language), the rest are all Uyghur teachers with *Min kao Han* backgrounds. Those teachers usually studied in Han schools at an early age and some even graduated with science majors from universities in Han regions. Since they studied specialized science majors in *Putonghua* themselves, so they seldom encounter problems with *Putonghua* teaching, nor do they have difficulty explaining science textbooks printed in Chinese to Uyghur students; therefore communication between them and students is easy and effective.

As was introduced by the deputy director of teaching affairs at this school, the newly enrolled students of junior middle school just started to know *Putonghua* at grade three in primary schools. They know little about *Putonghua* words, and are unable to make sentences; one-third of them cannot write their names in Chinese characters; and 70 percent of them claim that they can understand nothing in class. Facing the actuality that freshmen have low *Putonghua* levels, the school took the approach of gradually increasing the proportion of *Putonghua* in teaching by increments; in grade one of junior middle sector, 50 percent of teaching using *Putonghua* in class while the other 50 percent was taught in Uyghur language; in grade two, 70 percent using *Putonghua* and 30 percent Uyghur language; in grade three, the proportion turned to 80–90 percent *Putonghua* to 10–20 percent Uyghur language. Under these conditions of gradual transition, better effects may be obtained on both the linguistic and psychological adaptation of students. Although at present the government dictates that no Uyghur language is allowed in bilingual classes, this rigidity can neither be effectively realized, nor would the effect be practical. The implementation of these regulations should take a matter-of-fact approach to the problem of bilingual education.

According to the principal of Shufu Experimental Middle School, only those Uyghur students who fail to enter the Han No. 2 Middle attend bilingual classes there. With their low *Putonghua* levels, these students negatively influence the teaching quality of the bilingual classes. As was stated by the Han teachers in Kashgar Experimental Middle School, Uyghur students generally felt difficulties in their studies in the bilingual classes due to their low *Putonghua* levels. 95 percent of students at grade three in middle sector failed to pass science exams, and the language barrier in their studies would not be overcome until they reached grade three of senior high sector.

Han schools have strong teaching staffs and supportive *Putonghua* environment, so setting up bilingual classes in Han schools is superior to a certain degree for improving students' *Putonghua* levels. There are also obvious advantages to setting up bilingual classes in minority schools where teachers have a good knowledge of minority languages and can help students with low Putonghua ability to better understand the science lessons. In summation, presumably the best place for bilingual classes is the combined Han and minority schools. Nevertheless, in southern Xinjiang, where few Han people settle, Han schools are only located in the county seat, so most rural schools cannot operate on this condition.

Problems reflected in the practice of bilingual education in the Kashgar Prefecture

How to develop bilingual experimental classes

First, to develop bilingual classes, basic conditions must be met and the unrealistic goals of the "administrative achievement project" may not work. The first condition is having a certain number of qualified teachers who have mastered two languages and are familiar with the methods and techniques of bilingual teaching. The second condition is that the enrolled students (according to grade) must have the basic *Putonghua* ability necessary to sit in class and communicate with teachers. In addition, the other conditions of running a school, such as classroom buildings, library, equipment, laboratories, and operating budget, must be satisfied. In some bilingual classes set up in minority schools, the conditions have yet to mature. After graduation from the middle school, several ordinary classes in Kashgar No. 6 Middle School have been converted directly into bilingual classes in the senior high sector. The students in these classes had no previous language base for studying science in *Putonghua*, so the effect was predictably negative.

Of the bilingual class students in the senior high sector of Kashgar Experimental Middle School, 80 percent began to study their specialized courses with *Putonghua* as the language of instruction from grade one of junior middle sector, and 20 percent beginning to study these courses in *Putonghua* from grade one of senior high sector. The unbalanced *Putonghua* levels within the same class led to difficulties in teaching. To avoid this problem, when enrolling students for bilingual classes the school should present *Putonghua* exams with identical papers and correcting demands as strict criteria in order to formulate the size of the class according to the number of qualified students.

When bilingual classes were first established in the Kashgar prefecture, the exam selection system led to a perfect effect. In recent years, though, school enrollment was implemented in accordance with school district rather than exam performance, which resulted in the failure to assure the quality of students and the decline of effective teaching. A teacher in Shufu No. 4 Middle School contends,

> The opposite effect would result if bilingual education were carried out without taking into account the *Putonghua* ability and learning performance of students. To students with very poor foundation in *Putonghua*, bilingual class is hell, so they hate their courses. Therefore, bilingual education should be directed to students above the average performance.

Considering the *experimental* nature of bilingual experimental classes, it is suggested that the exam selection system be resumed so as to control the quality of students. Qualified teachers are in great demand since the establishment of many bilingual classes. When the Experimental Middle School was rebuilt, the chief of the County Bureau of Education explained, "20 or so teachers were selected from more than 300 teachers who applied, but the schools remain unable to find enough qualified teachers." Only 9.6 percent of the Uyghur teachers have once attended bilingual training programs. The principal of Kashgar No. 27 Middle School believes that teachers graduating from *Min kao Han* or *Han kao Min* adapt to bilingual teaching best. Nonetheless, there are too few graduates of *Min kao Han* in southern Xinjiang to satisfy the needs of middle schools there.

Second, the demand that no minority language should be used in science courses in bilingual class is one of the indicators for teaching evaluation. Nevertheless, in the meetings many teachers pointed out that Uyghur language should be used to supplement the explanation of major content and terminology when most students have a low *Putonghua* capacity and there are no enough qualified teachers for bilingual education. Also, in the teaching of mathematics, physics, and chemistry, both the improvement of *Putonghua* ability and the learning of knowledge of these subjects should be taken into consideration. The approach presented by Kashgar No. 1 Middle School, namely increasing the proportion of *Putonghua* teaching in science classes according to different grades, deserves reference. It has been argued that in terms of the application of *Putonghua* in bilingual classes, taking a realistic and practical approach and seeking positive results are the top priority.

Third, along with the overall development of bilingual teaching, a learning series will be gradually set up, so that after graduating from preschool bilingual class, the student will enter bilingual classes in primary school before further attending the bilingual classes in middle and high schools successively. When students have built a solid foundation of language learning, the effect of bilingual classes should visibly improve. With the present model of forcefully promoting the establishing bilingual classes simultaneously in schools of different levels and directly transferring minority students from the normal classes at lower grades into bilingual classes in higher grades, this can only act as a temporary special measure during transitional period.

Considering the present employment situation, as long as the attendees in schools are transferred into bilingual experimental classes, their *Putonghua* level will be more or less improved, which may have positive consequences on their employment prospects. As the deputy Director of the Bureau of Labor and Employment of the Kashgar Prefecture said, "Advancing bilingual classes has marked effects on solving problems of unemployment. Speaking even a little *Putonghua* will make the employment of students easier." There are concerns of some teachers, specifically the worry about that "bilingual class may improve their *Putonghua* level but diminish the quality of subject courses (e.g., math) learning for Uyghur students." The key reason for these concerns lies in the lack of qualified students and teachers for bilingual education, which leads to the decline of the teaching and learning quality in bilingual classes. A special employment survey of relevant graduates could accurately measure whether bilingual education exerts positive or negative influences on employment of students.

Fourth, the teaching of minority languages in bilingual classes of primary schools deserves attention. As was understood from the teacher's colloquia of Kashgar Prefecture, in the past, Uyghur language was taught from grade one in primary minority schools and *Putonghua* was taught from grade three. At present, however, *Putonghua* is taught from grade one in bilingual classes and Uyghur language is taught from grade three. The teachers said that, "The Uyghur alphabet is taught when pupils have just begun to make some progress in aural *Putonghua*, which might confuse them to a certain extent." Since the development of bilingual teaching aims to make students "master both *Putonghua* and native language," reducing the function of native language teaching is incompatible with the original intention of this policy.

Finally, as for the prospect of bilingual teaching in primary and middle schools in Xinjiang, some think that bilingual teaching can supplement the deficiencies of both *Min kao Min*, which results in low-level *Putonghua* and difficulties in the job market, and *Min kao Han*, which results in students not knowing much about their native languages. They even believe that with good development prospects, bilingual education may become the mainstream in minority schools. Therefore, parents decide to send their children to bilingual classes.

Meanwhile, some parents consider that it costs too much to attend bilingual classes (extra textbooks and reference materials), and the teaching quality cannot be ensured due to the fact that the teaching staff is not always qualified in *Putonghua* and students are enrolled according to school district rather than being exam-selected. As a result, many Uyghur parents with good incomes send their children to Han schools. The principal of Shufu Bilingual Experimental Middle School once said, "Only those Uyghur students who failed to enter No. 2 Middle School (Han school) will come to us." Even some teachers of bilingual classes clearly express the opinion that their first choice is to send their children to Han schools. To be sure, if the teaching quality of current bilingual education fails to improve on time, its status and popularity in the mind of the public will be damaged.

Protect minority groups' enthusiasm for participating in bilingual education

During home-visits to students, we got the sense that the Uyghur populace had enormous enthusiasm for learning *Putonghua*. In Shufu County, we were even told that some Uyghur peasants planned to persuade their children who had been in grade two in minority primary schools to quit and turn to bilingual preschool classes. The idea, of course, was rejected by kindergartens by the regulations. We once visited a middle-aged peasant who lives in a rural area 9 kilometers away from county town but persists in sending his children to a bilingual experimental school (No. 4 Middle School) in town. At first, he ferried his children to and from school every day by motorcycle; then, in 2002, he rented a house near the school and the whole family moved there. He takes care of their farm and does odd jobs in the slack season. Both of his two older daughters studied in bilingual classes in middle schools and entered *Nei gao ban* in 2006 and 2007 successively; his two younger daughters are now studying in bilingual classes in primary and middle schools. He takes great pride in this situation. According to teachers at No. 4 Middle School, there are many students there whose parents rent houses in the town to support them. In another case, a Uyghur student who entered the *Nei gao ban* in 2007 graduated from the Bilingual Experimental Middle School in the town. He lives in a village 8.5 kilometers away from the town, but persists in riding his bicycle to and from school every day. The distance is so great that even his parents and neighbors were surprised at his perseverance. According to a *Min kao Han* student, his parents encourage him to learn *Putonghua* and when he asks for something, his father, as a rule, will reply, "I'll buy it for you if you can name it in *Putonghua.*"

The ethnic relationships and religious issues are complex and sensitive in Xinjiang, and the central government and people all over the country show great concern for the stability and development of Xinjiang. It should be noted that the enthusiasm shown by Uyghur people who send their children to Han schools or bilingual classes is very valuable, and the availability of these classes offers an important historical opportunity for people to strengthen inter-ethnic communication and promote national unity. Despite strong governmental financial support, a scientific and practical attitude must be held on the concrete implementation of bilingual education in each area, and people should learn from their practices and adjust their running methods appropriately. The majority of people attach the greatest importance to actual practical results; therefore we should do the best to maintain, consolidate, and encourage the enthusiasm of minority students on learning *Putonghua* by means of continuously enhancing the practical effect of bilingual classes, improving their opportunities in job market and personal career after the students' graduation.

Teacher training for bilingual classes

The training of bilingual teachers is the key to improving the existing bilingual experimental classes and further developing them. According to many schools in Kashgar, after bilingual classes were set up, it became easy to find teachers for courses in grade one of junior middle school, while both the number and the ability of teachers for classes in higher grades failed to satisfy the needs of the school. Thus the difficulty of running bilingual classes increased. Only 9.6 percent of the total minority teachers of the Shufu County have attended bilingual training programs. Bilingual teachers of the Kashgar Prefecture are selected and sent to Urumqi for a year of training. The expenses for the training are paid by the government, but traveling expenses are borne by teachers themselves.

According to some teachers, they have to deliver a cautionary deposit when attending the training programs, which put great pressure on them. It is understandable that this measure was issued by the government in hopes of driving teachers to attend the training programs actively and perform well. However, if the standard of assessment deviates in practice, then the negative consequences may emerge, and an unhealthy trend could develop.

In our informal discussions in Kashgar City and Shufu County, the school teachers stated on several occasions that training of bilingual teachers failed to yield good results. The main problems and suggestions for improvement follow:

1   In the current training program, Uyghur teachers who speak low-level *Putonghua* are trained together, so they have no language surroundings in which to improve their *Putonghua*. It is suggested that those teachers be sent to key primary and middle Han schools in the nearby area or city to attend classes for a year and practice *Putonghua* teaching under the guidance of Han teachers will greatly improve their daily *Putonghua* and quality of their teaching.

2   Some Uyghur teachers who act as trainers in the programs do not speak fluent *Putonghua* or uphold professional knowledge themselves. Some trainees have said, "Some teachers have a *Putonghua* level no higher than my own." Thus it is suggested that trainers be selected on more critical grounds.

3   Some of the teaching approaches in the training class are totally HSK exam-oriented, and do not paying attention to the development of trainees' practical ability to teach, answer questions, and organize discussions in *Putonghua*. Due to the fact that such courses are directed to teachers of bilingual classes, innovative teaching methods should be introduced.

4   Bilingual teaching is a specialized field with its own particular techniques and teaching methods. A teacher who knows the target language (*Putonghua*) and knows about mathematics, physics, and chemistry will not necessarily make a qualified bilingual teacher. Han teachers need to be trained to teach minority students whose native languages are not *Putonghua*. Because Han teachers who are able to speak Uyghur language would have improved communication with students, they need to learn Uyghur. On the other hand, the training of Uyghur teachers should not only demand that they can speak *Putonghua*, but also that they specifically master *Putonghua* as it applies to the teaching of science courses.

5   Some training programs failed to complete the prescribed content because, although the teachers were highly paid, they did not follow the planned curriculum. It is recommended that the curriculum be restrictively implemented, the program be extended to two years, more teaching practice be added under the guidance of skilled trainers, and strict assessment be applied to the progress and results.

6   Since many minority teachers fail to pronounce *Putonghua* correctly, it is recommended that high-quality audio courses be recorded and distributed to schools for students to learn and master standard pronunciation. This method is highly recommended because of its low cost but high effectiveness.

HSK for minority teachers

HSK is an exam designed to test *Putonghua* level, popularized generally in the minority schools of the Xinjiang Autonomous Region. From 1998, the HSK performance of minority senior high school graduates in the Region began to be connected with their college entrance examination. The total performance of students on the college entrance examination would be increased by 5 points for reaching level three on the HSK, 10 points would be added for level four, 15 for level five, and 20 for level six. Students' performance in bilingual experimental classes would factor into their score on the HSK.

The demands of the Autonomous Region government placed on minority teachers are currently as follows: After being trained, full-time bilingual teachers who teach in primary, middle, or high schools should reach level six, seven, and eight respectively on the HSK. Since this is a rigid index that determines whether the teachers can keep their jobs or not, they would need to attend various *Putonghua* training programs for the relevant certificates of the HSK.

Nevertheless, the above-mentioned demands fail to be completely practical, and most local educational bureaus do not follow the criteria issued by the Autonomous Region government. Currently, teachers who meet the HSK criteria account for less than 35 percent of the total number of bilingual teachers in Shufu County. As was stated by teachers in the colloquia, there are a total of 11 levels on the HSK and teachers in courses other than *Putonghua* in primary minority schools of rural areas should reach at least level three, and *Putonghua* teachers should reach at least level five. Many teachers on the job failed to reach the requisite level, though. Moreover, many teachers hold fake certificates.

With the aim of getting the certificate and passing the quality assessment, or to reach the level of the language test required for promotion, black market HSK certificates have appeared in Urumqi with prices ranging from RMB 2,000–3.000. As a result, of the 28 teachers in a primary school, 5 reached level seven, 5 level six, 15 levels three to five, and 3 remained below band three. It is estimated that of the 28 teachers, 13 hold false certificates.

The phenomenon of black market certifications deserves great attention from educational authorities in Xinjiang, and reasonable required standards or indexes should be made in accordance with the reality and practice in each area, on the basis of field investigation, to check on teachers' performance. Different criteria may be presented in different areas (southern Xinjiang, northern Xinjiang, the middle area) and on different levels. A realistic attitude is demanded rather than a declaration of fixed criteria. Commensurate with the continuous improvement of the quality of, and renewal of the teaching staff, the index may be raised gradually until the indexes of the whole region become unified.

When bilingual education is actively promoted, the mode of **Min kao Han** *should not be ignored*

None would deny the fact that, from the prospect of the minority schools in Xinjiang, the main goal should be to develop bilingual education in order to improve the *Putonghua* ability and professional level of the teachers. In addition, the enthusiasm of minority people for sending their children to Han schools should also be supported. In every colloquium and home-visit, it was understood that the local Uyghur parents (notably in families located downtown, of which the children stay in *Putonghua* surroundings and have the ability to speak *Putonghua*) generally prefer sending their children to Han schools. For example, No. 12 Primary School in Kashgar (Han school) planned to recruit only 45 students in 2007. There were 475 applicants in total, most of whom were children of Uyghur officials. Such cases are common in every township in southern Xinjiang. In the view of many Uyghur parents, there are obvious advantages to students attending Han school: First, students can totally master *Putonghua* which is very useful in social communication and future career. Second, students use *Putonghua* textbooks and attend Han schools' exams, and therefore may learn science courses better. The parents, on the other hand, having a certain cultural knowledge, can coach their children on learning Uyghur language at home so that the children's native language would not be abandoned. Third, there are many preferences for students of *Min kao Han* when it comes to the college entrance exam that still maintain their priority when students attend the exam for *Nei gao ban* in Han schools.

About 90 percent of students in bilingual classes will choose *Min kao Han* at the time of college entrance exams. That is, they will attend the exam in *Putonghua*. The students do so because schools that enroll *Min kao Han* students outnumber those that enrolling *Min kao Min* students, so the *Min kao Han* students will have a much wider range of selection on universities and majors. They can also apply for the entrance examinations of more universities, and award marks may be added to their performance. It is generally thought that *Min kao Han* and *Han kao Min* graduates are well-suited for teaching bilingual classes. As such, the number of Han schools should be increased, and *Min kao Han* programs should be actively developed at least as far as generally developing bilingual classes for Xinjiang in the future. Furthermore, more preferential policies and great encouragement should be applied to *Han kao Min* students. The minority education in Xinjiang has developed various different modes at the same time, such as *Min kao Han*, *Min kao Min*, *Han kao Min*, and bilingual classes, according to the requirement of the local job market and the wishes of the minority people.

The stimulating impact exerted by Nei gao ban *on bilingual education*

In 2000, the central government began to implement the program of "Xinjiang high school classes in other provinces of China" (*Nei gao ban* for short). Students in *Nei gaoban* classes are selected among minority students who graduated from junior middle schools in each area of Xinjiang, in accordance with their performance in *Putonghua* and mathematics. A certain quota of students is enrolled every year, and 5,000 students (10 percent of which are Han students) have been enrolled each year recently. The enrolled students are sent to *Nei gao ban* teaching centers in selected best high schools in big cities in coastal areas; after one year's preparatory study (to enhance their *Putonghua*, mathematics, and English), they are assigned to ordinary classes in the schools individually or assigned to "Xinjiang class in group," depending on their performance and specialty in either humanities/social sciences or sciences. They are then enrolled individually in the college entrance examination, and all of them may enter universities or colleges according to their adjusted scores and preferences. At present, minority parents generally intend to send their children to *Nei gao ban* for the following reasons: First, *Nei gao ban* is among the best high schools in China with the most satisfying teaching conditions, teaching staff, and teaching results. Second, the reduction of tuition for *Nei gao ban* students may greatly alleviate their families' economic burdens. Third, their level of *Putonghua* and specialized courses will improve noticeably. Fourth, graduates of such schools can usually enter the best universities in China, which, as a rule, promise good prospects for employment. Students in middle schools who are selected and sent to *Nei gao ban* must pass certain exams, and attendees of *Min kao Min*, *Min kao Han* and bilingual classes all have different requirements. Now the annual selection of *Nei gao ban* has become a major event for schools and educational departments in Xinjiang.

The Bureau of Education has issued a definitive admission index for *Nei gao-ban* or *Qu nei chu zhong ban* for each school to evaluate the teaching performance in their best classes. In addition to *Nei gao ban*, there is also a *Qu nei chu zhong ban* (intra-regional junior middle school class) in Xinjiang. Quality minority students are selected based on their primary school departure examinations and sent to study in key middle schools within the Region. Some 5,000 students were enrolled in *Qu nei chu zhong ban* in Xinjiang in 2006. Those who fail to reach the index will be fined. One primary school principal explained that the enrollment index of *Qu nei chu zhong ban* has been issued to the best class in each primary school, and the school that fails to fill its quota will be fined RMB 200 each. The admission rate of students in bilingual classes to *Nei gao ban* is usually high, notably that of the first bilingual class, which was enrolled via exam selection. According to data from Kashgar No. 1 Middle School, of the 40 graduates of bilingual classes from the middle sector of this school, 36 (90 percent) were enrolled into *Nei gao ban* in 2000; the figure was 17 out of 102 graduates in 2006; in 2007, 24 students of the 83 graduates passed the *Nei gao ban* exam and were waiting for their health check during our visit. The opportunity to enter *Nei gao ban* is a major motivation for minority parents to actively send their children to bilingual classes. 2008 is the first year that students of the first *Nei gao ban* graduated from universities, so people are now generally concerned with their employment conditions and developing prospects. *Nei gao ban* has aided in promoting bilingual education in Xinjiang and will continue to exert influence in the future.

A new phenomenon appeared in recent years. Namely, a few students of *Nei gao ban* chose to return to their hometowns in Xinjiang to resume classes and take college entrance exams there because of the fear that they might not be enrolled in best universities upon their graduation from *Nei gao ban*. Schools in the Kashgar Prefecture welcome those students because their attending the college entrance exam in Kashgar can raise the admission rate of the local schools. Nevertheless, due to the fact that they also fill the local admissions quota, the dissatisfaction of local exam candidates should be taken into consideration.

Teaching materials for bilingual education

Teachers universally complained that there are no unified textbooks for preschool bilingual classes in Xinjiang. Now the materials for Han kindergarten, which seldom connect with local society and everyday life of Uyghur community, are used in Xinjiang. As a result, teaching materials need to be revised to boosting children's interest in order to satisfy teaching demands.

Not only native language textbooks but also those of every other subject now taught in bilingual classes are also identical with those of Han schools. Due to the different skill levels of the teachers, minority teachers in primary and middle schools have been avoiding or mentioning only parts of the content of some subjects (math, physics, chemistry and biology), and even refusing to cover some sections in exams. With the implementation of new bilingual teaching modes, teachers have more difficulties applying *Putonghua* to teach the content that was previously hard to teach in their native language. In response, the investigative report by the Autonomous Region Bureau of Education advises that:

> In accordance with this practical condition, it has been a necessity to research and develop specialized textbooks for each subject that are suitable for promoting bilingual teaching in primary and middle schools in our region. It might be taken into consideration that textbooks published by People's Education Press and Beijing Normal University Press are still taken as the blueprint, although some difficult and profound content should be canceled. Additionally, the learning and understanding of basic knowledge should be further emphasized; native language should be marked in brackets after technical terms so as to facilitate teachers and students to use them in teaching and learning. It can also be taken into account that textbooks may be complied by attaching glossaries of the two languages at the end of the textbooks.
> (Xinjiang Uyghur Autonomous Region Bureau of Education, 2007).

Three successive sets of mainstream Chinese textbooks have been compiled and officially published by educational publishers, and the most recent, 1998 version also needs to be revised in accordance with the developing conditions in Xinjiang and the nation at large. As was determined by the teachers of Kashgar No. 1 Middle School (Uyghur school), bilingual classes now use the Chinese textbooks compiled by People's Education Press, which are too difficult for Uyghur students in southern Xinjiang. On the other hand, those textbooks compiled by the Autonomous Region for minority schools are too simple—their level for grade six of primary school is lower than that of grade one in other provinces. A better effect would be achieved if the textbooks published by People's Education Press were revised by taking away with the section on ancient Mandarin and adding sections about daily life and local communities in Xinjiang.

Other problems with bilingual education

In the colloquia and interviews, teachers also reported some other problems pertinent to bilingual education. First of all, the curriculum set-up, class arrangement, and teaching materials lack a unified set of demands. Assessment of teaching quality is applied without unified criteria and methods. And furthermore, the structure, content, and degree of difficulty of exams remain to be normative. In the view of the teachers, the *Experimental Scheme of Bilingual Teaching (Draft),* issued by the Xinjiang Education Bureau in 1998, needs to be revised according to the changing conditions in recent years on the prescriptions and demands as regards many facets of teaching. In particular, curriculum set-up, teaching language, class arrangement, and demands for exams of different levels need to be standardized.

Two tendencies deserve attention here: First, the regional differences between southern and northern Xinjiang are ignored, and unified regulations are formulated that may be alienated from the realities of each area, leading to their failure to be implemented in some areas. Second, unified and normative teaching demands are lacking, which has led to the messy teaching situation. To overcome these two tendencies, the suggestion was made that on the basis of field investigations and surveys, the whole region be divided into several "administrative precincts of bilingual education," and that each precinct determine a set of teaching plans and assess methods to deal with the main content as consistently as possible, only permitting differences on a few aspects.

Second, there are serious problems with the students' tuition burden. It is reported that tuition is RMB 1200 per year for senior high school students, and textbook fees are RMB 230 per year. For students in senior vocational schools, the tuition is RMB 2000 per year, and the textbook fee is RMB 300 per year. What is more, in senior vocational schools, students from poor families account for 90 percent of the total student body. In the Kashgar and Hotan prefectures, the rural per-capita net income in 2005 was only RMB 1,699 and RMB 1,296 respectively (State Statistical Bureau of Xinjiang Uighur Autonomous Region, 2006, p. 222). As such, the above-mentioned fees are truly beyond the reach of rural families. The subsidy offered by the government to each poor student in boarding high schools is RMB 1,000 per year (RMB 100 per month for 10 months). Each apprentice in senior vocational schools may be offered RMB 1,500 per year as a subsidy from the government. The students who enrolled in jointly run vocational schools in the eastern and western regions of China (enrolling 3,000 persons each year) receive a RMB 2,000 subsidy per year offered by the program. These subsidies are greatly needed by minority students in southern Xinjiang to engage in and complete their education. We hope that the central government will reinforce its support for the courses of minority education in

Xinjiang by enlarging the scope and the amount of the financial subsidy. And we can say for sure that investing in education, notably minority education, is a most suitable expenditure for the central government and the nation.

Teachers reported that the textbook fee for each pupil in primary school is RMB 75 each semester. The books are bought collectively by the County Bureau of Education, but some books, like those for the course of Information Technology, were never offered due to the lack of teachers. This kind of phenomena should be avoided by the authorities by listening to the reports and complaints from the schools.

Finally, rural teachers currently take on too many non-teaching jobs in addition to their teaching tasks, and as a result their workload is too heavy. One major aspect of the problem is that the Bureau of Education and town/*xiang* government dually supervise rural primary schools. When there are certain tasks for the town/*xiang* departments, those tasks are then assigned to teachers directly. For example, the teachers must participate in the matter of managing employment services organized by county or town/*xiang* governments, reporting rural surplus laborers, and persuading the laborers to register or participate in the labor training and exchange programs. These tasks are made worse because if the teachers fail to finish the assignment, they must forfeit part of their wages. On top of these outside jobs, teachers must undertake the work of campus greening and cleaning, and of keeping campus watch. Each teacher will be on duty for 24 hours every 25 days. As a result, teachers often hire someone to do the duty and they have to pay him themselves. When teachers do not have enough time for study and teaching preparation, the teaching work of the whole school is surely affected. Thus it is advised that the Bureau of Education carry out special investigation into these problems and improve the working conditions of rural teachers and provide necessary subsidies.

Conclusion

In the process of modernization, sciences, technology, economics, and military affairs have developed as the objective measures of a country's relative standing in the global community. Competition between countries has become much more serious than ever before in human history, and the nations that are left behind in sciences and economics face many difficulties to survive. To stand strong in the international community and to catch up with the developing pace of the whole world, a country must devote major efforts to developing education. For any country (notably developing countries), the preservation of traditional cultural heritage and native languages is not enough to survive in the modern world. It is also necessary to learn about sciences, technology, management, social sciences, law, and other modern knowledge to catch up with the progress of globalization. Only by mastering universal knowledge and techniques can China have the possibility to develop into a modernized nation, and thus engage in dialogue, cooperation, and peaceful coexistence with other countries of the world under equal circumstances.

To obtain and master modern knowledge, and to enable a nation to be intellectually creative, the government and people must address the question of which language is most efficient and effective for use in school education. China is a multi-ethnic nation. Many ethnic groups in China have their own languages and cultural traditions. According to a sociological viewpoint, language basically has two functions: one is to act as the carrier of history and culture for a group, and the other is to serve as the tool for communicating and acquiring new knowledge from others. To remain current in the most advanced sciences and technologies in the world, China needs English education as a tool for study and application; Similarly, *Putonghua*, the common inter-ethnic language of the nation of China, is the most useful tool for people to communicate and receive basic knowledge in and out of the classroom. 95 percent of the population speaks *Putonghua* because it was chosen as the common language. While each minority group in China must make efforts to learn its native language, the opportunity for improvement and development through learning *Putonghua* should by no means be ignored.

The Chinese *Constitution* guarantees all minority groups the right to preserve and develop their languages. When a member of any minority group in China wishes to study in school using his/her native language as the language of instruction, the government should provide a school for them. In the case that there are too few students with such a wish and establishing and maintaining such a school is too inefficient, the government could arrange for those students to attend a boarding school in another region. In our field survey around the minority areas in China, this is the common arrangement.

Over the course of more than a century of development, with the hard work of tens of millions of teachers and scholars, Han schools have become an institution for research on *Putonghua* teaching and knowledge, publishing at a high level internationally. The *Putonghua* educational system cultivates tens of millions of Han, Hui and Manchu students, and has also offers an important ladder for the development of minority education. From the perspective of eventual employment prospects, in particular, mastering *Putonghua* and expressing specialized knowledge by means of *Putonghua* are important conditions for minority students to develop on the grand stage of China. A Uyghur scholar emphasizes: "In contemporary China, not knowing *Putonghua* means self-enclosing" (Hasimu, 2002). In every minority settlement area where we have conducted field surveys throughout the country, the local population's enthusiasm for learning *Putonghua* was noticeable. In addition, local governments actively promote *Putonghua* teaching in order to improve the employment conditions of minority graduates. *Min kao Han*, and the new type of bilingual education in Xinjiang are cases of exploration and practice on this account.

Many Uyghur students have also fully realized the importance of learning *Putonghua*. In one interview, a Uyghur student in Kashgar No. 2 Middle School said:

> Language is a tool, so learning *Putonghua* well is highly important for us to get to know the outside world ... We could get only a few high-quality versions of Uyghur language reference books before, while many Chinese reference materials can be found easily with wider coverage and a higher quality.

Therefore, we have to learn *Putonghua* well in order to do well in the college entrance examination.

When I was in Kashgar in 1997, I had a totally different feeling from what I have in 2007. I now feel that we should care for and maintain the active and enthusiastic approach to supporting the Uyghur populace in learning *Putonghua*, and we must contribute to efficiently running the bilingual education in Xinjiang by virtue of a realistic attitude and collective endeavor.

The Xinjiang Autonomous Region government is far-sighted in attaching great importance to bilingual education and being determined to "start at an early age." This is a measure of vital importance that can lay the foundation for the long-term stability and social development of the Region. When we made surveys across the Kashgar area, we could sense the force and influence of the government on promoting this work everywhere. We felt at the same time that some targets might seem somewhat beyond reality in some areas. For example, the Autonomous Region government proposes that *Putonghua* will be applied in all the primary and middle schools for everything except native language classes before 2012. Since the problem of insufficient qualified teaching staff cannot be practically settled in time, the goal of setting up bilingual classes in rural primary and middle minority schools presumably can hardly be attained.

Therefore, it is clear that many issues remain to be discussed in determining how to promote and develop bilingual education in Xinjiang, and many relevant problems remain to be solved. The various extant modes of bilingual education in each area need to be taken into account due to the great regional variation in Xinjiang. Southern Xinjiang, with its low population density and high minority proportions, is a special area. There is a great need for the Autonomous Region government to make special programs for educational development in the three prefectures of southern Xinjiang. It is also suggested that Han schools in some minority areas of Xinjiang should open Uyghur language courses for Han students and students of *Min kao Han* because such courses would benefit those students in developing and obtaining employment locally. In addition, due to the fact that many poor counties are incapable of offering financial support for the local bilingual education, sufficient financial support must be provided by the central government to satisfy the needs of the local populace.

People's high enthusiasm and great expectations notwithstanding, the road needs to be covered step by step. Integral programming is needed, and differences between the planning indicators of different areas should be apparent. Gradual exploration of experiences is still needed to promote the smooth development of minority education in each area of Xinjiang. Presumably, Deng Xiaoping's adage of "groping forward by feeling for stones in the river bed to cross a river" still applies here. Carrying out subject surveys, interviewing principals and teachers who work in school campus and classrooms of bilingual education, and talking with parents and students participating in bilingual courses so as to understand their thoughts and attend to their ideas and suggestions are the necessary paths for us to objectively understand the situations and thoughts of the people involved. Only when we persist in making systematic and deep studies, can we have the right to speak and determine practical methods and paths toward the development of minority education.

In recent years, many scholars concerned with the minority education in Xinjiang have made deep and systematic studies and published their findings (Hasimu, 2002; Wu, 2004). This chapter serves to put order to the materials gathered based on a short-term field study, and may still contain some immature views. Therefore, critiques and comments from readers are sincerely expected.

Acknowledgments

This chapter first appeared in *Front. Educ China* 2009, 4(2): 188–251 DOI 10.1007/s11516-009-0012-3. © Higher Education Press and Springer-Verlag 2009. (Edited version is reprinted with permission from Springer.)

The chapter was translated by Zhang Lin from *Beijing Daxue Jiaoyu Pinglun* 北京大学教育评论 (Peking University Education Review), 2008, (2): 2–41, revised by Daniel Weisman.

The author would like to thank Li Xiaoxia, a researcher in Xinjiang Academy of Social Sciences whose as yet unpublished thesis on the affirmative action policy on college entrance examinations in Xinjiang provided thorough information. His thanks are also devoted to the documents and reports on investigation of bilingual education by the Education Bureau of the Xinjiang Autonomous Region and relevant literature as well as survey data from other sources.

References

Census Office of Xinjiang Uyghur Autonomous Region (2002). *Tabulation on the 2000 Population Census of Xinjiang Uygur Autonomous Region*. Urumqi: Xinjiang People's Publishing House.

Hasimu, M. (2002). *Experimental study on teaching in Putonghua in minority middle schools of Xinjiang*. Urumqi: Xinjiang University Press.

Li, X. X. (2007). Analysis of the preferential policies to minority examinees in the entrance examination of universities and colleges in Xinjiang. Unpublished manuscript.

Ma, R. (2000). The distribution of minority groups in Kashgar, Xinjiang. *North West Ethno-national Studies*, 2, 1–9.

Ma, R. (2008). On bilingual education from sociological perspectives. *Journal of Yunnan Nationalities University (Social Sciences)*, 1, 11–17.

Ma, T. (1983). *Brief history of Chinese Islam sect and Menhuan system*. Yinchuan: Ningxia People's Publishing House.

Sautmen, B. (1999). Expanding access to higher education for China's national minorities. In G. A. Postiglione (Ed.), *China's national minority education* (pp. 173–210). New York: Falmer Press.

Simayi, Z. (2003). Success of education and minority education: A case study of bilingual education system in Xinjiang University. Unpublished master's thesis. Beijing, Peking University.

State Statistical Bureau. (2006). *Statistical yearbook of China*. Beijing: Chinese Statistical Press.

Wright, S. (2004). *Language policy and language planning*. New York: Palgrave Macmillan.

Wu, J. F. (2004). Study on minority preparatory education in universities and colleges in Xinjiang. Beijing: Nationalities Publishing House.

Xinjiang Uyghur Autonomous Region Bureau of Education. (1998). *Education yearbook of Xinjiang (1998)*. Urumqi: Xinjiang People's Publishing House.

Xinjiang Uyghur Autonomous Region Bureau of Education. (2007). *The survey report of minority bilingual teaching in Xinjiang Uyghur Autonomous Region*. Unpublished report.

Xinjiang Uyghur Autonomous Region Bureau of Statistics. (2006). *Statistical yearbook of Xinjiang (2006)* Beijing: China Statistical Press.

Zhang, T. L., & Huang, R. Q. (1993). *The evolution of Chinese minority population*. Beijing: Ocean Press.

Zuliyati Simayi (2003). Success of education and minority education: A case study of bilingual education system in Xinjiang University. Master's thesis of Department of Sociology at Peking University.

4 A brief report on bilingual education for the Dongxiangs

A new initiative

Yisu Zhou

Introduction

Dongxiang Autonomous Country (DAC) is the area for the Dongxiang ethnic minority group in northwestern China. According the 2000 census, there are 513,805 Dongxiang people nationwide, 451,622 (or 87.89 percent) of whom live in the Gansu Province. Most (215,144) reside in Gansu's Linxia Hui Autonomous Prefecture,[1] DAC (National Bureau of Statistics, 2003). Others live in the nearby counties of Hezheng, Guanghe, and Linxia, and a small number reside in Xinjiang Province (National Bureau of Statistics, 2003). Not many Dongxiang people speak Mandarin. For example, according to Qin and Ma (2004), 85 percent of Dongxiang people speak only Dongxiang in their daily lives.

Education achievement levels of the Dongxiang are the lowest in China, with the lowest completion rates of elementary and secondary education and consequently the lowest college entrance rate (Chen, 2006). While China's adult illiteracy rate has dropped to less than 10 percent, 62.88 percent of the Dongxiang adults are illiterate[2] (National Bureau of Statistics, 2003) (Table 4.1). One study estimated the average years of education received by Dongxiang people to be only 1.98 (Qin & Ma, 2004) while the national average is 8.5 (Ministry of Education, 2007). Moreover, student dropout rate is more than 10 percent at the elementary level (Lu & Chang, 2006).

While poverty is recognized as a key factor that has constrained educational development in Dongxiang, language also matters a great deal. However, little empirical research has been conducted to understand the role of language issues in educational development until recent years (Lu and Chang, 2006; Wang & Postiglione, 2008). Dongxiang language is a member of the Mongolian-Altaic language family. Phonologically, it is a toneless with no vowel length distinction. /j/ and /q/, /g/ and /k/ are in phonemic contrast while head-initial fricatives /f/ and /h/ are kept in the word initial position. The lexical stress is on the first syllable (Dongxiang County Annals Editorial Committee, 1996). Many Mandarin-speaking Dongxiang people have difficulty with coronal nasal and velar nasal as well as various tones. Syntactically, the basic word order of the Dongxiang language is Subject–Object–Verb, which has a reversion of the Mandarin verb and object position. These differences between the two languages sometimes cause

Table 4.1 Adult illiteracy among the Dongxiang

	Male	*Female*	*Total*
Population aged 15 and over	173,748	168,591	342,339
Illiterate population	87,236	128,023	215,259
Ratio of illiterate population to population aged 15 and over (%)	50.21	75.49	62.88

Source: National Bureau of Statistics (2003, p. 190).

difficulty for native Dongxiang-speaking students in their studies in Mandarin at schools (Chen, 2006).

More importantly than the phonetics or syntax of the language, however, may be that the Dongxiang is among the 29 ethnic minority groups that have only oral languages.[3] This situation complicates classroom instruction. Historically, local schools adopted the sink-or-swim model of language acquisition. Dongxiang students enter an all-Mandarin (second language) learning environment without overt Dongxiang language (first language) support. For native-speaking Dongxiang students, there is virtually no transitional stage from using first language (L1) at home to the second language (L2) in school. Prior to entering the first grade, Dongxiang students have very limited exposure to Mandarin because the majority of Dongxiang families only speak the Dongxiang language at home (Qin & Ma, 2004). Nor do they learn Chinese in preschools because, as is the case with many other inland areas of China, preschool is not part of the free compulsory public education in DAC and can only be afforded by a small number of families (Zhang, 2009). In primary and secondary schools, however, the national standard textbooks written in Mandarin are used as the official medium of instruction is Mandarin. Though teachers are mostly ethnic Dongxiang locals (Wang & Zhou, 2005) and they occasionally use Dongxiang language to assist teaching, it is a great challenge for Dongxiang students to learn in Mandarin.

Dongxiang language borrows a large number of Mandarin vocabulary (Bao, 2007), but students tend to imitate the pronunciation of words and often use the wrong characters. According to Wang and Postiglione (2008), this is due to the lack of written scripts. Local teachers report that the five-year elementary curriculum takes about eight years for Dongxiang students to finish and graduate (Wang & Zhou, 2005). Recent studies suggest that Mandarin language proficiency, time spent on schoolwork, and attitude toward school are significant predictors of students' academic performance in Dongxiang (Lu & Chang, 2006; Wang and Postiglione, 2008), explain some of the challenges Dongxiang students face.[4]

The new initiative

The importance of literacy in increasing student achievement has been addressed in academic research (Baker, 2001). International studies have suggested the importance of first language literacy in second language literacy acquisition. Research indicates that teaching in minority students' mother tongue does not hinder their acquisition of a second language. In fact, proficiency in the students' mother tongue is "a strong predictor of their second language development" (Cummins, 2001, p. 17). One approach applied to do this is that of bilingual education, a common model adopted in ethnic minority education (Cummins, 2000). Bilingual minority students have been found to perform consistently better than their monolingual counterparts in schools where such programs are successfully implemented (Thomas & Collier, 1997, cited in Finifrock, 2010). The Chinese state recognizes that "every ethnic minority is free to use and develop their language" in the Constitution (Coulmas, 1999, cited in Geary & Pan, 1999), but this constitutional right has been enjoyed by the minorities such as the Mongolians, Koreans, Tibetan, and the Uyghurs, who have long histories of written languages. Students from these groups are more likely to have bilingual options in their schooling (Geary & Pan, 2003). For example, in elementary schools in southern Gansu, *Yuwen* (Chinese Language Arts) textbooks have been translated into the Tibetan language. Tibetan students use their mother tongue to study at school for the first three years, and after fourth grade, both Mandarin and Tibetan are used in class for instructional and assessment purpose (Du, 2006). Some schools also extend the typical five-year elementary curriculum for one or two more years to adjust for students' learning pace (Du, 2006). In other cases such as in Qinghai, several schools offer experimental courses for Math and Science in Tibetan (Wang & Postiglione, 2008). Sometimes bilingual education goes beyond middle school and continues through to high school or college education. In recent years, experiments aimed at providing bilingual education to minorities with written scripts developed in the 1950s also caught the attention of researchers (Finifrock, 2010; Geary & Pan, 2003).

However, little is known about minorities with no written scripts. To address this gap, several initiatives have been implemented in recent years to popularize compulsory basic education and improve the learning ability of Dongxiang minority students. Of particular interest here is one initiative that gets to the heart of the persisting debate in academic circles regarding the use of mother tongue education as a medium of instruction. In July 2007, scholars and the DAC government held the first conference on bilingual education in DAC. The conference announced a "unanimous approval of gradual implementation of bilingual education in county elementary and secondary schools" (Chen, 2006). The first step was to experiment at *Nalesi* (or *Narisi*) Central Elementary School. The experiment was designed for two waves, each with one class in *Nalesi*, starting from 2002–2005 and 2004–2007. The aim of the experiment was to evaluate the effectiveness of using a transcript system to help L2 acquisition.

Because no written scripts of Dongxiang language exist, there are no local-language-based textbooks available for Dongxiang students. The innovation of this initiative is to use a Romanized transcript system as a linguistic tool to mark down the oral language. Then educators use the transcripts to annotate the Mandarin-based textbook in the Dongxiang language, for both Chinese Language

Arts (*Yuwen*) and Math. The transcript system itself does not create any new linguistic features such as grammar or vocabulary; neither does it have any intrinsic meaning. It serves as a linguistic tool to connect oral language with written scripts. The educational purpose of this initiative was thus twofold: to provide Dongxiang people a written form of their language and to facilitate Dongxiang students in their learning of Mandarin using the written scripts.

In 1998, a book entitled *Applied Transcript for Dongxiang Language* (Ma & Chen, 2001) was published. This book introduces a transcript system for Dongxiang language. Most of the transcript's linguistic structure is based on *Pinyin*, another Romanized script providing pronunciation and tone of a *Hanzi*. After that, a Dongxiang–Mandarin Dictionary was also published using this transcript system. The initiative also included publishing new textbooks. In 2002, the first experimental textbooks consisting of Dongxiang folklores and fairytales were put into use in preschool classrooms. The idea was to create an acquisition phase of L1 at preschool and extend it to include a transitional phase to L2 before they enter first grade. These students were taught to read in L1 with this transcript system. They were also exposed to simple Mandarin characters during the same year. In elementary school, textbooks based on the national curriculum were marked with transcripts, which enabled teachers to use the transcripts to explain the Chinese meaning of each word and sentence in the Dongxiang language. It is analogous to other areas where Chinese in textbooks are marked in *Pinyin* in early grades. The initiative requires teachers to use the Dongxiang language as the instructional language in the first grade and to use both Dongxian and Mandarin in the second grade. When students enter third grade, textbooks are no longer annotated by transcripts and teachers mainly use Mandarin to teach. Later, Dongxiang students are treated no differently from Han or Hui students. In this bilingualism with monoliteracy model (Dai & Cheng, 2007, p. 84), Dongxiang is used only to explain Mandarin textbooks as a "helping language." Therefore, only Mandarin literacy is developed in classrooms (e.g., no Dongxiang language course is offered; no Dongxiang language-based literacy textbooks are created or used in elementary classrooms).

In 2004, the Educational Research Office (*jiaoyan shi*) of DAC assessed all the students who participated in bilingual education at the end of their first grade in both Chinese language and math subjects. They compared Dongxiang students who received bilingual education (experimental group) with those who did not (control group). The results showed no dropout in the experiment class (group), yet in control groups, the dropout rate is 4–5 percent overall and it was worth noting that it was 13 percent for girls. The test results also show that average passing rate for the experiment class is 10 percent higher than those of the control groups in *Yuwen*. This is equivalent to a five-point average difference on a 100-point scale. For Math, the experimental class had a 2 percent higher passing rate than the control groups (Chen, 2006). Though self-selection effect[5] could not be ruled out, the results show the potential to improve instruction and stimulate student learning. Teachers who participated in bilingual education confirmed the effectiveness of such practices. Teachers also reported that students showed a strong motivation for learning after acquiring the transcript system.

Challenges and discussion

The evaluation of the bilingual experiment shows its advantage in increasing achievement and reducing attrition rates among Dongxiang students. These results seem to confirm other international findings of successful bilingual preprograms (e.g, Cummins, 2001). Researchers, however, have reported problems with the experiment as well. Wang and Zhou (2005) found that although the transcript system greatly improved instructional quality, student participants still reported difficulty in learning Mandarin. Lower grade elementary school teachers reported having spent substantial amount of time explaining the textbook content in Dongxiang and Mandarin. They argued that because the Dongxiang language is so different in syntax from Chinese that simultaneous use of both languages in the classroom can cause confusion. Some teachers claimed that there are many Mandarin expressions such as idioms or complex reading materials in *Yuwen* class that could not be effectively translated into Dongxiang (Wang & Zhou, 2005).

These issues deserve some discussion here. They either resemble generic issues commonly found in bilingual programs or are specifically tied to local contexts. For one, curriculum development is still in early stages. Dongxiang students use the same textbook as Han students except that they are annotated throughout with transcripts. International studies have shown that instruction has maximum utility if the instructional material matches student's cognitive ability (Daly, Martens, Kilmer, & Massie, 1996). Yet according to the teachers who participated in the program, there seems to be a gap between content difficulty in the national textbook and students' learning ability. Using annotated curriculum may not fully address the learning needs of Dongxiang students. In addition, Zhang and Wang's ethnographic study (2006) found that current use of Mandarin textbooks is not connected to the religious value or cultural heritage of the local community. They found that the local community wished to incorporate Dongxiang history and Islamic tradition into the curricula (Zhang & Wang, 2006), but the usage of only national curriculum is unlikely to fulfill these wishes. No content knowledge is specifically designed for Dongxiang students with the exception of literacy textbooks used in preschools. The irrelevance of the curriculum might limit their interest to learn L1. After all, schoolwork is still centered on Mandarin-based textbooks. Some parents already chose private institutions, many of which were located in local mosques, as the way for their children to acquire knowledge on religious texts and local history (Zhang & Wang, 2006). Some empirical evidence is needed to show whether new textbooks specifically tailored for Dongxiang students aid learning and their parents' choice of schools for them.

Teacher quality is another question that deserves discussion. Bilingual education raised the bar for teaching in Dongxiang schools. In the current experiment, teachers participated in a two-month workshop to learn to use transcripts in teaching, but little effort has been made to help teachers solve issues in classroom teaching. Bilingual teaching requires more than the use of transcripts to explain textbooks. Despite the specific concern about classroom practices, teacher quality overall has been a concern in Dongxiang for quite a while. As in many other rural areas in China, the majority of teachers in DAC graduated from a local secondary level normal school. One study showed that Dongxiang teachers trained in this institution are not very fluent in Mandarin. Most teachers speak "Dongxiang-styled Chinese" which refers to their toneless accent (Wang & Zhou, 2005, p. 33). Only 85 percent of teachers are fully certified by the education bureau (Wang & Zhou, 2005). Such issues raise concern because these teachers are probably going to participate in the bilingual program later. In addition, teachers considered good at teaching often managed to get transferred to urban areas for better benefits. Schools have to hire para-professions (*daike jiaoshi*) to fill vacancies left by teacher turnover (Lu & Chang, 2006). These conditions impose potential threats to the bilingual program because an ill-prepared teaching workforce is less likely to successfully implement bilingual teaching.

The bilingual initiative in Dongxiang also unveils tensions in the school finance mechanism under the current fiscal system. The Ford Foundation supported the first two experiments in DAC. Initial funding was US$50,000, which helped them to complete two rounds of pilot experiments. The cost for future implementation has been greatly reduced because textbooks with transcripts have been created. Since 2007, the Oxfam Hong Kong branch continued to fund this project until 2010 to expand the initiative to more schools: eight sites within DAC. The total cost for this expansion is US$70,000, yet over the county, there are 156 primary schools, 80 percent of which are eligible for bilingual education. The total student population that needs to be covered is 5,000. For a full implementation of bilingual education, many other resources will be needed, financial support and teacher training in particular. For example, teachers need to engage in special workshops or professional development programs that help them master skills needed in bilingual teaching. If the one-year preschool program is considered preferable, extending compulsory education to preschool will also need financial support. Textbooks need revision and periodical updates. One estimate suggests additional financial support will need to be around 10 million RMB (about US$1.5 million), but DAC, with more than 90 percent of its population engaged in subsistence agriculture, is not likely to have the fiscal capacity to sustain bilingual education by itself.[6] Under the current system, major responsibility for financing schools (including teacher salaries, professional development, curricula designs) is undertaken by the county. A new program like bilingual education would only burden local communities unless additional grant aid can be added by provincial or central governments.[7] As a part of current state aid to relieve the financial hardship of rural schools, the "two exemptions and one aid" (*liang mian yi bu*) policy has been implemented since 2005. This policy is directly funded by the central government as a first step to provide free elementary education, but as Zhang and Wang (2006) pointed out, local educators believe additional efforts are needed to reach the same goal of enrolling every school-aged child in school and providing them with quality education. While efforts in recent years aim at providing equal access to rural students, not enough has been done to ensure achieving equal educational outcomes.

The implication of the bilingual education initiative is far-reaching. First, the language issue connects broad socio-economic policies in Dongxiang. Acquiring Mandarin is of practical concern for the Dongxiang community. Due to a harsh natural environment, people living in DAC and nearby counties have historically engaged in subsistence agriculture for survival (Zhang, 2007). In recent years, substantial numbers of Dongxiang people have migrated to metropolitan areas such as Lanzhou, Jiuquan, and Baiyin for better employment opportunities, but low educational attainment and Mandarin proficiency limited those opportunities to so-called "3D" (Dangerous, Difficult, Dirty) low-end jobs (Ma, 2004). When completion of middle school education becomes the national standard, job market conditions increasingly demand fluency in Mandarin and increasingly English as well (Finifrock, 2010). Successful implementation of bilingual education can improve local human resources and increase the chances of graduates securing better employment when they enter the labor market.

Second, lessons learned in piloting bilingual education in Dongxiang could also inform similar practices for other ethnic minority groups. For example, Muslim minorities such as the Salar and the Bao-an people face similar challenges, in which they only have oral language without written scripts. They are small in population, low in economic development and also have a large number of illiterate adults. Presumably, Dongxiang-type of bilingual education could work for them as well. But different from Dongxiang, Salar and Bao-an people live in even more isolated mountainous regions. Their students typically attend single-teacher facilities, where a multi-grade integrated classroom is very common. To develop bilingual education for them would require more resources and collaboration among county, provincial, and central administrations. Finally, bilingual education can shed new light on adult literacy programs also as the growing number of illiterate adults has been a concern of local communities. If the bilingual program can be modified and extended to the illiterate adult population, it might be able to provide practical help to Dongxiang people.

In summary, the bilingual education experiment in Dongxiang draws attention to the educational issues of ethnic minority people that have not been traditionally a focus in education policy-making in China. This chapter discussed the new practices in Dongxiang and also their challenges. The experiment supports the contention that L1 acquisition increases students' L2 literacy and math achievement, though more empirical studies need to be conducted to evaluate the effectiveness and adequacy of this experiment on a larger scale. As discussed in this chapter, bilingual education in rural areas such as Dongxiang needs support from a variety of sources. A stand-alone policy is not likely to succeed. These findings correspond to international literature on bilingual education, in which researchers suggest that curriculum development, personnel training and finance are essential parts of a successful bilingual program (Baker, 2001). Nonetheless, this initiative provides new possibilities for people in Dongxiang.

Acknowledgments

The author would like thank the Graduate School of MSU for a grant that made this work possible and Zhong Chen from Cornell University for providing technical help on the Dongxiang language.

Notes

1 Linxia Hui Autonomous Prefecture (*Linxia Huizu Zizhi Zhou*) includes one municipality (City of Linxia) and seven nearby counties: Guanghe, Linxia, Kangle, Hezheng, Yongjing, Dongxiang (DAC) and Jishishan, with a total population of 1.96 million. The population consists of five large ethnic minority groups of Tibetan, Salar, Bao-an, Hui, and Dongxiang with 11 other small groups.
2 According to official Chinese Statistics, illiteracy refers to "population who are unable or have difficulty in reading" (http://www.moe.edu.cn/edoas/website18/73/info29073. htm). In the adult literacy program, literacy refers to the ability to recognize and use 1,500 Chinese characters in rural areas and 2,000 Chinese characters in urban areas. (http://www.chinaliteracy.org/script/infodetail.jsp?id=36andbid=1).
3 A version of written scripts called *Xiao Jingwen* is used for religious purposes in various places. It uses Arabic characters to annotate Dongxiang language, but was not widely used after 1949. See Dongxiang County Annals (1996, p. 498) for reference.
4 The authors used factor analysis to construct one composite measure of language factor, which includes variables such as student's Chinese efficiency, the language environment at home and on campus, and exposure to Chinese, etc. See Wang and Postiglione (2008, p. 175), Table 3.
5 It is not clear what criterion is used when selecting students for the treatment condition. It is possible that more motivated families participated in the treatment.
6 In 2006, the fiscal revenue in DAC was about 16 million RMB, 6.7 million of which are discretionary funds. The revenue funds a broad array of public expenditures with education being only one of them.
7 A World Bank report of May 24, 2010 on fiscal sustainability in nearby Jishishan Country reveals that most of the county fiscal revenue is used to pay teachers' salaries and the daily operation of schools. According to this report, county level government would not be able to afford additional education services.

References

Baker, C. (2001). *Foundations of bilingual education and bilingualism* (3rd ed.). Clevedon: Multilingual Matters Ltd.
Bao, S. (2007). Jieci Ancang de Xiaoyong Tanxi: Yi Dongxiang Yu Zhong de Hanyu Jieci Weili [The investigation of hidden effectiveness of the borrowed words: A case study of the borrowed words in Dongxiang language from Chinese]. *Journal of the Second Northwest University for Nationalities*, 76(4), 30–35.
Chen, Q. (2006). *Dongxiang Shehui Yanjiu* [Dongxiang society study]. Beijing: The Ethnic Publishing House.
Cummins, J. (2000). *Language, power and pedagogy: Bilingual children in the crossfire.* Clevedon: Multilingual Matters Ltd.
Cummins, J. (2001). Bilingual children's mother tongue: Why is it important for education? *Sprogforum*, 19(February), 15–19. doi: 10.1080/13670059808667672.
Dai, Q., & Cheng, Y. (2007). Typology of bilingualism and bilingual education in Chinese minority nationality regions. In A. Feng (Ed.), *Bilingual education in China: Practices, policies and concepts* (pp. 75–93). Clevedon: Multilingual Matters Ltd.

Daly, E. J., Martens, B. K., Kilmer, A., & Massie, D. R. (1996). The effects of instructional match and content overlap on generalized reading performance. *Journal of Applied behavior analysis*, 29(4), 507–518. doi: 10.1901/jaba.1996.29-507.

Dongxiang County Annals Editorial Committee. (1996). *Dongxiang County annals.* Lanzhou: Lanzhou Culture Press.

Du, S. (2006). *GanQing ZangZu Xiandai Jiaoyu Fazhan Yanjiu* [Modern educational development for Tibetans in Gansu and Qinghai]. Beijing: The Ethnic Publishing House.

Finifrock, J. E. (2010). English as a third language in rural China: Lessons from the Zaidang Kam-Mandarin bilingual education project. *Diaspora, Indigenous, and Minority Education*, 4(1), 33–46. doi: 10.1080/15595690903442272.

Geary, D. N., & Pan, Y. (2003). A bilingual education pilot project among the Kam People in Guizhou province, China. *Journal of Multilingual and Multicultural Development*, 24(4), 274–289. doi: 10.1080/01434630308666502.

Lu, G., & Chang, B. (2006). Yingxiang Dongxiang Zu Xiaoxuesheng Xueye Chengji Yinsu de Diaochayanjiu [Factors affecting Dongxiang pupils' achievement]. *Journal of Northwest University for Nationalities*, 5, 146–152.

Ma, G., & Chen, Y. (2001). *Dongxiang-Chinese dictionary*. Lanzhou: Gansu Ethnic Press.

Ma, T. (2004). Dongxiang Nongcun Laodongli Zhuanyi Tedian jiqi Sikao [Characteristics of rural Dongxiang migrating labor]. *Journal of Northwest University for Nationalities*, 1, 92–94.

Ministry of Education. (2007). *Guojia Jiaoyu Shiye Fazhan "Shiyiwu" Guihua Gangyao* [National Strategy of Education Development in the Eleventh Five-Year Plan]. Beijing. Retrieved from http://www.china.com.cn/news/txt/2007-06/04/content_8340435.htm.

National Bureau of Statistics. (2003). *Tabulation on nationalities of 2000 population census of China*. Beijing: The Ethnic Publishing House.

Qin, Z., & Ma, G. (2004). *Dongxiang: A survey in Hanzeling village, Dongxiang county, Gansu province (Dongxiang Zu: Gansu Dongxiang Hanzeling Cun Diaocha)*. Kunming: Yunnan University Press.

Wang, J., & Postiglione, G. A. (2008). China's minorities without written scripts: The case of education access among the Dongxiang. *Journal of Asian Pacific Communication*, 18(2), 166–189. doi: 10.1075/japc.18.2.04pos.

Wang, J., & Zhou, F. (2005). A reflection on bilingual teaching for ethnic minorities in China: Taking Dongxiang nationality as a case. *Journal of Northwest Normal University [Chinese]*, 42(1), 32–36.

Zhang, G. (2009). Guanyu Xibei Shaoshuminzu Ertong Chuoxue Yuanyou de Shehuixue Kaocha [A sociological study on school dropout among western minority students]. *Journal of Northwest University for Nationalities*, 3, 125–130.

Zhang, L. (2007). *Dongxiang: A study on poverty and anti-poverty issues* [Dongxiangzu: Pinkun yu Fan Pinkun Wenti Yanjiu]. Beijing: The Ethnic Publishing House.

Zhang, L., & Wang, X. (2006). Shanqu Dongxiangzu Xiaoxuesheng Chuoxue Wenti de Sikao yu Diaocha: Yi Dongxiangzu Zizhixian Beiling Xiang weili [Dropping out of schools among Dongxiang students: A case study in Beiling township]. *Ethno-National Studies*, 2, 1–10.

5 China's minorities without written scripts

The case of education access among the Dongxiang*

Jiayi Wang and Gerard A. Postiglione

The Chinese state sees language policy as an essential determinant of ethnic minority educational progress. The use of minority language as a medium of instruction is viewed as a way to increase attendance rates and strengthen socialization into a national identity. However, the policies differ for those ethnic minorities with or without a commonly used written script. Among the minorities without a script are the 300,000-strong Dongxiang, an ethnic group with the lowest level of literacy and school access in China. There has been little systematic research on the role of language in school access for Chinese minority groups without a written script. This and Zhou Yisu's Chapter 4 about the Dongxiang aim to provide insights into the schooling of script-less minorities. In fact, there is a need for more research and analysis of the Dongxiang (and similar groups without a written script), especially with reference to their learning styles and school discontinuation. This research identifies the major difficulties in school-based learning for Dongxiang speaking children. Specifically, it explores local perspectives on how language and other factors are related to school enrollment and achievement. In order to accomplish this, the research combined a variety of data gathering methods, including survey questionnaire, open-ended and in-depth interviews, field visits, observations, and case studies to analyze the difficulties of language transition faced by Dongxiang ethnic minority children. The results reveal that native language does not cause schoolchildren to discontinue their studies. However, it does have an important indirect influence, especially on the education of girls. The research results also show that Dongxiang ethnic minority schoolchildren in the early years of schooling struggle to understand their teachers when they teach through the medium of Chinese. This results in poor school performance, a decline of interest in learning, a frustrated sense of achievement, and a decline in self-respect. Many students drop out as part of a vicious cycle that sees a reproduction of poor conditions for learning.

Language transition in China: education and minority language in China

Language is an essential factor in China's ethnic minority schooling (Fei, 1980, 1989, Lam, 2005, Gladney, 1996, Hansen, 1999, Harrell, 2001, Heberer, 1989).

As the gap in educational attainment between most of China's ethnic minorities and Han Chinese becomes more glaring, attention is focused on native languages and the medium of instruction in schools (Fang, Wang, & Linda, 2001; Postiglione, 2006).

The Constitution guarantees the rights of ethnic minorities within the 148 autonomous areas of the country to use their own languages (Ma, 1985; Mackerras, 2003). Of China's 55 state-designated ethnic minority groups, 53 have at least one spoken language. Some like the Mongols, Tibetans, Dai, Uigurs, Koreans, Kazak, Xibe, Uzbek, Kirgiz, Tatars, and Russians have had their own languages in fairly common use for generations.

Others like the Yi, Miao, Naxi, Jingpo, Lisu, Wa, and Lahu had written scripts that were not in common use. The rest were without a script. The Chinese government aided in the development of phonetic scripts for the Zhuang, Buyi, Miao, Li, Lisu, Naxi, Hani, Wa, and Dong, and it reformed the languages of the Lahu, Jingpo, and Dai, and postponed the reform to replace the Arabic script of the Uigur and Kazak with a Romanized one (Ma, 1985; Wang, 1994; Yu, 1995). There are 12 minority scripts used in both primary and secondary school textbooks, and nine more are being piloted in the schools (Zheng, 2002). China produces 3,500 textbook titles in more than 30 ethnic minority languages. The use of minority languages as a medium of instruction is viewed as a way to increase attendance rates and strengthen national socialization (Banks, 1994).

Although the provision of education for ethnic minorities at all levels has increased, most minorities' level of educational attainment is below the national average. Moreover, the role of language has not been ignored in the literature (Lam, 2005; Lee, 2001; Postiglione, 2002; Trueba and Zou, 1994. National policies have addressed the issue of language and education with varying levels of success. Stites (1999) studied policies and practices regarding four of the main minority languages used in education: Zhuang, Yi, Uyghur, and Tibetan, as examples to examine China's efforts to develop a viable bilingual system of education. Those children in these four language groups will spend most of their lives within a linguistic environment different from that of the Han Chinese majority. Although the Chinese state has gone to great lengths to accommodate minority languages, the debates and complexities of Chinese language policies and their implementation within different contexts point to the need for field-based studies of different groups (Zhou & Fishman, 2003; Zhou & Sun, 2004).

The case of Tibetan education is particularly illustrative of the dilemma of ethnic education in China, as shown by Upton's research (Upton, 1999). Her fieldwork in the Abba region of Sichuan convinced her that China has done well in certain respects in the way it has handled minority language, though not always as well as most Tibetans seem to want or expect. Few Tibetans advocate not learning any Chinese and an increasing number want to learn Chinese fluently because their daily survival and access to broader occupational opportunities may depend upon it. Moreover, some would like to study as much English in school as do Han Chinese students. In Tibetan areas of China, dual track education (Tibetan and Chinese) is generally available in the urban areas, but after the third grade most courses are taught in Chinese with only language and some Tibetan "culture" courses taught in the Tibetan language (Wang & Zhou, 2003). However, there are many variations. In the Kangding area of Sichuan, for example, there are opportunities to learn all courses (science, math, history, etc.) in Tibetan up through senior middle school, although interest drops as the students prepare for the national college and university entrance examinations in Chinese. In Qinghai's Tibetans regions, some schools offer instruction solely in the Chinese language while others offer all courses in Tibetan. There are also experimental courses that use Tibetan as the language of instruction for all the science and math subjects. Those advocating the trial programs want to make Tibetan a language of science and modernity so that Tibetans can use their own language as the main form of communication, as well as increasing their opportunities to go into higher education since they will learn better and thus perform better on the college entrance examinations. This same argument is used by those who advocate introducing Chinese in the early years, because that too will enable children to do better on the standardized tests. Most children in rural and nomadic areas have little opportunity to use Chinese in daily life, and their Chinese is often too poor to pass examinations. Thus, the dropout rate is high in many places and problems remain, including a lack of qualified teachers.

While the Tibetan case is illustrative, most minorities do not have a written script. Therefore, the two-track model is not feasible for most minorities. Many schools employ a transitional bilingual teaching model, under which the spoken minority language is used as the teaching medium alongside the Chinese language school textbooks in the first and second year of primary school, as part of a process of transition by grade three to complete Chinese medium teaching.

Language continues to be a major issue in ethnic minority education (Postiglione, 2001). Debate has increased among specialists and policy-makers in China as has the literature on the subject. The main research topics include: the theories and principles of minority bilingual teaching, the guiding role of contemporary psycholinguistics, ethnolinguistics, sociology and anthropology; research on socio-cultural background, and social environment of Tibetan, Uyghur, Mongol, and Yi language education (Stites, 1999; Upton 1999; Teng 2000); and, bilingual teaching models (Fang, Wang & Linda, 2001; Dai, Teng, Guan, & Dong, 1997). Yet, research on groups without a commonly used native script has been scarce.

Since the 1980s, scholars have conducted research on the Dongxiang religious and mosque education. However, as a result of an experimental project in the Narisi school that employs a phonetic form of Dongxiang language in preschool and early primary school teaching materials, there is evidence of the positive value of native language as a medium of instruction (Qi, 2004). Given the amount of study of transitional bilingualism globally, the Dongxiang constitute a valuable case study (Baker, 2001). This research focuses on the difficulties of language transition for Dongxiang children and the impact on learning and school discontinuation. According to a 2001 survey of Dongxiang county, the adult illiteracy rate was over 80 percent among people 15 years old and above;

the enrollment rate of school-aged children was 81 percent, 61 percent for school-aged girls, and the dropout rate for primary school students was 10 percent. Dongxiang County is locked in by mountains, with poor transportation and communication facilities and droughts almost every year, leaving it with a low agricultural output and a lack of industrial production. The Dongxiang ethnic group has a strong belief in Islam, and a spoken language in common use (Dongxiang County Annals Editorial Committee, 1996). However, they have no official written script. Local intellectuals and some officials in Dongxiang County have attributed much of the educational difficulties to the bottleneck created by language-related factors.

Research methodology

Field methods

This chapter is based on a study of the role of language in learning difficulties. Specifically, it explores local perspectives about how language and other factors relate to school enrollment and achievement. The research combined a variety of data-gathering methods, including survey questionnaires, open-ended interviews, in-depth interviews, field visits, participatory and non-participatory observations, literature analysis, and case studies to analyze the difficulties of language transition faced by Dongxiang ethnic minority children.

Dongxiang schools and sample selection

Dongxiang County has 184 schools, of which 171 are primary schools (Table 5.1). These include 25 county and township level central primary schools, 78 village primary schools, and 68 teaching points. The student population numbers 31,769, of which 27,438 are in primary schools. Following the principle of stratified random sampling, this research sampled selected schools where bilingual teaching is a serious problem. The sampling was guided by these factors: First, since the location, teaching conditions, teaching staff quality, size and language environment of teaching points, village schools and central schools differ, so we selected three sample schools from the teaching points, three from village schools and three from central schools, respectively, with the purpose of making the samples more representative. Second, since the issue of transitional bilingual teaching and second language learning is more serious in the remote areas of Dongxiang County, the research also selected ten sample schools from the remote and "backward" areas. Third, the Dongxiang Normal (Teacher Training) School is the major institute for training Dongxiang primary school teachers. Its students come from the villages of Dongxiang County. They are generally among the most outstanding Dongxiang ethnic minority students. Since their past experience as a student in Dongxiang is valuable to this research, 100 of them were surveyed by questionnaire (Table 5.2).

The research instruments included questionnaires, interview outlines, classroom observation record forms, and a Chinese language-level assessment form.

Table 5.1 Basic information about the sample schools

School name	Location	Students			Teachers			Local communities		
		Total	Female	% of Dongxiang ethnic minority	Total	Female	% of Dongxiang ethnic minority	Population	Language	Location
Teaching point A	Heizhuang Village, Nale Township	139	30	100.0	3	0	100	1,502	Dongxiang	Poor traffic conditions
Teaching point B	Xinxing Village, Yanling Township	81	17	100.0	2	0	100	1,206	Dongxiang	Poor traffic conditions
Teaching point C	Gaojia Village	92	26	100.0	4	1	100	UN	Dongxiang	Along the Suoda Highway
Village Primary School A	Beizhuangwan Village, Longquan Township	139	43	90.4	5	1	80	1,411	Basically Chinese	The nearby township is inhabited by pure Han people speaking Chinese
Village Primary School B	Waziling Village, Wangji Township	119	40	100.0	4	2	100	785	Dongxiang	Along the highway, easy access, greater communication with the outside world
Village Primary School C	Beizhuang Village, Chuntai Township	145	20	93.0	7	2	75.6	1,400	Dongxiang	Within mountains, only one road leading to town
Central Primary School A	Mianguchi Township	190	71	100.0	7	0	100	UN	Dongxiang	1 kilometer from the highway
Central Primary School B	Yanling Township (China Daily)	369	85	99.6	16	6	77	UN	Dongxiang / Chinese	7 kilometers from the county town
Central Primary School C	Chuntai Township	138	39	100.0	8	5	50	UN	Dongxiang	2 kilometers from the highway
Dongxiang Normal School	Dongxiang County	135	UN	UN	UN	UN	UN	—	Chinese/Dongxiang	County town

Notes

Some of the figures are collected from school investigations and some from questionnaires.

UN = unavailable.

Table 5.2 Distribution of subjects

	Mianguchi Central School		Zhongbao Central School		Chuntai Central School		Beizhuangwan Village School		Waziwan Village School		Beizhuang Village School		Heizhuang Teaching Point		Xinxing Teaching Point		Gaojia Teaching Point	
	T	F	T	F	T	F	T	F	T	F	T	F	T	F	T	F	T	F
Primary schools students (721)	78	14	249	41	85	15	73	13	61	14	59	9	55	7	30	0	33	8
Faculty members (65)	9	0	14	7	10	5	7	3	8	4	7	2	3	0	4	0	3	1
Parents (120)	16	9	23	15	3	3	14	4	15	6	9	2	15	11	18	10	6	4
Normal school students	119*																	
Government officials	51**																	

Notes
*Dongxiang 91, Female 35.
**Dongxiang 40, Female 8.

1. "T" for total number of subjects, "F" for number of female subjects.
2. Fewer female subjects due to enrollment limitations. Generally speaking, the higher the grade, the smaller the number of female students. That is, the first-year groups see the largest number of female students. With this group excluded in the survey, it naturally follows that female subjects are of a very small number in this table.
3. 721 students are of Dongxiang origin, the other 11 are of Hui origin.
4. 120 parents are all of Dongxiang origin. As in the most households, the bread-winners are the male family members, the majority of the surveyed family member are female.

The research team spent two days conducting a pilot investigation. The aim was to revise the research instruments and refine the five interview outlines, three focus group interview outlines, the classroom observation outline, five forms of survey questionnaire and one Chinese-level assessment form. Using these tools, a task force conducted the following data gathering: Interviews: individual interviews with nine Head Teachers, individual and focus group interviews with 46 teachers, individual and focus group interviews with 97 students, interviews with 27 villagers, nine village heads, and seven officials and intellectuals.

Questionnaires

Some 723 students, 53 teachers, 51 officials, 120 villagers, and 119 Dongxiang Normal School students were surveyed. In accordance with a Chinese language-level assessment form, the teachers rated the Chinese level of the investigated students in his or her class.

Classroom observation

The task force participated in 22 periods of class observations, with the aim of comparing the teaching of different courses and of teachers with different Chinese levels in teaching points, village schools and central primary schools and collecting information about the teaching language, teaching methods, and student learning. The task force kept observation records about all the classes they attended, and used photographs to record the second-grade Chinese language lessons. Student case studies: two excellent students and two students with learning difficulties were chosen from the village primary schools and teaching points for the case studies. Investigations on their learning in classrooms, schools and families were carried out with the purpose of comparing students with different Chinese levels and school performances and finding out the impact of language on their leaning.

The research process was divided into three stages: (1) formulating research tools; (2) conducting field visits; and (3) analyzing the data. During the field visits, the task force was divided into three groups according to the investigations and interviews in central primary schools, village schools, and teaching points, respectively. To improve reliability of the questionnaires, the research team ran checks throughout the entire survey process.

Questionnaire structure

While taking account of the language factor, the research team also adopted a panoramic perspective and included questions related to the campus environment, social context, and family conditions.

Order of presenting questions

To guarantee that the subjects remained independent in filling out the questionnaires, the questionnaires were entitled "Survey on the Basic Education Conditions in Dongxiang County." In arranging the order of the questions, great care was taken to avoid the subjects' awareness of the actual focus of the research team—the language issue. Instead, the survey started with topics not directly related to the language and then gradually shifted to the language factors.

Language barriers

The research team engaged students from the Dongxiang Normal School as interpreters since they are versed in both Chinese and Dongxiang languages and familiar with survey process. The questions were read to students in their native language.

Reliability estimates of the 42 questions in the questionnaire arrived at an Alpha Coefficient of 0.7758, a high level of reliability. Table 5.3 shows the general reliability and that of the individual factors after some components are excluded, and takes the student questionnaire as an example. Here language factors referred to the students' Chinese efficiency, the language environment at home and campus, and exposure to Chinese. Study time showed whether the students are often absent due to reasons like cold weather, school–home distance, language difficulties, household chores, etc. Attitude refers to the psychological inclination towards the school, study and the language of Chinese formed in the context. Culture and career reflects their attitudes towards school and religion, which to a large extent shows their cultural inclination and future career. In-class support examines whether the teachers offer language or substantive support to help the students understand the subject matter. Table 5.4 shows that the reliability coefficients are higher than 0.6 except for all factors except "Culture and Career."

Findings

Factors influencing students' academic performance

First, to determine whether the influence of Chinese proficiency on academic performance is significant or not, analysis of variance had been carried out by taking the former as the independent variable and the four examination test results and the mean of the aggregate score as the dependent variables. We found that the influence of the Chinese proficiency level on the four examination results and the mean result are all highly significant (Table 5.5).

Table 5.6 shows that the shaping factors of Chinese and Mathematics subjects. The major shaping factors for Chinese are study time and Chinese proficiency level. For Mathematics, it is proficiency, attitude and in-class support. Language has significant influence only on the 2002–2003 first-semester Chinese test result; its influence on other test results is not very significant. The shaping factors of the four test results are not the same, possibly because the subjects are measures at different grade levels. Although these are results of a unified examination, the level of difficulty at various grades levels may differ and that is why the findings do not concur. If the mean of the four test results are taken as the dependent variable, the interference of the test paper difficulty level with the research results can be avoided.

Therefore, we conclude that the major shaping factors of the students' academic performance are time, Chinese proficiency, and attitude. The Dongxiang language factor does not appear to have a direct effect of the students' academic performance.

Table 5.3 Factor analysis of the student questionnaires

	Language factor	Study time	Attitude factor	Culture and career	In-class support
38. Can you understand the teacher who speaks only Chinese?	.708				
15. Do you know Chinese?	.685				
19. Can you catch classroom Chinese ?	.653				
20. Do you chat with your classmates in Chinese after class?	.579				
22. Do you have discussions in Chinese in class?	.576				
23. Do you understand the texts?	.436				
43. Can your parents speak Chinese?	.421				
21. Have the teachers ever encouraged you to speak Chinese after class?	.387				
27. Is Chinese used in class?	.366				
07. Do you read books other than textbooks?	.336				
32. Have you ever skipped any class because of cold weather?		.743			
33. Have you ever skipped any class to help with household chores?		.729			
31. Have you ever skipped any class out of transportation reasons?		.696			
35. Have you ever skipped any class for language reasons?		.677			
45. Do you often skip classes for health reasons?		.566			
41. Have you ever skipped any class hours for scripture reading?		.440			
09. Are you fond of going to school?			.685		
10. Do you like your school?			.585		
06. Do the teachers care about you?			.479		
18. Are you fond of having classes?			.469		
39. Do you parents care about your academic performance?			.381		
14. Are you fond of speaking Chinese?			.359		
25. Are you willing to learn Chinese?			.306		
42. Does scripture reading mean much to you?				.673	
40. Do you like reading scripture?				.539	
29. Have you ever thought seriously about passing entrance examinations?				.426	
37. Does your Chinese teacher ever explain the texts in Dongxiang dialect?					.690
26. Do the teachers speak Dongxiang dialect in class?					.663
28. Do the teachers use the teaching tools in class?					.388
08. Are there sufficient stationary available for you?					.287

Notes: The survey questionnaire numbers are included with the respective questions.
    1. Rotating method: Varimax with Kaiser Normalization.
    2. The rotation takes iterations.

Tables 5.6 and 5.7 show the results of the regression equation with the mean value of the examination results as the dependent variable and language, time,

Table 5.4 Alpha coefficient for the questionnaire and factors

	Language	Study time	Attitude	Culture and career	In-class support
Alpha coefficient	.7516	.7750	.6171	.4039	.6066
Alpha aggregate	.7758 (29 items)				

Table 5.5 Analysis of variance for the Chinese proficiency level

	Degree of freedom (df)	F	Sig.
Mean	4	7.214	.000
2001–2002 second-semester Chinese	4	5.614	.000
2001–2002 second-semester Maths	4	3.430	.009
2002–2003 first-semester Chinese	4	8.341	.000
2002–2003 first-semester Maths	4	7.294	.000

Table 5.6 Step-wise regression

Dependent variables	Factors taken into equation	Degree of freedom (df)	F	Significance (sig)
Mean	Time, proficiency and attitude	390	19.605	.000
2001–2002 second-semester Chinese	Time, proficiency	415	36.576	.000
2001–2002 second-semester Maths	Attitude, time, proficiency and in-class support	413	8.954	.000
2002–2003 first-semester Chinese	Time, proficiency, language	472	19.585	.000
2002–2003 first-semester Maths	Proficiency, attitude and in-class support	475	11.523	.000

attitude, culture and career, in-class support and Chinese proficiency level as the independent variables entering through coercion. Table 5.7 indicates that time, attitude, and Chinese proficiency levels are significant factors shaping students' academic performance. With reference to the standard regression coefficient Beta, the shaping factors of the students' academic performance can be sequenced as follows according to significance of influence: time, Chinese proficiency, attitude, in-class support, language, and culture and career.

Factors influencing the Chinese proficiency level

Initial regression analysis shows that the influence of the language factors (including the students' ability to understand the Chinese language, family and campus language environments and exposure to Chinese on the students'

Table 5.7 Results of enter regression

	B coefficient	Standardized beta coefficient	T	Significance
Constant常数项	44.697		22.745	.000
Language	−.725	−.044	−.923	.357
Time	−4.189	−.257	−5.347	.000
Attitude	2.301	.138	2.886	.004
Culture and career	−5.841E-02	−.004	−.075	.940
In-class support	−1.300	−.078	−1.651	.100
Chinese proficiency	2.087	.160	3.282	.001

academic performance) is not very significant. To determine how language factors work on Chinese proficiency level, the Chinese proficiency level may be treated as the dependent variable and language, time, attitude, culture and career, and in-class support as independent variables. Putting these into regression equation, the results are represented in Table 5.8.

Thus, time and language are two most significant shaping factors with a significance value of .05. It is clear from the standardized Beta coefficient that the shaping factors of the Chinese proficiency level can be sequenced according to the significance of the influence as follows: time, language, attitude, culture and career, and in-class support.

The influence of other background factor on the academic performance and Chinese proficiency level

In addition to the above-mentioned factors, sex and ethnicity of students, and the age, education, length of teaching, title, language use, and language attitude of the teachers, can also affect students' academic performance. We took the above-mentioned factors as the independent variables and the mean of the examination results of the students as the dependent variable and subjected them to multivariate analysis to determine the significance of the factors on academic performance. Table 5.9 demonstrates the results from the analysis.

Table 5.9 shows that teacher-related independent variables have a significant impact on the students' academic performance, whereas the impact of the sex and ethnicity of the students on their academic performance is not very significant. This phenomenon may have something to do with the distribution features of the survey subjects. More than 98 percent of those surveyed are of Dongxiang origin. How frequently the parents speak Chinese at home also has significant impact on the students' academic performance while how they view schooling does not. Variance analysis also shows that parents' attitude towards Chinese and Chinese study does not have much impact on the academic performance of the students.

As there are a large number of items, the related statistics are not shown in great detail. The significant factors are analyzed to determine whether the impact of these factors on the academic performance is negative or positive. The results

Table 5.8 Regressional analysis of the shaping factors of the Chinese proficiency

	B coefficient	Standardized Beta coefficient	T	Significance
Constant常数项	2.831		51.563	.000
Language	.133	.106	2.433	.015
Time	−.181	−.145	−3.309	.001
Attitude	8.804E-02	.070	1.607	.109
Culture and career	−5.292E-02	−.042	−.965	.335
In-class support	4.824E-03	.004	.088	.930

Table 5.9 Analysis of variance for the impact of background factors on students' academic performance

Source of the independent variables	Independent variables	Degree of freedom (df)	F	Significance (sig.)
Students	Sex	479	2.027	.155
	Nationality	481	.161	.688
Teachers	Age	443	9.826	.000
	Education	481	15.573	.000
	Professional title	481	6.834	.000
	Frequency of the use of Chinese in class	433	10.047	.000
Parents	Speak Chinese at home?	54	3.688	.018
	Household financial status	54	4.177	.010
	Is schooling important?	54	1.274	.293

are shown in Table 5.10. Age, education, and professional title of the teachers are factors that have significant negative impact on the students' academic performance. The higher the age, education, and title the teachers have, the lower the students' academic performance tends to be. How frequently the teachers use Chinese in class correlates significantly with the students' academic performance, that is, the higher the frequency the better the performance. By contrast how frequently parents use Chinese at home does not have very significant impact on the students' performance. The household financial status has significant negative impact on the students' academic performance.

Major findings

Our analysis leads us to the following findings:

1 Students' comprehension of Chinese, the campus and family language environment, and exposure to Chinese are not directly linked to the students' academic performance.

Table 5.10 Correlation between the background factors and students' academic performance

	Teachers' age	Teachers' education	Teachers' title	Frequency of in-class Chinese use	Do parents speak Chinese at home?	Household financial status
Correlation coefficient	−.129	−.257	−.128	.160	−.192	−.405
Significance (Sig).	.006	.000	.005	.001	.616	.002

2   Factors that have a direct impact on the students' academic performance are students' attendance rate, their Chinese proficiency and their attitudes towards schooling.
3   Although language factors such as language comprehension ability, language environment and exposure to Chinese have no direct impact on the students' academic performance, they are closely related to the students' Chinese proficiency.
4   Attendance rate is also an important shaping factor of the students' Chinese proficiency level.
5   Teachers' age, education and professional title have a significant impact on students' academic performance; and the more frequently the teacher's use Chinese in class, the better the students' academic performance.
6   Among all family-related factors, household financial status is the most significant shaping factor of the students' academic performance. In general, our aggregate data seems to show that the better-off the household, the better the students' academic performance.

Discussion

Language, academic performance and dropout rate

Language factors, such as Chinese language environment, are not a direct influence on the students' academic performance. However, this does not mean that language-related factors have no impact on students' academic performance at all. If the impact of such factors as language environment on the students' Chinese proficiency is taken into account, it is rather clear that language-related factors work on the academic performance through Chinese proficiency. Time, attitude, in-class support, and Chinese proficiency, in combination with teacher and family background, affect the students' academic performance. From the standardized Beta value listed in Table 5.8, it is obvious that Chinese proficiency is the most important shaping factor, second only to time. And language-related factors are the most important shaping factors of the Chinese proficiency level after time. Qualitative analysis comes to the same conclusion, i.e. language-related factors do

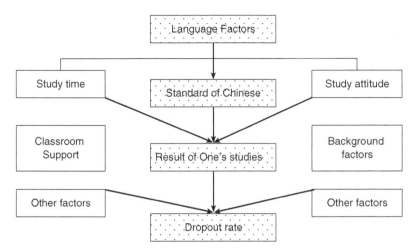

Figure 5.1 Factors that affect the dropout rate.

not have a direct impact on the academic performance, yet they can work on academic performance indirectly by affecting the Chinese proficiency level first. Figure 5.1 demonstrates the relationship between these elements.

Survey information gained from questionnaires of students of the Dongxiang Normal School students (prospective teachers) indicates that only 18.2 percent of them believe that their old school classmates' dropout rate had nothing to do with the difficulties they came across in their study. Meanwhile, interviews with dropouts also showed that some children lost self-confidence because of poor academic performance. They left school out of the dual pressure of study difficulty and household financial constraints, either to help with the farm work or do odd jobs outside their hometown. It is well justified to hold that language factors had an impact on the students' Chinese proficiency and through that, on the academic performance and dropout rate, as is shown in Figure 5.1.

Language and Chinese proficiency

Table 5.9 shows that the standardized Beta coefficient of the language factors is .106 in the regression formula where Chinese proficiency level serves as the dependent variable. In other words, the higher the coefficient, the higher the Chinese proficiency level. Language factors are embedded in questions like "Can you understand Chinese?" or "Do you have difficulty in catching what the teachers say in class in Chinese?" Such questions to some extent indicate students' Chinese proficiency level. Other questions such as "Do you discuss in Chinese in class?" or "Do you chat with your classmate in Chinese after class?" show how and in what situation Chinese is used by the students. As language factors and Chinese proficiency are two overlapping concepts, it is hard to tell whether the two are causally bound; however, the correlation can be easily verified through regression.

The impact of other factors on academic performance

Academic performance is subject to the influence of the following factors: time, attitude, teachers' age, education, professional title, and household financial status of the students.

In the regression analysis, the standardized Beta coefficient for the impact of time factors on students' academic performance is − .257. According to the survey, time factor-related questions are mainly related to insufficient attendance due to home–school distance, cold weather, household chores, language barrier, scripture reading and health-related reasons. There are five different options for each item ranging from "never" to "always," the marks for which range from 1–5 points. In other words, the lower the attendance rate, the poorer the students' academic performance, and vice versa.

This coincides with interview findings. As it is often the case in Dongxiang, students are exposed to the language context of Dongxiang dialect after school. Chinese is rarely used at home and in a social context. On the one hand, the Chinese class offered at the school familiarized students with the basics of Chinese grammar and enhanced their understanding of the subject matter. On the other hand, Chinese is commonly used as the teaching language and most teachers have a very high Chinese proficiency level, which creates an enabling environment for the use of Chinese. Campus life is definitely good for the enhancement of language use. Absence from class means insufficient exploitation of the language learning environment at the school, which in most cases has hindered the enhancement of the students' Chinese proficiency levels and of their academic performance in general (He & Wang 2004; Wang & Zhou 2005).

Attitude-related factors refer to how fond students are of their schools, their schooling, their class-hours and Chinese learning within the social context (e.g. how much parents care about the education of their children). In the regression formula where the academic performance acts as the dependent variable, standardized Beta coefficient of this factor is .138. To put it in another way, the more motivated the students are towards their school life and their learning, the more likely for them to gain better academic achievements. According to behavioral motivation theory, good academic performance in return will have a positive impact on the students' attitude towards study. Factor analysis demonstrates that how much care parents give to education and the teachers to their students are two important contributing elements to the attitude-related factor. To some extent, this means that the formation of the students' attitude toward academic study and language learning is prone to the influence of the parents and teachers. If parents care more about their children's studies, and the teachers care about their students' performance, the students are likely to take more interest in their study, and be better motivated towards their study and campus life.

According to the analysis of variance and relevant calculation, teachers' age, educational background, and professional title can have significant impact on students' academic performance; or to be more specific, there is a negative correlation between the two. This conclusion differs rather significantly from common belief that these factors are positively correlated with student's academic performance, as years are often associated with rich experience and education and title with professionalism. The findings in some way indicate that there are problems with the existent staff appraisal mechanism which relies heavily on the teachers' education background. It is for this reason that some teachers seek follow-up education just for the sake of obtaining a diploma, which in practical terms leads to the prevalence of examination-oriented follow-up education. Higher educational level may not bring about increased professional standards. Besides, the long-standing scarcity problem of the teaching resources has led to the sharp increase in the number of *minban* (non-accredited) teachers. Although this problem has been addressed by the government in recent years, this does not change the fact that non-accredited teachers are not professionally competent due to lack of formal training. The present professional accreditation and promotion system based on the length of teaching years is very likely to lead to the acquisition of high titles by some teachers without matching competence. This is likely to be the very reason that analytical findings fail to meet expectations. It may take greater research efforts to get a fuller picture of the real situation.

Another important research finding is that household financial status also has a bearing on the students' academic performance. It is commonly believed that economic factors are the major deterrents of educational development, higher enrollment rates and higher educational quality in backward areas like Dongxiang County. The financial status of the household is directly linked to children's growth. It is conjectured that a better-off household can afford more reference materials and stationary and greater exposure to TV and radio broadcasts. However, the situation turns out to be quite the opposite: there exist a negative correlation between the financial status of the household and the students' academic performance. That is to say, the better off a family is, the poorer the child's performance. This contrasts with the findings of our quantitative data above. We found that in the aggregate, there was a positive relationship between family income and academic performance. However, when we interviewed people, we also discovered that in a number of families the relationship was not viewed in this way, and that language was perceived as being a key factor.

How does language affect learning and academic performance?

Our analysis indicates that students' academic performance for the subjects of Chinese and Mathematics are prone to significant influences by different factors. To some extent this finding is useful in clarifying the internal mechanism of how language influences academic performance. As is shown in the research findings of Table 5.6, students' academic achievements on the subject Chinese are under the impact of such factors as time, Chinese proficiency and language, while with regard to Mathematics the shaping factors are Chinese proficiency, attitude, and in-class support. By in-class support, we refer to whether relevant teaching tools are used in class and whether the analysis indicates that students' academic performance in the subjects of Chinese and Mathematics are subject to significant influences by different factors. To some extent this finding is useful in clarifying the internal mechanism of how language influences academic performance.

As is shown in the research findings of Table 5.6, students' academic achievements in the subject Chinese are influenced by such factors as time, Chinese proficiency, and language, while with regard to Mathematics, the shaping factors are Chinese proficiency, attitude, and in-class support. By in-class support, we refer to whether relevant teaching tools are used in class and whether the teachers are able to explain the subject matter in the Dongxiang dialect. Such a difference may be explained by the fact that the spoken language without its written form becomes a barrier in students' second language acquisition with its unique phonetic system whereas written languages can hardly interfere with each other. Chinese teachers of grade 2 no longer need to explain everything in the text in Dongxiang dialect as students can understand the subject matter based on the information they get from the written words in the textbook. Mathematics teachers have to explain the abstract subject matter in greater detail. The phonetic system of the mother tongue often prevents the students from understanding what the teacher is explaining orally if it is done in Chinese. The process of knowledge intake will be very difficult if the teachers do not render corresponding assistance (either to give an explanation in Dongxiang dialect or to resort to teaching tools).

In fact, this supposition had been verified in the qualitative study, which shows that the mistakes a student made in his composition are related to the interference of the phonetic system of the local dialect. This is illustrated in a composition we found of one Dongxiang ethnic minority student at grade four of a primary school:

敬爱的奶奶您好！
多日没见到您，身体海（还）好吗？请（听）说你病了，病的（得）很眼中（严重），你上医远（医院）吗？你如果上了医远（医院），你要养好神气（身体），我是四年级的学生，我不像远来（原来）那样，选在（现在）我很东时（懂事）。选在（现在）我们上课海（还）在半学起（学期），快要方假（放假）了，方假（放假）以后我一进（一定）回来看你的。

From: Beizhuang Villege School of Chuntai, Dongxiang, Nov. 26, 2003.
(Note: words in parentheses are the correct ones added by the researcher.)

Analysis of the composition show that its grammatical structure is not terribly inaccurate on the whole and the feelings it tries to express are sincere and unaffected. However, serious mistakes exist in the usage of words. Of the 95 characters of the whole composition, there are 16 mistakes concerning the usage of words (characters), of which 15 mistakes are the result of the phonetic influence of Dongxiang language on the pronunciation of Chinese words.

Dongxiang language has no differentiation of the four tones found in standard Chinese, and only has the level tone. Because of this, schoolchildren make no differentiation of the four tones while speaking Chinese. Consonants such as "q" and "t" are not distinguished in the Dongxiang language, and that is why students make no distinction between "体" (body) and "气" (air), and "请" (please) and "听" (listen) in Chinese. What's more, the identification of Chinese characters and words requires one to establish links between pronunciation, graphic form, and meaning; whereas in Dongxiang language there is no graphic form but only pronunciation and meaning. This difference easily leads to the incorrect usage of words. The composition above, as a typical example, displays the influence of the Dongxiang pronunciation on the learning of Chinese. Many Dongxiang people have experiences of language difficulties in learning. A certain Dongxiang language expert once talked about his study in primary and secondary schools. He said: "I basically didn't understand my teacher's Chinese in my pupil days. In the school, I translated Chinese into Dongxiang language first of all and then thought about it. But sometimes I failed to translate all the words."

According to the questionnaires issued to teachers, most of them, accounting for over 77 percent of the total respondents, admitted that students in Dongxiang County had difficulties in Chinese learning. In respect to the question of "Is the Chinese level of the students the main cause influencing their school performance?," 45 percent somewhat agreed and 25 percent totally agreed. In the questionnaires issued to students, to the question of "Does your Chinese have any influence on your school performance?," 13.5 percent of them answered that their Chinese did not affect their school records at all, 15.1 percent thought it did not affect their school records, 18.4 percent believed it had some influence on their school records, 23.2 percent said that it did influence their school records, and 29.7 percent thought that their Chinese has a great influence on their school achievement. Moreover, parents and teachers held similar opinions regarding the relationship between language learning and school performance.

We therefore come to the conclusion that students are prone to misunderstand and misrepresent the subject matter under the influence of the phonetic system of their mother tongue. If more data can be gathered in the study of students' reading, listening, and writing abilities it could be a step forward in the verification of the presupposition.

Conclusion

Language, learning, achievement, and enrollment: a vicious cycle

The Dongxiang children's poor Chinese ability is the key reason for their poor school performances. Once the students' school performances drops, parents become disappointed with school education and rethink their investments (money, time, and spiritual expectations). Therefore, they take some "abandoning" measures such as transferring educational fees to household affairs, occupying children's normal study time (for example, having children to stay home and help with housework), a lowering of expectations due to their failure of educational investment, which eventually leads to dropping out of school.

Thus, we can draw the conclusion that although the language factor does not directly cause schoolchildren to drop out or be obliged to discontinue their studies, it has an indirect influence on the Dongxiang pupils (especially on girls). Language serves as an important factor leading to Dongxiang children's dropout rate. Dongxiang children are generally not proficient in Chinese and their teachers' Chinese level is not high either. Therefore, they cannot understand their teachers' Chinese teaching, which results in poor school performance, decline of interests in learning, frustrated sense of under-achievement, and harm to their self-respect. The overall result is a self-perpetuating vicious cycle that begins with inadequate recognition of the importance of language as a factor in learning for unscripted minorities.

The pattern above not only has relevance to the case of the Dongxiang ethnic minority in China, but also to other ethnic minorities in China that have a spoken language in common use but no written script, and live in remote poor rural areas of the country with a high concentration of members of their own ethnic group. Such groups generally have very low levels of educational attainment and high dropout rates. Given such a situation, language becomes an important resource for group solidarity and survival amid poverty and deprivation. It would be foolish to expect these groups to give up their native language for practical use in everyday life. However, educational policies on language usage and the medium of instruction often operate as if this is the case. Language-related factors deserve greater attention than they are currently accorded both in policy and practice as well as in research and innovative planning.

Acknowledgements

*The authors thank the *Journal of Asia-Pacific Communication* for permission to reprint sections of "China's minorities without written scripts: The case of education access among the Dongxiang," *18*: 2 (2008), pp.166–189.

This research was initiated by Gansu Basic Education Project, launched in 1999 in the Linxia Prefecture of Gansu. This project aimed to promote the development of the basic education in the four counties, raise the enrollment rate and improve educational quality. Since October 2002, the task force of Northwest Normal University has been cooperating with three officials from the Dongxiang County Education Bureau and nine native Dongxiang students from the Dongxiang Normal School in the research of the 10 sample schools of Dongxiang County.

References

Baden, N. (1996). The school curriculum from a multicultural perspective: Building a common spirit for peace and development, unpublished manuscript, 1996. [See also Baden, N. (1994). Zangzu jiaoyu de chulu [The way out for Tibetan education]. Xizang yanjiu. Tibetan Studies, 3, 44–50.]

Baker, C. (2001). *Foundations of bilingual education and bilingualism* (3rd ed.) Clevedon: Multilingual Matters Ltd.

Banks, J. (1994). *Multiethnic education.* Boston: Allen and Unwin.

Dai, Q., Teng, X., Guan, X. & Dong, L. (1997). *Zhongguo shaoshu minzu shuangyu jiaoyu gailun* [Introduction to bilingual education for China's minorities]. Liaoning Nationalities Press.

Dongxiang County Annals Editorial Committee. (1996). *Dongxiang County annals.* Lanzhou: Lanzhou Culture Press.

Fang, J., Wang, K., & Linda, S. (2001). *Dangdai zhongguo shaoshu minzu shuangyu-jiaoxue lilun yu shijian* [China's contemporary ethnic minority bilingual education theory and practice]. Xian: Shaanxi Jiaoyu chubanshe.

Fei, X. (1980). Ethnic identification in China. *Social Science in China*, 1, 97–107.

Fei, X. (1989). Zhonghua minzu de duoyuan yiti geju [Plurality and unity in the configuration of the Chinese nationality]. *Beijing Daxue Xuebao*, 4, 1–19.

Gladney, D. (1996). *Muslim Chinese, ethnic nationalism in the People's Republic of China.* Cambridge, MA: Harvard University Press.

Hansen, M. H. (1999). *Lessons in being Chinese: Minority education and ethnic identity in Southwest China.* Seattle: University of Washington Press.

Harrell, S. (2001). *Ways of being ethnic in Southwest China.* Seattle: University of Washington Press.

He, X., & Wang, J. (2004). Dongxiang nutong xuexi kunnan jiqi shixue chuoxue — yuyan yingsu yingxiang yanjiu [On Dongxiang minority girls' learning problems and dropping out from schools: A perspective on the language system]. *Northwest National Minorities Studies*, 43(4), 179–184.

Heberer, T. (1989). *China and its national minorities: Autonomy or assimilation.* Armonk, NY: M.E. Sharpe.

Lam, A. (2005). *Language education in China.* Hong Kong: Hong Kong University Press.

Lee, M. J. B. (2001). *Ethnicity, education and empowerment: How minority students in Southwest China construct identities.* Aldershot: Ashgate Press.

Ma, Y. (1985). *Questions and answers about China's nationalities.* Beijing: World Press.

Mackerras, C. (2003). *Ethnicity in Asia.* New York: Routledge Curzon.

Postiglione, G. A. (1999). *China's national minority education: Culture, schooling, and development.* New York: Falmer Press.

Postiglione, Gerard A. (Ed.). (2001). Bilingual education in China. Special Issue of *Chinese Education and Society*, 34(2).

Postiglione, G. A. (Ed.). (2002). Strengthening ethnic minority education: Research from an Asian Development Bank Technical Assistance. Special Issue of *Chinese Education and Society*, 35(3).

Postiglione, G. A. (Ed.). (2006). *Education and social change in China: Inequality in a market economy.* New York: M.E. Sharpe.

Qi, G. (2004). A report on the first year and a half of the bilingual education experimental class at Narisi Primary School, Dongxiang County. *China Education Forum*, 5(1).

Stites, R. (1999). Writing cultural boundaries: National minority language policy, literacy planning, and bilingual education. In G. A. Postiglione (Ed.), *China's national minority education.* New York: Falmer Press.

Teng, X. (2000). *Wenhua bianqian yu shuangyu jiaoyu* [Cultural change and bilingual education]. Beijing: Jiaoyu kexue chubanshe.

Trueba, H., & Zou, Y. (1994). *Power in education: The case of Miao University students and its significance for American culture.* Washington, DC: Falmer Press.

Upton, J. L. (1999). The development of modern school-based Tibetan language education in the PRC. In G. A. Postiglione (Ed.), *China's national minority education, culture, schooling and development* (pp. 281–340). New York: Falmer Press.

Wang, C., & Zhou, Q. (2003). Minority education in China: From state preferential policies to dislocated Tibetan schools. *Educational Studies*, 29(1).

Wang, J., & Zhou, F. (2005). A reflection on bilingual teaching for ethnic minorities in China: Taking Dongxiang nationality as a case. *Journal of Northwest Normal University*, 142(1), 32–36.

Wang, Y. (1994). *Zhongguo minzu yuyanxue lungang* [The study of minority languages in China: A critical introduction]. Beijing: Central University of Nationalities Press.

Yu, H. (1995). *Shuangyu yanjiu* [Research on bilingualism]. Chengdu: Sichuan University Press.

Zheng, X. (2002). *Woguo yiwu jiaoyu jieduan shaoshu minzu wenzi jiaocai jianshe diaocha yanjiu* [Research on China's ethnic minority language teaching materials development for the compulsory education years of schooling]. Beijing: Beijing Normal University manuscript.

Zhou, M. L., & Fishman, J. (2003). *Multilingualism in China: The politics of writing reforms for minority languages, 1949–2002*. Berlin: Walter de Gruyter.

Zhou, M. L., & Sun, H. K. (Eds.) (2004). *Language policy in the People's Republic of China: Theory and practice since 1949*. Norwell, MA: Kluwer Academic Press.

6 Bilingual education in China

The case of Yunnan

Linda Tsung, Ge Wang, and Qunying Zhang

Background

Over the past thirty years the world has witnessed China's rapid growth into a regional and global economic power. However, a number of frontier provinces in China's western region are still struggling to eliminate poverty and to improve the literacy of school-aged children. Yunnan is a case in point. According to The State Council Leading Group Office of Poverty Alleviation and Development (SCLGO) (2007) report, 65 percent of Yunnan's poor people (1.47 million) concentrate in ethnic minority areas where 56 of its 78 impoverished counties are also to be found. These 56 counties are among the most poverty-stricken counties not only in Yunnan but also in China.

In general, basic education in Yunnan lags behind that in the rest of China, and basic education in Yunnan's ethnic minority communities is nearly ten years behind that in its non-ethnic minority communities. The fifth national population census in 2000 (National Bureau of Statistics of China, 2002) revealed that the average years of schooling in China was 7.27, but in Yunnan it was only 5.96 years, ranking 29th among China's 31 provinces and autonomous regions. In their survey Xu and Wu (2007) found average years of schooling among the Lahu, Va, Bulang, Dulong, and Nu minority groups to be 3 years or less. Illiteracy and semi-illiteracy among these minority groups constitutes 15.9 percent of the national level (the 4th place in China) and 25.4 percent of the Yunnan provincial level.

Yunnan is the most typical multi-ethnic province in China. Fifteen of the 25 recognized ethnic minorities are unique to Yunnan. Others, such as the Mosuo, are awaiting official identification and still others have applied for and are awaiting re-identification. In addition to the Hui, the Manchu and the Shui, who commonly use the Han language for daily communication, the remaining 22 minority groups speak more than 26 languages. Table 6.1 displays the language use pattern of 15 major ethnic minority groups in Yunnan.

The inability to function in Putonghua (Mandarin) is another tremendous disadvantage that the minority people have in seeking better education and career prospects. For instance, 85.99 percent of the Dulong people are unable to understand *Putonghua* (see Table 6.1), and among the whole ethnic minority population in

Table 6.1 Fifteen distinctive ethnic minority groups and their language use in Yunnan

No.	Ethnic group	Mono-lingual population by 2005	%	Bilingual population by 2005	%	Speakers of a 3rd language (non-native nor Han) by 2005	(%)
1	Achang	10,060	49.23	7,516	36.78	2,857	13.98
2	Bai	414,891	36.64	615,333	54.35	102,000	9.01
3	Bulang	36,106	61.75	17,215	29.44	5,152	8.81
4	Dai	483,168	57.55	316,628	37.72	39,700	4.73
5	De'ang	7,132	58.00	4,591	37.33	574	4.67
6	Dulong	3,984	85.99	649	14.01	0	0
7	Hani	649,024	61.29	408,782	38.61	1,000	0.001
8	Jingpo	60,979	65.59	31,997	34.41	0	0
9	Jinuo	5,836	48.79	6,126	51.21	0	0
10	Lahu	202,277	66.48	89,981	29.57	11,998	3.94
11	Lisu	384,058	79.70	96,826	20.09	1,000	0.21
12	Naxi	110,465	43.91	131,127	52.12	10,000	3.07
13	Nu	6,971	30.45	4,525	19.76	11,400	49.79
14	Pumi	6,749	27.85	10,289	42.45	7,200	29.70
15	Va	198,466	66.46	83,489	27.96	16,656	5.58

Source: Tsang, Yang, & Qiu (2005).

Yunnan, only 12 percent can communicate in *Putonghua*. In light of these dismal statistics, bilingual education is one of the best vehicles for ethnic groups to obtain the basic early education they highly need as it "contributes to enhanced mutual understanding and respect as well as political and economic equality" (Teng & Wen, 2005, p. 268). With more than 50 years of development, which has been considerably rapid in the past 30 years, bilingual education is universally believed to be a critical means not only for facilitating the transmission, maintenance, and development of native languages and cultures, but also for realizing the equality of different nationalities. Thus, as the frequency and intensity of communication grow both within and between Yunnan and its foreign and provincial neighbors, and as local peoples see for themselves the social, economic and political advantages of bilingualism, the importance of early bilingual education in constructing a prosperous future will become increasingly apparent.

Literature review

Research into bilingual education in Yunnan

During its half-century of development, bilingual education has undergone numerous trials, hardships, revivals and honeymoons "in response to the political realities of the country" (Feng, 2005, p. 530). Over the past 20 years, research into bilingual education in Yunnan has flourished both at home and abroad from various perspectives. There have been macro studies examining chronicles and synchronic studies focusing on the history, policies and challenges of bilingual education (Feng, 2005, 2007; Lam, 2007; Lin, 1997; Qi, 2007; Teng, 2001; Teng & Wen, 2005; Tsung, 2009). Micro studies have focused on the practice of bilingual education in school and classroom settings as well as on methodology, teacher training and textbook usage (Li & Hu, 2004; Tao, 2002; Xu, Tao, & Guo, 2003; Xu & Wu, 2007; Zhuang & Lai, 2002; Tsung, 2009). Further, a number of case studies have focused on current bilingual education practices targeting specific ethnic minorities in particular schools (He, 2002; Jiang & Zhou, 2004; Tsung, 1999; Tsung & Wang, 2008; Yang & Song, 2006; Zhu & Xiao, 2005). Furthermore, an impressive number of young scholars in Yunnan have begun studying bilingual education from interdisciplinary perspectives. For instance, Hu (2004) investigated the influence of bilingual education on the development of ethnic minority girls and has proposed a number of measures to improve their disadvantaged conditions; Yang (2004) investigated the use of Yi on bilingual government websites; and Li (2007) analyzed the features, functions of and phenomena and cultural psychology related to bilingual education among Yunnan's minority nationalities.

Types of bilingual education in Yunnan

Zhu (2003) identified four types of bilingual education in China: (1) common bilingual education; (2) special bilingual education; (3) auxiliary bilingual education; and (4) higher bilingual vocational education. Zhu also observed that bilingual instruction may be delivered via ethnic languages, *Putonghua* or both (Zhu,

2003). Teng and Wen (2005) identified two approaches of bilingual education programs: Transitional Bilingual Education (TBE) and Language Maintenance Bilingual Education (LMBE). Dai and Cheng (2007) also proposed seven models of bilingual education in terms of approaches.

During the 1950s, Yunnan adopted TBE to help monolingual ethnic minority students' transition from their native language to *Putonghua*. Students received instruction in their native language during years one and two at primary school and then began receiving instruction in both their native language and in *Putonghua* during year three. In their final year at primary school, *Putonghua* was used as the dominant medium of instruction. Although TBE seemed an ideal pathway to Yunnan's ethnic minority education, it has various problems. For instance, Teng and Wen (2005, p. 268) observed that TBE was "fragmented" and there was a "lack of continuity," often forcing students to master a new language before they had fully mastered their own native language. Furthermore, over the past few decades and even today, few teachers have acquired the bilingual competency and teaching experience needed to deliver effective instruction in two languages. Consequently, students often failed to gain full mastery of either their own native language or *Putonghua* and many even lost interest in school learning. There were reports (Teng & Wen, 2005) of a large numbers of students dropping out in years four and five due to the failures of TBE.

Intending to follow up and contribute to this growing body of research, the present study based on two empirical studies conducted in 1999 and in 2008, compares changes in 10 years of bilingual education policies and implementations, discusses the latest developments in bilingual education in Yunnan and identifies a number of gaps between current policies and practice. The following section depicts the methodology of the present study.

Methodology

Field Study 1

This research adopted a mixed-method approach to collecting multiple sources of data. Study 1 was designed to understand policy implementation and outcomes of bilingual education in primary schools in Yunnan during the 1990s. The study was conducted between 1995 and 1999 in four primary schools located in Lijiang, Ninglang, Zhongdian and Luxi counties. The four schools provided Naxi–Han, Yi–Han, Tibetan–Han and Dai–Han bilingual programs respectively. Data were drawn from a survey of 162 fifth year students and in-depth interviews with four principals and 22 teachers. The interviewees, 15 males and 11 females, were from six nationalities: Han, Naxi, Yi, Dai, Tibetan and Jingpo. Among the teachers, 13 were employed as *Gongban* (government-employed) teachers and nine as *Minban* (community-employed) teachers. Only one teacher had a university degree while the majority of teachers (14) had two-year diplomas, nine teachers had only junior or senior high school education, and two teachers had three-year diplomas. The majority of teachers (13) had between five to ten years of teaching experience, four teachers had more than ten years of teaching experience, and nine teachers had between one to four years of teaching experience.

Field Study 2

Follow-up studies were planned in 2008 to be conducted in the same four schools, but only one school, the Shangri-la Bilingual Primary School (SBPS) in Zhongdian, had continued the bilingual program (Tibetan–Han). Field study 2 was undertaken in this school in May 2008. The principal, the vice-principal, two Tibetan language teachers and one fourth-year student were interviewed to trace the latest developments in bilingual education in Zhongdian. The principal was responsible for the strategic development of the SBPS whereas the vice prin-cipal is in charge of teaching affairs.

The most important informant in Study 2 is a female Tibetan teacher who had taught in SBPS over ten years. She received her Tibetan education in Aba Prefecture in Sichuan province and was recruited as a full-time Tibetan teacher ten years before. In addition to teaching Tibetan literacy to approximately 200 students from year four to year six, she also served as the head a teacher of Tibetan teaching group, a campus radio hostess, and a Tibetan dance teacher.

One Tibetan language class was observed to provide additional information about the bilingual program. In order to obtain a wide array of views from vari-ous stakeholders, the researchers also approached and interviewed one official at the Department of Ethnic Minority Education of the Yunnan Provincial Education Committee. In brief, Study 2 sought to examine the development of bilingual education in Yunnan during the past decade, explore any possible gaps between current policies and practice, and envision prospects for bilingual education in Zhongdian and Yunnan as a whole.

Data analysis

Interview data were transcribed verbatim and interviewees' responses were grouped according to answers to specific interview questions. Major issues were identified by a content and thematic analysis and then transcripts were reana-lysed to identify comments on these emerging themes and issues. Class observa-tion data and notes were summarized and used as an aid when analysing and interpreting the interview data.

Findings

Types of bilingual programs

The finding of Study 1 revealed four types of bilingual education programs in Yunnan

Type 1: Naxi–Han bilingual program. The Naxi–Han bilingual program has operated for students in first to third grades since 1983. In the first three years the Naxi language was the main medium of instruction to study the Han language, Maths, Arts, Music, Sports and Ideology, and Character Building. Teachers estimated that they used the Naxi language as the medium of instruction in the first grade 90 percent of the time and 70 percent of the time in the second grade. In the third grade, the Naxi language was used 40 percent of the time. In forth to sixth grades, Naxi was essentially eliminated as Han teachers took up the classes and the medium of instruction switched to Putonghua Only (see Figure 6.1).

Type 2: The Yi–Han bilingual program. The Yi–Han bilingual and biliteracy class took a different approach from the Naxi–Han program. In the first grade, the medium of instruction was Yi. The Yi script lesson was taught for 14 periods and the Han language for six periods per week. In the second grade, the Han language lesson increased to 10 periods per week and the Yi script dropped to eight periods. In the third grade, the time for the Yi script lesson was six periods and for Han it was nine periods. Mathematics was taught through Yi, while other subjects were taught in Putonghua. This pattern was maintained until the sixth grade (see Figure 6.2).

Type 3: The Tibetan–Han bilingual program. School 3 was located in the town centre of the Zhongdian County in Diqing Tibetan Autonomous prefecture. The school, established in 1980, was a boarding school with 273 students, 73 percent of whom were from Tibetan families. The school only took students from Grades 4 to 6. Some 95 percent of the parents were farmers.
The Tibetan–Han Bilingual program in the school required that the Tibetan language be used as the medium of instruction for Tibetan Language and Culture. Putonghua was the medium of instruction for other subjects. Between 1989 and 1993 the Tibetan language was a compulsory subject for all the students in Grades 4 through 6. The Tibetan language was taught for 14 periods per week. One Tibetan teacher said that in order to fulfill the requirement set by the Tibetan language syllabus he needed even more periods (see Figure 6.3).

Type 4: The Dai–Han bilingual program. The Dai–Han bilingual program was in Luxi county, Dehong Dai and Jingpo Autonomous Prefecture. The school had 413 enrolled students, 97 percent of whom were students of the Dai nationality in Dehong. Most students came from farming families. The medium of instruction in the school was Putonghua, except for the Dai language lesson (see Figure 6.4). Dai language textbooks were produced locally by the Education Department of the Dehong Dai and Jingpo Autonomous Prefectures. The school's objectives were to help Dai children learn Putonghua and to develop children's cognitive skills. Students received 30 bonus marks for Dai language learning in their high school entrance examination.

Bilingual and monoliteracy programs use one minority language such as Naxi plus *Putonghua* as mediums of instruction and develop literacy in Chinese. These programs serve as forms of transitional bilingual education. Bilingual and biliteracy programs, also called *shuangyu shuangwen* or *shuangyuwen*, are forms of

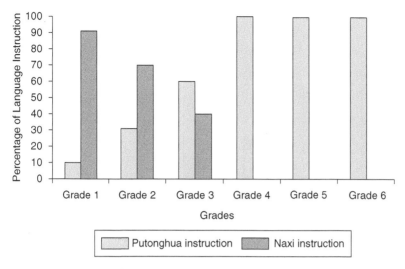

Figure 6.1 Naxi–Han bilingual program in School 1.

maintenance bilingual education that involve the development of oral competency and literacy in both languages (one minority language and Chinese). In these programs, minority languages function both as languages of instruction and as subjects to be studied.

The findings of the study indicate that language maintenance bilingual education (LMBE) is a popular program among ethnic groups with long-standing native languages and writing systems such as Tibetan and Dai. Language maintenance programs introduce minority languages as subjects, not merely as mediums of instruction. Given the diversity in linguistic and cultural features of its minority nationalities, such as the diversified scripts, oral traditions, religions, etc., Yunnan presently employs two main bilingual education programs: *the bilingual and monoliteracy* such as Naxi–Han bilingual programs and *the bilingual and biliteracy* such as the Tibetan and Yi programs.

Development of bilingual textbooks and bilingual schools

There was clear evidence in Study 1 that a shortage of bilingual textbooks was a serious problem. For example, the Yi–Han bilingual textbooks were bought from Sichuan Province. Therefore, it was costly in terms of transportation and time. In Study 2, however, we observed that the development of bilingual textbooks has dramatically improved in the past 10 years.

The data from Study 2 further revealed that bilingual education has experienced rapid development over the past few years in Shangri-la (Zhongdian), where several years ago only one Tibetan class was offered to about 20 students

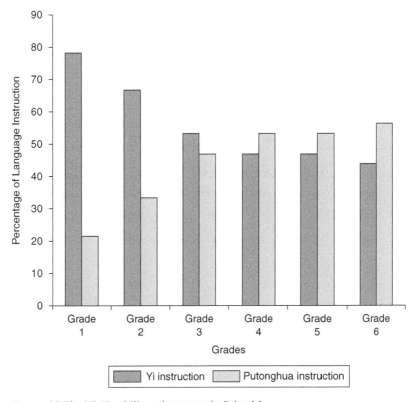

Figure 6.2 The Yi–Han bilingual program in School 2.

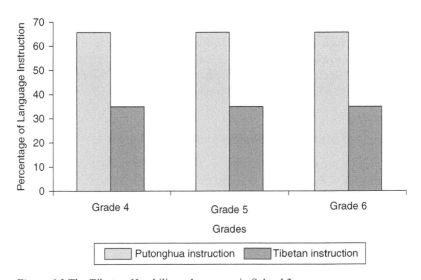

Figure 6.3 The Tibetan–Han bilingual program in School 3.

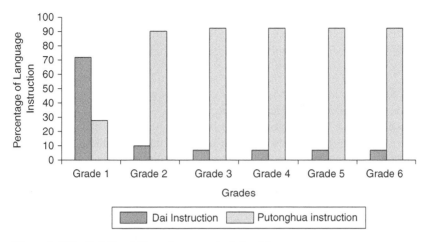

Figure 6.4 The Dai–Han bilingual program in School 4.

at a primary school. It now has five Tibetan classes with an enrollment of 250 students at its Shangri-la primary school. We also found that local civil servants must take a Tibetan language tests in order to qualify for some government positions.

Gaps between policy and practice

Although bilingual education in Yunnan has achieved great progress in recent years, there are still many problems concerning policies, perceptions, textbooks and teacher education which need to be solved. The interview data reveal that many ethnic minority parents have a great deal of difficulty affording the additional expenses of bilingual education due to their poor socio-economic conditions. In 2005, the average net income among ethnic minorities in Yunnan was RMB 2,041 (The State Ethnic Affairs Commission, 2006). If the net income of an average family is RMB 2,041, the maximum amount for a typical farming family of four with two children would be around RMB 500 per person. Deducting the ever-increasing cost of production (fertilizer, pesticide, etc.) and living, the remaining amount is not enough to cover the cost of education.

Moreover, the majority of the ethnic minority population in Yunnan lives on farming. According to the latest report from the National Information Center (2007), the Consumer Price Index (CPI) of farmers in Yunnan was 3.9 percent from January to May in 2007, which is even higher than the 3.4 percent CPI of city dwellers. Meanwhile, the production costs of farming in 2007 were 2.9 percent higher than the previous year. In light of these statistics, if compulsory education, which covers primary and junior high schooling, is not provided free of charge, it will increase the financial burden on farmers rather than alleviate it.

Local schools, however, cannot settle the huge deficits that bilingual education incurs without subsidies from local and/or central governments. During an interview for Study 2, the vice-principal of SBPS explained that whereas the school can accommodate a quota of 300 boarding students based on subsidies from the three levels of governments (municipal, county, and township), SBPS had to pay RMB 240,000 to cover the costs of an additional 120 boarding students. As a result, SBPS was forced to reject scores of school-aged Tibetan children due to limited accommodations and teaching resources.

Since 2001, the Chinese government has implemented an education-funding policy called *"liangmian yibu"* (two exemptions and one subsidy), by which children of compulsory education age from poor rural families were exempted from tuition fees, textbook costs, and the boarding students are gradually subsidized with living expenses. The central government is responsible for providing free textbooks while the local government takes charge of the tuition fees and the subsidies for boarding students. In 2006, this policy was expanded to cover all the rural children of compulsory education age and as many as 48.8 million students had benefited from the policy in that year alone. The data for this study, however, indicate that the government policy of later years has not been so successful. The gaps between policy and practice may be attributed to many contributing factors, some of which are perceived by the authors to be more important than others and so they are addressed in the following sections.

Perceptions of and attitudes towards bilingual education

The practice of bilingual education programs is to a great extent influenced by the attitudes and beliefs of local administrators and parents. The study revealed the existence of two detrimental mentalities: the "great Han mentality" Lin (1997) and the "pragmatism mentality." It is reported that the local Tibetan middle school rejected one of the top students from SBPS not because his Tibetan was poor—he in fact earned the highest mark in Tibetan on the secondary school enrollment exam—but because he failed in Chinese and Mathematics. The Tibetan middle school decision-makers were worried that the students' low scores in Chinese and mathematics might affect the overall scores of Tibetan students in that examination. The "pragmatism mentality," which is also detrimental to the practice of bilingual education in ethnic minority communities, is found among some local administrators of bilingual education programs and many ethnic minority parents. This mentality reflects the belief that *Putonghua* (Mandarin) is more important and beneficial for one's academic record and future job opportunities.

Religion education or school education?

Religious and cultural factors also seem to impact on the attitudes and actions of ethnic minority parents and their children. There have been reports by interviewees of temples and public schools in some areas of Yunnan competing to attract school-aged students. Interviewees reported that two years ago in Dehong Prefecture, some Burmese monks offered some free instruction of Dai script but the teaching was cut short as the monk was invited to another temple. The Dai classes were very popular and large; many local Dai children were enrolled.

When students encounter difficulties with studies in public schools, they often quit and attend temple or church schools instead. Their parents thus become willing to provide financial support to temple or church schools rather than to public schools. The findings from Study 1 revealed that most Dai are Hinayana Buddhists and that it was quite common for Dai parents to send their children to a temple to study their own language. It is in fact a custom to send teenagers to temples to study the Dai script. The Dai prefer to donate money to build temples for worship and services rather than to establish schools. Study 1 also revealed the challenge that temple education poses to public school education. One Tibetan teacher argued:

> The Tibetan language is an important part of the cultural heritage of the Tibetan people. Parents wish their children to maintain both our written and oral traditions. This is the reason why parents send their children to monasteries. Parents set more value on Tibetan education than Han education. An educated Tibetan must be literate in Tibetan script. I teach children our Tibetan culture. They are very motivated to learn the Tibetan language.

Given that language is the carrier of culture, the teaching/learning of language and culture are inseparable. Language instruction without delivery of cultural knowledge will confuse and lose learners. Hannum and Park (2002, p. 11) observed that:

> Messages about the value of minority culture—negative and positive—transmitted through schools can have powerful effects on the academic engagement and achievement of minority students. Minority children in remote rural settings often find a vast distance between their experiences of daily life and the contents of school learning.

When ethnic minority students encounter difficulties learning or adjusting to school, they are apt to go to the temple or church to seek comfort. In this sense, religious influences may cause students to drop out of public schools.

It is also worth considering that some foreign political and religious forces along Yunnan's national boundaries are seeking to attract school-aged children to various ideologies promoting visions of transnational homogeneous languages and cultures. It is reported that some (anti-unitary China) forces are seeking to recruit ethnic minority students, broadcasting propaganda in minority languages, organizing (clandestine) training classes and awarding native language books. In this sense, bilingual education has become a battlefield for promoting intercultural understanding, safeguarding national unity and preserving frontier stability.

Textbook issues

One Tibetan language class was observed in Study 2. It was a 45-minute lesson of Tibetan language. The topic of that lesson was "The Spring is Coming." The female teacher, who was very experienced in organizing her teaching, successfully linked the teaching content with the view of Spring held by the Tibetan community as well as the students' real experiences. However, teachers noted that problems concerning the quantity and quality of textbooks remained unsolved. The number of bilingual textbooks, reference books, and readers is far below the demand. Bilingual textbooks are generally of very poor quality. Currently, there are only about 60 bilingual textbooks for 11 ethnic minority languages and most of these have been compiled or translated for students in years one, two, and three. As most of these bilingual textbooks focus on the development of *minwen* or mother tongue literacy and do not cover other subjects like mathematics and liberal arts, native speakers of other languages do not make use of them. Reference books written in ethnic minority languages are almost unavailable.

Teachers we interviewed expected that, in addition to literacy, other knowledge such as ethnic fable, folklore, festivals, can be introduced in the mother tongue and should be part of the school-based curriculum contents. The majority of the existing minority language textbooks are either too old or inappropriate. For instance, the latest year-one literacy textbook for Dai students was published in 2005 by the Yunnan Press of Nationalities of Kunming contains the following poem and story about snow.

> It snowed all day and all night. The houses, trees and the ground were all covered in white. Mummy Rabbit had to go out seeking food. She built a snow child rabbit to play with her baby rabbit … the snow child saved the baby rabbit from the big fire but he melted as it was too hot.
>
> *(Translation of an excerpt from Lesson 19, Snow Child)*

Given that Dai students live in a tropical environment and have never seen snow before, it is very hard for them to imagine what snow looks like and to relate it to their daily lives.

With respect to these problems, more effort is needed in revising old textbooks and compiling new ones with particular attention to both structure and content. For instance, bilingual textbooks should contain topics relevant to the lives and cultures of ethnic minorities. They could, if possible, integrate practical knowledge concerning farming, local cuisine, holidays and festivals, and local handicrafts. Above all, local schools should be given greater autonomy in developing regional textbooks or selecting from national ones. Local teachers should be empowered and encouraged to compile minority language textbooks and reference books which have more relevance to the customs, emotions, and social lives of their students.

Teacher shortages and teaching quality

As with textbooks, the quantity and effectiveness of bilingual teachers are another worrisome problem. According to the survey by Tsang, Yang, and Qiu

(2005), 10,635 of Yunnan's 12,936 bilingual teachers were monoliterate while only 2,301 were biliterate, and only 5.6 percent of Yunnan's 218,969 primary school teachers were bilingual.

Given the increasing number of bilingual programs and growing student enrolment, bilingual teachers, especially biliterate ones are in great demand. In reality, however, students often complain that their teachers are either proficient in *Putonghua* but not in their native languages or are proficient in their native languages but not in *Putonghua*. Thus, there will be a growing need for more and better-trained, especially bilingual/biliterate teachers, in the coming years. Take the Shangri-la Bilingual Primary School, for example, the school is experiencing a serious shortage of qualified teachers for its bilingual program and it now has only two Tibetan language teachers to teach more than 250 students in two courses.

Unfortunately, few newly graduated teachers are willing to work in such bilingual schools, as most are located in remote and poorly resourced mountainous areas with very harsh living conditions. Moreover, low salary, slim chances for promotion and limited training opportunities also plague the recruitment of competent bilingual teachers. At the same time, many in-service bilingual teachers are not fully competent in both languages, and the number of bilingually competent teachers is gradually decreasing. Over the past three years five newly recruited male teachers have left Shangri-la Bilingual Primary School after a short period of teaching in the school, as indicated by one respondent in the study.

Curriculum deficiencies

Despite the increasing number of bilingual students, SBPS is faced with the possibility of having to reduce the number of Tibetan language classes it offers per week while confronting the overwhelming task of teaching six textbooks in three years. Whereas ten years ago students had seven Tibetan classes per week, they now have only five classes per week. Respondents in the study reported that students cannot finish all the textbooks as required within the given period of study. Similar situations were also found with other bilingual schools, which led us to suspect that the minority students are only able to complete one or two textbooks in three years.

After graduating from elementary school and enrolling in Tibetan middle school, students have to study Tibetan from the beginning. Teachers rightly see this as a waste of time and resources while students who do not study Tibetan well in elementary school may interpret it as a second chance to catch up with others. Moreover, yearly changes in textbooks and little or no communication between in-service native language teachers and test writers render bilingual education even more difficult.

Conclusion

The latest studies (Luo, 2007; Yunnan Education Committee, 2008) report that by the end of 2008, bilingual education in Yunnan would have been implemented in 4,056 schools involving a total of 157,979 students or 6.3 percent of the 2,489,662 primary students enrolled in 74 county cities. The present study also reveals that bilingual education has made progress in Yunnan, and yet it still faces many practical barriers and challenges. In the long run, more rational plans and strategies are needed to integrate national policies and local needs. As Sposky (1980) argues, "The choice of language education policy is among the most critical and complicated issues facing the modern society" (p. xiii). For Yunnan in particular, we hope that policies and practices can serve to broaden the spectrum of bilingual education in terms of age, gender, subjects and communities; to improve the quality and efficiency of fundamental education; and to benefit the political, economic, cultural and religious interests of ethnic minority people.

It is well known that the costs of bilingual education are substantially higher than the costs of monolingual education because the former requires additional funding for developing courses, writing and translating textbooks, and training teachers. However, bilingual education is not only a program of instruction, but also a yardstick for measuring a government's policies for protecting the languages and identities of individual ethnic minorities as well as its commitment to humanitarian concerns and social justice in general. Policy-makers should always strive to balance fairness and justice, the welfare for the majority versus that for the minority, and economic gains versus social justice.

Given the diverse challenges, successful promotion of bilingual education in Yunnan needs both policy support and substantial and sustained financial aid. Both central and local governments should allocate more money to support bilingual programs and should take measures to alleviate the financial burden that bilingual education imposes on ethnic minority families. It is essential for China as an emerging global economic power to regularly review bilingual education policies and practices in order to promote more rational and humanistic approaches to encourage and nurture prosperity in both majority Han and minority ethnic communities.

After decades of development, bilingual education in Yunnan is facing new challenges and opportunities as China strives to become a powerful and prosperous nation in an increasingly globalized world. As education is both a tool for and a reflection of cultural diversity (UNESCO, 2003), it is hoped that through this model of instruction, ethnic minority students can not only gain greater access to new knowledge and skills but also develop their citizenship (Li, 2007) in order to function more freely and effectively within and beyond their cultural boundaries and participate fully in their local, national and global communities.

References

Dai, Q. X., & Cheng, Y. Y. (2007). Typology of bilingualism and bilingual education in Chinese minority nationality regions. In A. Feng (Ed.), *Bilingual education in China: Practices, policies, and concepts* (pp. 75–93). Clevedon: Multilingual Matters.

Feng, A. (2005). Bilingualism for the minor or the major? An evaluative analysis of parallel conceptions in China. *Journal of Bilingual Education and Bilingualism*, 8(6), 529–551.

Feng, A. (Ed.). (2007). *Bilingual education in China: Practices, policies, and concepts.* Clevedon: Multilingual Matters.

Hannum, E., & Park, A. (2002). Educating China's rural children in the 21st century. *Harvard China Review*, 3(2), 8–14.

He, Z. K. (2002). Yunnan gongshanxian dulongzu nuzushuangyu jiaoyu xianzhuang yu duicsikao [Pedagogical condition and strategy of bilingual education of the Drung and the Nu in Gongshan County Yunnan Province]. *Dali Xueyuan Xuebao* [Journal of Dali College], 1(5), 24–27.

Hu, Y. P. (2004). Shaoshu minzu nütong yu shuangyu jiaoyu [Minority nationality girls and bilingual education]. *Zhonghua Nüzi Xueyuan Xuebao* [Journal of National Women's University of China], 16(3), 19–24.

Jiang, L. H., & Zhou, X. Y. (2004). Yunnan gaoxiao shuangyu jiaoxue duice fenxi [On the countermeasures for improving bilingual teaching in the universities in Yunnan Province]. *Yunnan Shifan Daxue Xuebao* [Journal of Yunnan Normal University], 2(5): 62–64.

Lam, A. S. L. (2007). Bilingual or multilingual education in China: Policy and learner experience. In A. Feng (Ed.), *Bilingual education in China: Practices, policies, and concepts* (pp. 13–33). Clevedon: Multilingual Matters.

Li, F. J. (2007). Yunnan shaoshu minzu shuangyu jiaoyu zhong de wenhua xintai yanjiu [On the cultural psychology in the bilingual education of Yunnan minority nationalities]. *Yunnan Shifan Daxue Xuebao* [Journal of Yunnan Normal University], 39(1), 128–131.

Li, L. J., & Hu, F. W. (2004). Shilun Yunnan bianjiang diqu minzu jiaoyu de xianzhuang, chengyin ji duice [Discussion on the present situation, problem causes and coping strategies of ethnic education in the southwest frontier regions]. *Honghe Xueyua Xuebao* [Journal of Honghe University], 2(4), 89–92.

Lin, J. (1997). Policies and politics of bilingual education in China. *Journal of Multilingual Multicultural Development*, 18(3), 193–205.

Luo, J. (2007). Zhanzai xinde lishi qidian shang tuidong wosheng shuangyu jiaoxue gongzu zai shang xin taijie [The historical standpoint: Promoting bilingual education in Yunnan]. *Yunnan Jiaoyu* [Yunnan Education], 10, 17–19.

National Bureau of Statistics of China (2002). *Zhongguo 2000 Nian Renkou Pucha Ziliao* [Tabulation on the 2000 Population Census of the People's Republic of China]. Beijing: Zhongguo Tongji Chubanshe [China Statistics Press].

National Information Center (2007). Yunnansheng 2007 nian 1–5 yue jumin xiaofei jiage shuiping jianxi [An analysis of CPI in Yunnan from January to May of 2007]. Retrieved on November 22, 2008, from http://party.cei.gov.cn/index/dqbg/showdoc. asp?blockcode=DQBGYNFX&filename=200707032442.

Qi, D. C. (2007). *Yunnan minhan shuangyuwen jiaoxue lilun yu shijian* [Theory and practice on the Min-Han bilingual education in Yunnan). Kunming: Yunnan Nationality Press.

Sposky, B. (1980). Foreword. In E. G. Lewis (Ed.), *Bilingualism and bilingual education: A comparative study* (pp. xiii–xv). Albuquerque: University of New Mexico Press.

Tao, T. L. (2002). Yunnan shuangyu jiaoxue de fazhan xuanze [The options for bilingual education in Yunnan]. *Zhongguo Minzu* [China Ethnicity], 10, 20–21.

Teng, X. (2001). Objects, characteristics, content, and methods of research in ethnic minority bilingual education in China. *Chinese Education and Society*, 34(2), 54–75.

Teng, X., & Wen, Y. H. (2005). Bilingualism and bilingual education in China. In N. K. Shimahara *et al.* (Eds.), *Ethnicity, race, and nationality in education: A global perspective* (pp. 259–278). Hillsdale, NJ: Lawrence Erlbaum.

The State Council Leading Group Office of Poverty Alleviation and Development. (2007). *2006 nian Yunnan nongcun pinkun renkou jianshaoliang ju quanguo di'er* [The poverty alleviation in Yunnan ranked second in 2006]. Retrieved on November 9, 2008, from http://www.cpad.gov.cn/data/2007/0627/article_334846.htm.

The State Ethnic Affairs Commission of the PRC. (2006). *2005 nian shaoshu minzu diqu nongcun pinkun jiance jieguo* [Poverty report on the ethnic minority inhabiting areas 2005]. Retrieved on December 23, 2008, from http://www.seac.gov.cn/gjmw/xwzx/2006-07-10/1170411119478198.htm.

Tsang, M. C., Yang, C., & Qiu, L. (2005). *Yunnan shaoshu minzu jiaoyu: fazhan, tiaozhan hezhengce* [Minorities, education in Yunnan: Developments, challenges and policies]. Retrieved from Columbia University, Teacher's College, Center of Chinese Education website on November 17, 2008, from http://www.tc.edu/centers/coce/pdf_files/a11.pdf.

Tsung, L. (1999). Minorities in China: Language policy and education. Unpublished PhD thesis, the University of Sydney.

Tsung, L. (2009). *Minority languages, education and communities in China*. New York: Palgrave Macmillan.

Tsung, L., & Wang, G. (2008). Bilingual education in Yunnan: Gaps between policy and practice. *Paper presented at Conference on Minority Language Education in China: Issues and Perspectives*, April 19th, 2008, The University of Hong Kong, Hong Kong.

UNESCO. (2003). *Education in a multicultural world*. Retrieved on April 8, 2008 from http://unesdoc.unesco.org/images/0012/001297/129728e.pdf.

Xu, J. S., & Wu, Z. F. (2007). Yunnansheng minzu jiaoyu zhengce kaocha baogao [A survey on the educational policy for ethnic minorities in Yunnan]. *Guangxi Minzu Daxue Xuebao* (Journal of Guangxi University for Nationalities), 21, 12–16.

Xu, Z., Tao, T., & Guo, Y. (2003). Shuangyu jiaoxue shi kefu Yunnan shaoshu minzu jujuquxuesheng yuyan zhangai de youxiao tujing [Bilingual teaching is an effective way to overcome language obstacles for students of ethnic minority compact communities in Yunnan]. *Minzu Jiaoyu Yanjiu* [Journal of Research on Education for Ethnic Minorities], 14(5), 39–46.

Yang, Q., & Song, Y. (2006). Bai-han shuangyu beijingxia yingyu jiaoxue yanjiu pingshu [A survey of English teaching in the Bai-Han bilingual context]. *Dali Xueyuan Xuebao* (Journal of Dali College), 6(9), 70–73.

Yang, X. L. (2004). Yi–Han shuangyuban zhengfu wangzhan kaitong gaishu [Brief introduction to government Yi-Chinese bilingual website]. *Xinan Minzu Daxue Xuebao* (Journal of Southwest University for Nationalities), 30(2), 245–249.

Yunnan Educational Committee. (2008). Shaoshu minzu diqu shuangyu shuangwen jiaoyu jianjie [Brief introduction to the bilingual and biliteracy education in the areas where ethnic minorities live]. A news briefing.

Zhu, C. X. (2003). Shuangyu xianxiang yu zhongguo shaoshu minzu shuangyu jiaoyu tizhihe jiaoxue moshi [Bilingualism and the system and teaching mode of bilingual education of ethnic minorities in China]. *Minzu Jiaoyu Yanjiu* (Journal of Research on Education for Ethnic Minorities), 14(6), 73–77.

Zhu, W. X., & Xiao, X. (2005). Yizu diqu shuangyu jiaoyu leixing xianzhuang yanjiu [A study of the present situation of bilingual education types in the Yi nationality areas]. *Minzu Jiaoyu Yanjiu* [Journal of Research on Education for Ethnic Minorities], 16(5), 87–92.

Zhuang, W. L., & Lai, Y. (2002). Minzu diqu jiaoyu xianzhuang yu duice yanjiu [A study of the current practice and strategy on education for ethnic minority communities]. *Xinan Minzu Daxue Xuebao* [Journal of Southwest University for Nationalities], 23(5), 21–31.

7 Language hegemony in its relation to Chinese marriage migrants' mothers' adaptations to and educational involvements in Taiwan

Yi-Hsuan Chelsea Kuo

Background

Taiwan has always been a multi-cultural society where various languages are spoken: Taiwanese, Hakka, the aboriginal languages, and Mandarin, imposed by the KMT as the national language in 1945. The emergence in the late 1980s of the so-called "foreign brides," or female marriage migrants (FMMs), as more and more Taiwanese men are seeking marriage partners from Southeast Asian countries and from mainland China, has slowly reshaped the linguistic landscape. The number of Taiwanese men marrying internationally has indeed been rising rapidly in recent years. In 2003, for example, 31.9 percent of Taiwanese men, or 1 out of 3.1, married women from counties other than Taiwan (Ministry of the Interior, 2004). The number dropped in recent years due to the restrictions put in place in 2003 by the Ministry of Interior, but remains at a relatively high level: 14 percent in 2008 and 18.8 percent in 2009 (Ministry of Interior, 2010). Taiwan, however, is not at all unique when it comes to inter-national marriage. This burgeoning phenomenon in such East Asian countries as Korea, Japan, and Taiwan[1] (Asakura, 2002; Kim, 2006; Lee, 2003; Nakamatsu, 2003; Ochiai, Ishikawa, & Liaw, 2006; Piper & Roces, 2003), one that is more accurately denominated inter-national hypergamy, is brought on by the unequal developments of capitalism within an age of globalization.[2] It occurs when a nation's disadvantaged men seek to "import" marriage partners from their region's less "developed" countries (H. R. Wang, 2001; Xia, 2002).

International hypergamy is a completely understandable trend given the need that Taiwanese men of lower socio-economic status have to get married and raise a family. It must be noted, nevertheless, that it has quickly become tainted by that patrilineal ideology which Taiwan shares with the rest of Asia. One sees this in the way giving birth to "children of new Taiwanese" (a term widely used by the Taiwanese to refer to the children born to FMMs) is thought to be the chief "duty" of these FMMs (Xia, 1997). Childrearing has in this way become a contentious topic in Taiwan. According to statistics from the Ministry of Interior, in the year 2003, 13.37 percent of Taiwan's babies were born to women immigrants from Southeast Asia—more than double 1998's figure of 5.12 percent (Ministry of the Interior, 2004). In other words in the year 2003, about 1 out of every 8 newborn babies was born to a woman immigrant from Southeast Asia or mainland China. Little wonder, then, that the Chinese and Southeast Asian mothers have been living under an intense spotlight, directed by the host society upon their childrearing skills and educational involvements with their children. At a deeper level, the influx of FMMs has served to further inflame that sensitive topic of cultural-linguistic identity which is never far from the minds of home-grown Taiwanese, as we shall see the next section.

Guo-yu: the story of the "national language"

It is noteworthy that these new immigrants to Taiwan are subject to an "assimilation process" forced upon them by the host society's integrationist ideology and one-size-fits-all language hegemony, notably similar to the one that once was imposed upon the native Taiwanese people. Just 60 years ago, Taiwanese people were confronted with the integrationist language policy brought by the Nationalist Party (the KMT) in their flight from Mainland China. They were forced to abandon their mother tongues—Taiwanese, Hakka, and the aboriginal languages—to speak a language not their own: the dominant dialect of the mainland, Mandarin with the standard Beijing accent. This enforcement has not been confined to the use of language itself, but also has entailed a series of deprivations of native history, culture, and language (Cheng, 1994). For decades, the so-called *guo-yu* (national language) policy was strictly imposed in the media, government agencies, and schools, with those Taiwanese children who did not follow it often being humiliated by their teachers and peers. Soon a cultural hierarchy was formed in keeping with the integrationist policy brought by the Nationalist Party, one that has placed the native Taiwanese languages and culture at the bottom and Chinese Mandarin and its culture at the very top.

This experience has given Taiwan a complex legacy of language and culture. Today, Mandarin has become the dominant language in Taiwan. The Mandarin spoken and written in Taiwan is, however, very different from that used in mainland China, mostly because so much of the native Taiwanese tongue has been adapted into the daily lives of the people. Most young people understand Taiwanese even if they do not speak the language fluently, and they have thereby enriched the content of Mandarin. Regardless of how it happened, Mandarin in Taiwan clearly has developed its own new genre and thereby become a cultural marker, something that the younger generations in particular identify with.

The ideal Mandarin used to be the one spoken strictly with a Beijing accent, with any deviation from that standard accent being deemed "inappropriate" or "vulgar." Today, what was once deemed the periphery has become the center. The Beijing accent has become "stilted," "alienated," or "aggressive," since it represents the ruling class's takeover. By contrast, speaking with a slightly Taiwanese intonation brings a cultural connotation of "cool," "vibrant," and "local," especially to the younger-generation Taiwanese. Thus one can doubt whether the process whereby the female marriage migrants are slowly immersed in the ongoing flow of "Taiwanese-ized Mandarin" is as analogous as it initially seems to be to the old imposition of Mandarin on Taiwan's native population. First of all, the Chinese female marriage migrants (C-FMMs) are confident that their cultural-linguistic, or even ethnic, affinity with the host society guarantees them a smooth adaptation when they come to the new land. Second, whereas the KMT's attempt to impose Mandarin on the Taiwanese people was a top-down effort, today's notably Taiwan-ized form of Mandarin has come into being more from the bottom up, as if naturally fermenting into existence over time.

An assimilationist view of the female marriage migrants of Taiwan

The influx of the FMMs occurred at a time when the cultural-linguistic identity of Taiwan came to fruition. All of it has simply revealed, however, the extent to which the assimilationist (also known as the integrationist) view continues to dominate the mainstream ideology, but this time it was directed not toward immigrants rather than native Taiwanese. The children of the FMMs are widely seen as being doomed to be low academic achievers given their mothers' distinctive cultural-linguistic status and, in most cases, the low socio-economic status of the receiving family. Such views often notably crop up in Taiwan's media (M. L. Chen, 2004; Gao, 2003), among government officials' (Han, 2004) and legislators' (H. G. Chen, 2004; Ke, 2006) discussions. It is also a topic of discussion among school teachers (S. Y. Wang *et al.*, 2006) and academics (Liu, 2002). It goes without saying that this radically assimilationist view has been proved invalid, in the context of numerous cases all around the world. In the United States, for example, study after study has tried to explain how it happens that so many immigrant children (e.g., Hmong, Vietnamese, Indo-Chinese) from low socio-economic families are high achievers first in school and then in the professional realm (Gibson, 1988; Ogbu, 1991; Zhou & Bankston III, 1998). We now know that given a positive context of reception, sufficient support from family and from an ethnic social network, and beneficial government policies and resources, children of any background can succeed (Portes & Rumbaut, 2001). It is equally clear that the stereotypes presented by the media and by certain government officials and legislators spring directly from their assimilationist viewpoint, which focuses obsessively on the FMMs' stocks of capital or lack thereof, and assumes that the FMMs' lack of cultural-linguistic affinity for the host society must necessarily hinder the development and academic success of their children.

The perceptions fostered by both conventional wisdom and academic research with respect to the female marriage migrants and their children in Taiwan only serve to reinforce the widespread assimilationist ideology. Typical in this regard are the many studies of the achievement gap which purport to show that the linguistic deficiency of the mother is the (in fact, untested) reason for the achievement gap between native Taiwanese students and students born to Southeast Asian female marriage migrants (SEA-FMMs) but not those of the Chinese

FMMs (Li, Hsu, & Su, 2006). When findings like these find their way into the hands of political and media pundits, they tend to further reduce this complex issue to ignorant claims such as the Southeast Asian mothers are deficient in Mandarin ability and thus must be incapable mothers.

Both the C-FMM and the SEA-FMM mothers are indeed seen by many as being incapable of helping their children advance in school, but the stereotypes are a bit different for each group. Granted, in both cases, one sees widely reflected in the newspapers and electronic media, and at times hears from government officials and legislators, the notion that the FMMs' cultural and/or linguistic differences, and low socio-economic status, produce incapable mothers. The SEA-FMM, however, have received especially vicious stereotyping, as in references being made to their "bloodline" or accusations, even by legislators, of having "genetic defects" (Ke, 2006), and with such factors being cited to discourage them from giving birth to too many children (H. G. Chen, 2004; C. Q. Wang & Chen, 2004; Zhu & Meng, 2004). These extremist views were quickly and strongly criticized by human right activists in Taiwan, and yet while most people do not agree with these racist comments, many "moderates" agree that SEA-FMMs' cultural-linguistic differences are to blame for the supposed problems they have in educating their children, problems the host society feels it cannot afford to take lightly (Ministry of the Interior, 2004; Yan, 2006).

"Learning Chinese" has come to be seen by many as the solution of, or even a panacea for, this "problem." At the instigation of the central government, many primary schools have set up night sessions in which FMMs can learn Mandarin, and the Ministry of Education even has a plan in place to force the FMMs to attend night schools (M. L. Chen, 2004; Han, 2004). In some counties the FMMs already are attending classes in primary schools right alongside their children, again with the encouragement of the government (X. T. Zhou, 2004).

Despite their displeasingly paternalistic overtone, these initiatives certainly are valuable in aiding these immigrants in their adaptation to the new society. Yet their subtext seems to be that language learning will in and of itself solve all of the SEA-FMMs' parenting problems. Such a focus allows those concerned to ignore the non-linguistic factors, which really means all the various ramifications of the cultural-linguistic differences that may be hindering FMM from getting involved in their children's education. Seductive, certainly, is the public discourse focusing on "language learning" as a panacea for all the problems encountered by the FMMs, but this is a myth that waits to be unraveled. The truth is that a mother's stock of capital "on paper" (be they Mandarin-speaking ability, or actual money) do not automatically translate into an ability to get involved in her children's education. In other words, when it comes to educational achievement, it is not language ability alone, but rather the whole "package" of educational aspiration and culture that matters. In particular, the acquisition of academic discourse has been shown to be closely linked to a family's cultural capital that facilitates learning (Lareau, 2000). Thus a mother's capacity to get involved in her children's educational lives can never be reduced to her sheer linguistic ability or lack thereof. As we will see in the next section, C-FMMs' linguistic ability does not always lead to the accumulation of assets in terms of cultural capital.

When the *Putonghua* meets the *Guoyu*: societal perceptions of the Chinese FMM

As for the Chinese FMM, although they are not accused of being genetically inferior, they still are not immune from being disparaged as incapable mothers due to their—or more accurately, their receiving families'—low socio-economic status. In addition, C-FMM often are subjected to other hostilities, or at least strong skepticisms, owing to the ongoing tension between Taiwan and China. Indeed, their intentions in coming to Taiwan, and/or their true devotion to their families, are more often called into question than is the case with the SEA-FMM (Z. R. Chen & Yu, 2005). One might think that because the Chinese-FMMs "speak the same language" as the members of the host culture, and thus they are the best possible candidates for assimilation. Something more like the opposite is true, however, for their *Putonghua* (Mandarin; the term used in Mainland China) is imbued with the unique yet varied "Mandarin accents" of the different provinces of China. These are vastly different from the Taiwanese *guoyu,* and they are immediately distinguishable in the ears of Taiwanese people. Hence, the C-FMM can be easily "otherized" in their daily lives, owing to that burgeoning trend of Taiwanese cultural identity we noted earlier, a trend that could even be seen as a form of nativism. In this context, the C-FMMs' use of *"Putonghua"* can be seized upon by native Taiwanese as a mere stick with which to beat the scapegoat: the C-FMMs evoke from native Taiwanese the resentments they feel toward China.[3]

There can be no doubt that the Chinese FMMs have been placed in a uniquely odd situation: that of Mandarin-speaking immigrants to Taiwan encountering members of a host society that is Mandarin-speaking and yet whose newly-formed cultural-linguistic identity has notably Taiwan-ized its native tongue. Suddenly the old, seemingly firm boundary-line between Taiwan's old and new cultures has been blurred by the inrush of Chinese FMMs, with two ironies having come along with them. First, these "new Chinese immigrants" who speak Mandarin with the Mainland accent represent, in the eyes (or the ears) of the Taiwanese, not modernity but rather the old ideology and culture brought along with the KMT government in 1949. Second, many Chinese FMM have been startled to discover, upon their emergence into the linguistic landscape of Taiwan, that a new Taiwan-centered hegemony has replaced the old Mainland-centered hegemony of 60 years ago. Regardless of how it is packaged, what they are up against remains the same old assimilationist, or integrationist, ideology.

Drawing upon my fieldwork in Taiwan, I argue that assimilation, especially in its most reductive form of an imposed common language, can never in itself be a panacea that completely solves the "problem" of immigration. I also believe that those who expect a common language to promote instant assimilation, forget how diversified any great language inevitably is and what a vast cultural weight it carries, beyond its merely utilitarian usage. Quite simply, language hugely impacts everyone's identity and worldview. In the ensuing pages we will look at how the C-FMMs' shared-language factor is having some unforeseen side-effects when it comes to shaping these women's worldviews and adaptation strategies, and thereby their educational aspirations for their children.

Escaping the stigma: Chinese FMM and the new cultural-linguistic identity of Taiwan

Given that the Mandarin accent of the Chinese FMMs tends to make them recognizable by the native-born Taiwanese, their full command of the language does not keep them from being subjected to certain stereotypes in their everyday lives. A study done by Chen and Yu (2005) has shown that the perceptions of Mainland-born FMM held by native-born Taiwanese tend to line up with the particular political inclination of a particular Taiwanese individual. More specifically, the more pro-Taiwanese-independence the person is, the more negative his or her attitude is likely to be toward the Chinese-FMMs and indeed toward all those immigration-related policies that help the C-FMMs, even though they also benefit the SEA-FMMs.

In the small village in the southern part of Taiwan where I conducted part of my fieldwork, I often heard people call these FMM *dalumei* (Mainland girls) out loud in public, which is considered disrespectful and rude. Sometimes, comments making fun of the Chinese FMMs' Mandarin accent were made right in front of the FMMs themselves. I heard remarks which suggested that these "Mainland girls" talk like "communists," that they sound very "aggressive," that as they come from a communist country which has no property rights. They, therefore, must be "poor", certain to become "gold-diggers" in Taiwan. Oddly enough, however, these derogatory comments from the villagers do not necessarily represent any real hatred of the Chinese FMMs. In their daily lives, people do get along quite nicely with one another, with the language factor being more a focus of interest than an excuse for intolerance. Chinese FMMs, or at least most of them, do become an integral part of their communities—chitchatting, gossiping with the neighbors, discussing with one another family business and their children's education.

Thus, while language-related stereotypes are harmful in theory, in practice the host society's often negative impressions of the Chinese FMMs rarely include any real doubts as to their capability in general and as mothers in particular, with the absence of such doubts being particularly notable in rural Taiwan. A number of comments came my way during my fieldwork—some from teachers and school staff members, some from "meddlesome people" who knew I was doing research on this topic; usually in private but sometimes in more public settings—to the effect that the Chinese FMMs, as compared to the Southeast Asian ones, experience fewer problems when getting involved in their children's education. Indeed one rural principal I interviewed in 2005, even suggested that C-FMMs make the *best* mothers: "Simply my own experience tells me that the children of the Mainland brides sometimes—sometimes—do even better than the native ones. The mothers are more capable; you know: those Mainlanders are very aggressive!"

That principal's viewpoint was echoed by others I talked with in this village. C-FMMs often were spoken of as being "diligent," "capable," and "active," even if, at times, those words were loaded with such negative connotations as "aggressive," "impolite," "calculating," or "mean-spirited." When it comes to these women's involvements in their children's education, however, those negative qualities seem to be seen by teachers, school personnel, family members, and neighbors as doing little to undercut the C-FMMs' basically positive, proactive attitude.

Thus, my field observations do suggest that Chinese FMMs are able to wriggle out of the net of stereotypes always being imposed upon FMMs when it comes to the hot-button issue of their capability as parents. Mothers who more or less speak the same language as their host families do seem to be free, or even in some way to *benefit*, from the stereotypes that are imposed upon FMMs—by schoolteachers and public discourse which the media greatly amplifies. And yet, the possibility remains that the C-FMMs' high Mandarin skills matter less in and of themselves and more as a kind of token of the broader cultural affinity they have established with their receiving families and society. Then too, as we shall see next, a sense of cultural entitlement, springing from the shared-language factor, can be as much a liability as an asset.

Proud of being ethnic Chinese: the Chinese FMMs' sense of entitlement

Although both my own observations and other studies have found some discrimination against, or at least stereotyping of, the Chinese FMMs, perhaps the most unexpected thing I unearthed in the course of my fieldwork was the complex nature of the situation the Chinese FMM find themselves in, one that their own confidence, or even hubris, with respect to the shared-culture-and-language factor has had a hand in creating.

The Chinese FMMs' proud sense of being "ethnic Chinese" showed up in most of the C-FMM in my fieldwork. Typical in this regard is the following comment made by Ting-hui, a Chinese FMM living in Taipei:

> I feel that the adjustment of the Mainland brides should be fine. The real problem is when the bride comes from Vietnam. I feel they are much worse than us! I read in the newspaper that [the children of SEA-FMM say such things as] "My mother does not talk," because their Vietnamese mothers do not speak Chinese, and therefore are being discriminated against.

Miao, another C-FMM living in the countryside, has this to say when asked to describe her new life:

Where should I start? Of course for us [the C-FMMs] we are not used to being treated this way—there's no freedom married into the family [being supervised by the in-laws and the neighbors] . . . It depends on who you ask. Those SEA-FMMs of course would think it is nice. For them Taiwan is good enough. They know nothing! They can't go anywhere. Staying home is their only option [Interviewer: why can't they go anywhere?]. They don't speak the language! They can go nowhere!

These kinds of comments are very prevalent among the C-FMMs: seeing themselves as more capable than their SEA counterparts who "know nothing" in Miao's words. Their pride undoubtedly is linked to their linguistic identity—being able to speak Mandarin gives the C-FMMs not only confidence, but also a sense of entitlement that is not seen in the SEA-FMMs. This confidence arises not only through comparisons with the SEA-FMMs but also, ironically enough, crops up when they compare themselves to the native Taiwanese. It is not at all unusual for C-FMMs, as opposed to the SEA-FMMs, to interpret their occasional unfriendly encounters with Taiwanese, or quarrels with neighbors or family members, as revealing not discrimination, but rather the local people's vulgarity. Jen, for example, a C-FMM with whom I became quite close over the course of my fieldwork, frequently complained to me about the need she felt to leave Taiwan, owing both to the lack of attractive job opportunities for her and to the supposed "low quality of the local people."

Rural people, you cannot reason with them, you know! They murmur about everything, complain about this and that, always! I feel the quality of the people here [in rural Taiwan] is very low. They do not make sense. You know, *rural people don't even talk clearly.* [Interviewer: What do you mean by that?] They don't even speak Mandarin well! You wouldn't know what they are talking about, but they sure love to talk!

It is clear that, in such cases, language is being used as a barometer to gauge one's level of culture and class. Mainlanders, it should be noted, are already well versed in the habit of stereotyping each other on the basis of the accents prevalent in the various provinces. When Jen asserts that "rural people don't even talk clearly," she is implying that rural people (1) speak Mandarin with a heavy Taiwanese accent and (2) are not cultured enough to enunciate clearly. In both ways, however, this C-FMM is reclaiming her right to be a cultural arbiter by putting down the heavy, Taiwanese-style Mandarin spoken by the rural villagers. After I had grown closer to Xiaotong, another C-FMM, she shared with me this comment which reveals what some FMMs think of the "Taiwanese-style" Mandarin: "Even macho men talk like sissies here [in Taiwan]. It really gives you goosebumps! Nobody in our place talks this way."

The C-FMMs' sense of superiority, by reason of being ethnic Chinese, to SEA-FMMs and even to homegrown Taiwanese, a sense that often is heightened by living in a relatively remote rural area of Taiwan, leapt out at me even more clearly in these comments made by another C-FMM, Surong: "Indeed, the material life here is better . . . but there is no culture. In our place [her hometown in Mainland China], even though the material aspect is not as good, all of the people are cultured.

Many of the Chinese FMMs, by envisioning themselves as not just equal, but even superior to the native-born Taiwanese, have almost literally risen above the stereotyping that comes their way from the host society. Their children supposedly even receive better treatment in school. This confidence has to with their sense of a cultural-linguistic link to, and even superiority over, the host society, but it grows slowly into something more like hubris as the C-FMMs decide that Taiwanese-style Mandarin is "peripheral," not "authentic" enough and hence less desirable.

One sees this cultural confidence, bordering on hubris, at work in Surong who, although she wants her son to be seen as being like everybody else, also fears that if he gets "too close" to the Taiwanese kids in the neighborhood, it will foster downward assimilation. So too when Siwei was telling me once about the way her co-workers made fun of her accent, I was surprised to hear her end by saying, "I don't laugh at their jokes. I am not used to their countryside vulgarity." And when Surong's neighbors say things like, "You are lucky [to have been able to] flee [from Mainland China] to Taiwan," she simply thinks that these nice people are as ignorant as they are amusing.

With respect to these women's educational attitudes, I believe their ethnic pride does lead them, or at least some of them, to worry less than the SEA-FMMs about their children possibly being discriminated against in school by students and teachers. I did, however, hear at least one Chinese FMM, Tinghui, express her distaste and unease about place of politics in her son's classroom:

> Sometimes their teachers are more pro-DPP [the party promoting Taiwanese independence], and they will say something . . . Because the teacher has his own [political] stance and thinking, he shares this with his students. But I don't think little kids should be influenced and polluted by political thought . . . I tell my son, "Don't be too serious about these things. When you grow up, just do your own stuff well."

One can hear the confident ring of those last words. And Tinghui does indeed possess an independent spirit, one that her pride in being Chinese may or may not have helped her to cultivate:

> From kindergarten right through primary school, whenever his teachers asked, "Whose mother is a foreign bride?" he always raised his hand. He did not feel inferior or embarrassed about it; to the contrary, he was quite proud. He was like, "Yeah, my mom is a foreign bride." . . . I feel that we gave him, ever since he was small . . . As parents, we need to give kids some values. Not to let him feel inferior just because his mother is a foreign [Chinese] bride. If I had a sense of inferiority, that would influence the kids. That would be wrong.

One can only admire Tinghui for wanting to keep pride strong, in both her and her son. Such pride does not represent an absolute asset for every C-FMM, however, as we shall see in the ensuing section.

The collision of two language hegemonies: the dark side of the C-FMMs' high self-regard

When it comes to the shared-language factor between the C-FMMs and the native Taiwanese, this study sees it as playing a part in creating that broader cultural affinity with the Taiwanese, which begins by stoking feelings of ethnic pride in the C-FMMs only to sometimes end by plunging them into disappointment. My initial interviews with and observations of these women led me to believe that when it comes to Taiwan's C-FMMs, their high regard for their own cultural heritage translates into a positive perception of their own ability, and thereby into a similarly positive perception of the role their own stock of capital and capacity in advancing the children's education. Gradually, however, I understood how this high self-regard and sense of entitlement that many of the C-FMMs share are by no means a pure asset. For by leading them to expect that they will get a great deal from Taiwanese life and be treated with respect, it often betrays them into sheer disappointment. Take Siwei, for example. Her fluent Chinese and her high-school diploma have not brought her the life she hoped for. When she first thought of marrying into Taiwan she envisioned "a prosperous life and a happy family, just like the ones seen on Taiwanese soap operas [the shows she watched back in Mainland China]" and the making of lots of money, but instead she has ended up "trapped" in a small rural community where there are only a few factory jobs, not the kind of service jobs she still hoped to find. Worse yet, her controlling in-laws did not allow her to go to Taipei to work. Instead, they demanded that she give birth to a lot of children and understand that her job is being a mother. This is how she vented her anger:

> I am completely stuck here, there is nothing that I can do! . . . My husband and his family treat me badly. I told them "You should have married a Vietnamese bride! You should not have married me!"

It is understandable that Siwei tries to cope with her unhappiness by implicitly stereotyping Vietnamese brides as being better able to endure bad treatment from their receiving families. Indeed, many of the people I met with during my fieldwork, and especially those living in rural Taiwan where people seem to feel freer to openly reveal their prejudices, suggested that the Southeast Asian brides are docile whereas the Mainland brides are capable and aggressive. Siwei had this to say when talking about the comments the local people made:

> Of course SEA-FMMs are docile. They have to stay here. They are actually happy to be here—comparing [Taiwan] to where they come from. Also their

culture-level is not that high . . . They don't understand the suppression they are put under and they honestly don't have the ability to reach for more. [Interviewer: Reach for more?] Language! And the culture. How do they go [to work] outside if they know nothing?

This confidence will soon turn into sheer disappointment for many of the C-FMMs, however, when they compare their own lives with those of the local Taiwanese. Tongying and Tiantian, for example, are two urban Chinese FMMs whose proud sense of being Chinese has been shattered by the harsh realities they face, owing to the low socio-economic status of their families and the sense of relative deprivation they experience by living in the city. These factors deprive them of the seemingly ethnic, but in reality largely language-based, pride they otherwise feel. The following comment, pinning all the blame on economic capital, was made by Tongying but is typical of many others I heard from the C-FMMs:

The problem is [our] being poor. I do not think my being a Chinese FMM is something the children need to know about, or something we should talk about with them. There is nothing special about being an immigrant. We are all Chinese.

It is clear to me that despite the seeming nonchalance of such comments, in fact these mothers' intentional subtractions of their own culture and heritage from their dealings with their children's education constitutes, in their own eyes, a step they must take in order to help their children assimilate fully into the "mainstream." Once, for example, when Tongying's daughter told her, while discussing an assignment in which the kids were to interview their mothers about their life-experiences and heritage, that the teacher had asked the students whose mothers were foreign brides, Tongying's response to her daughter was unequivocal: "Don't draw attention to yourself! We are the same as everybody else! Don't raise your hand [when the teacher asks whose mother is a foreign bride]! . . . [There is] nothing worth talking about [you being the daughter of a foreign bride]." She then turned her head to me and added, "We are all Chinese! There is no need to draw attention."

On the one hand, Tongying's insistence that "we are all Chinese" represents her deep-seated belief that both the native Taiwanese and the C-FMMs are indeed all Chinese who share the same language and culture, with the native Taiwanese presumably noting a difference but not finding it as a cause of discrimination. On the other hand, she subconsciously understand that things aren't quite that simple, for she feels a need to conceal her identity as a "foreign bride" from China, telling her children "not to draw attention to yourself!"

I can only assume it is the sheer harshness of their daily lives, within their very constrained contexts of reception that has led quite a few of the initially proud C-FMMs to seek to hide themselves away from all public scrutiny. What is beyond doubt, however, is that their "recessive" attitude toward their lives in

Taiwan in general leads them to sell both themselves and their kids very short, when it comes to educational issues. They do this by reducing their involvement to its two most basic elements: a bit of supervision, and scraping together whatever money they can to pay for cram school. Tongying spoke to the first of those factors when she told me this:

> Yes, I do ask them to keep their room neat, to wash their hands before eating, that kind of thing. That's about it. After I come back from work it is usually very late, and I don't have that kind of time to talk about useless BS with them. But when I am home, I make sure they do everything [personal hygiene and the daily chores] right.

Tiantian, another Chinese FMM living in the city, is even more passive in her approach:

> All I can do is give my daughter money and ask her to go out and play. I have nothing to offer her. I know nothing. I do not know even where to play in Taiwan. I just tell her to go out and play. . . . I can't do it well [educating my child], because I know nothing [about Taiwanese life].

Of course, cram school looms large in Taiwan's educational scene (virtually every mother I met during my fieldwork sent her children to cram school at one time or another), but the C-FMMs seem to have very different, though equally self-effacing, attitudes toward it. A woman like Tongying sees getting her child into cram school as being "the only good thing [I can do] for my children," whereas Tiantian seeks to do it simply so that "he [my son] won't be like me." Be such attitudes as they may, however, what is certain is that the C-FMMs' allegiance to an assimilationist ideology renders them relatively blind to the subtle language-ironies we looked at early in this chapter, the one borne out of the burgeoning sense of a "homegrown" Taiwanese identity and ensuring that "speaking Mandarin in a Taiwanese style" and thus becoming "one of us [Taiwanese]" is a goal very few Chinese-FMM will ever reach. They will rarely be out-and-out hated for speaking with a Mainland accent, but oftentimes they will be mentally pigeonholed as "foreigners" in the estimation of many native-born Taiwanese.

Conclusion

The present chapter began its life as an examination of how Taiwan's female marriage migrants, and especially the Chinese ones, are forging adaptation strategies that allow them to get involved in the lives of their children. It has evolved into an exploration of the complexity of cultural-linguistic identity, with the latter revealing its hidden power as the Chinese FMMs experience more challenges than they expected to have in aligning themselves with Taiwan's rather unique and multicultural mix.

I noted earlier in this chapter how Taiwanese cultural-linguistic hegemony has produced a prejudice against the Southeast Asian FMMs, evidenced by disparaging comments made by media and political figures regarding incapable and overly fertile mothers. Prejudice has also produced C-FMMs, like Miao, who are subconsciously rebelling against their disgruntled awareness that mistreatments and difficulties are in fact happening to *them*, the supposedly more favored immigrants from Mainland China who share the supposedly same culture and, above all, language with Taiwan. My findings suggest that this cultural-linguistic and even ethnic affinity that the Chinese FMMs feel with their Taiwanese hosts initially brings them a sense of confidence and pride. This pride, however, later comes close to buckling under the stress of immigrant life, especially when a Chinese FMM has married into a family that is unsupportive, economically deprived, or simply not well-off when compared to the native Taiwanese families.

When I first began to delve into this issue, I looked upon the language factor as being just one of many that the FMMs struggled to cope with, and a factor always likely to be reduced to its utilitarian function in the minds of many of Taiwanese social pundits as well as many of the women themselves. A further exploration, however, confirmed my belief in the fallacy of equating "perfect language skills" with "perfect integration" into the host society and its various factions and members. The unique linguistic-cultural relationship Chinese-FMMs have with the Taiwanese host society have made their integration an even more complex issue. The notably conflicted lives being lived by the C-FMMs in today's Taiwan, as they suffer from a new hegemony, teach us about a power history can turn a trend on its head within just a few generations. For whereas the old KMT-led attempt to impose standard Mandarin on the Taiwanese was overtly hegemonic and class-conscious, today's "Taiwanized" Mandarin is a bottom-up social growth that makes "standard" Mandarin speakers sound, to the ears of local Taiwanese, stilted and alienated in their approach to both language and life. It seems that linguistic-cultural hegemony is able to assume many forms, and to exert its power every bit as easily from below as from above.

Notes

1 In Korea, inter-national marriage comprised 13.6 percent of all the marriages registered in 2005, according to the Korean Statistical Information System (KOSIS). Marriages between Korean men and women coming from China, Southeast Asian countries, and the Commonwealth of Independent States (CIS) of the old Soviet Union increased 9.2 times over the period 1990–2005 (Kim, 2006). In Japan, the percentage of marriage represented by inter-national hypergamy slowly grew from 0.43 percent in 1965 to 0.93 percent in 1980, but by 2004 it had reached 5.46 percent, with Chinese wives having the largest number of 35.7 percent, followed by Brazilians (19.1 percent), Filipinos (14.3 percent), and Koreans (10.2 percent) (Ochiai, Ishikawa, & Liaw, 2006).
2 Scholars warn us against this viewpoint of reducing such marriages to the "mail-order brides" phenomenon, i.e., merely to a form of capitalist market exchange. By treating these brides strictly as victims, one can easily reinforce or replicate the Orientalist stereotype (Constable, 2003).
3 I owe this thought to an insight shared with me by Dr. Gulbahar Beckett.

References

Asakura, T. (2002). Foreign brides fill the gap in rural Japan: Bachelors looked abroad after eligible local girls fled village life for city. *Japan Times*. January 8. Available at: http://search.japantimes.co.jp/cgi-bin/nn20020108b9.html. Accessed on August 19, 2010.

Chen, H. G. (2004). Xin yimin kangyi qishi, Zhou Can-de daoqian [New immigrants protest at being discriminated against, Zhou Can-de apologizes]. *Zhongyang Ribao* [Central Daily News]. Section 5. July 13.

Chen, M. L. (2004). Waiji ji dalu peiou xintaiwan zhizi jiudu zhongxiaoxue renshu yu san wan [More than thirty thousand children of foreign and Mainland spouses study in middle and primary schools]. *Zhongyang Ribao* [Central News]. Section 14. October 13.

Chen, Z. R., & Yu, D.-L. (2005). Taiwan minzhong dui wailai peiou yimin zhengce de taidu [Attitudes of the Taiwanese toward policies on foreign spouses]. *Taiwan Shehuixue* [Taiwan Sociology], 10, 95–148.

Cheng, R. L. (1994). Language unification in Taiwan: Present and future. In M. A. Rubinstein (Ed.), *The Other Taiwan: 1945 to the Present* (pp. 357–391). Armonk, NY: M.E. Sharpe, Inc.

Constable, N. (2003). *Romance on a global stage: Pen pals, virtual ethnography, and "mail order" marriages.* Berkeley: University of California Press.

Gao, Y. Z. (2003). Haitong fazhan chihuan cheng yinyou [A hidden crisis: Children's development]. *Zhongguo Shibao* [Chinatimes], May, 8, Section A11.

Gibson, M. (1988). *Accommodation without assimilation: Sikh Immigrants in an American high school.* Ithaca, NY: Cornell University Press.

Han, G. D. (2004). Bushizi waiji peiou, ni qiangzhi buxi [Illiterate foreign spouses: Forced into adult education]. *Zhongguo Shibao* [Chinatimes], October 19, Section C8.

Ke, H. M. (2006). Liao Ben-Yan: Yingcha yueniang youwu yudu [Liao Ben-Yan: Vietnamese brides should be under investigation for bio-chemical poisoning]. *Lianhe Bao* [United Daily News], April, 1, Section A3.

Kim, D. S. (2006). The rise of international marriage and divorce in contemporary Korea. *Paper presented at the International Conference on Intermediated Cross-border Marriages in Asia and Europe*, Taipei, Taiwan, September 18–20.

Lareau, A. (2000). *Home advantage: Social class and parental intervention in elementary education.* Lanham, MD: Rowman & Littlefield Publishers, Inc.

Lee, H. K. (2003). Gender, migration and civil activism in South Korea. *Asian and Pacific Migration Journal*, 12(1–2), 127–153.

Li, C. H., Hsu, S. Y., & Su, X. F. (2006). The school performance of studies in rural Taiwan: A comparison between the descendants of immigrant and native brides. *Paper presented at the International Conference on Intermediated Cross-border Marriages in Asia and Europe*, Taipei, Taiwan, September 18–20.

Liu, X. Y. (2002). Kuawenhua chongji xia waiji xinniang jiating huanjing ji qi zinuu xingwei biaoxian zhi yanjiu [Foreign bride family environment and their children's behavior under cross-cultural conflicts]. Unpublished dissertation: National Chung-Cheng University, Min Hsiung.

Ministry of the Interior. (2004). Jiuer nian waiji peiou shenghuo zhuangkuang diaocha baogao [Report on the lives of FMM, year 2003]. Taipei: Ministry of the Interior.

Ministry of the Interior. (2010). Available at: http://www.moi.gov.tw/stat/news_content. aspx?sn=3748&page=0. Accessed August 19, 2010.

Nakamatsu, T. (2003). International marriage through introduction agencies: Social and legal realities of "Asian" wives of Japanese men. In N. Piper & M. Roces (Eds.), *Wife or worker? Asian women and migration* (pp. 181–201). Lanham, MD: Rowman & Littlefield Publishers.

Ochiai, E., Ishikawa, Y., & Liaw, K. L. (2006). Feminization of migration and cross-border marriages in Japan. *Paper presented at the International Conference on*

Intermediated Cross-border Marriages in Asia and Europe. Taipei, Taiwan, September 18–20.

Ogbu, J. U. (1991). Immigrant and involuntary minorities in comparative perspective. In M. A. Gibson, & J. U. Ogbu (Eds.), *Minority status and schooling: A comparative study of immigrant and involuntary minorities* (pp. 3–33). New York: Garland.

Piper, N., & Roces, M. (2003). *Wife or worker? Asian women and migration*. Lanham, MD: Rowman & Littlefield Publishers, Inc.

Portes, A., & Rumbaut, R. G. (2001). *Legacies: The story of the immigrant second generation*. New York: Russell Sage Foundation.

Wang, C. Q., & Chen, Y. L. (2004). Buyao sheng name duo [Don't give birth to that many]. *Zhongguo shibao* [Chinatimes], July 10.

Wang, H. R. (2001). Shehui jiecenghuaxiade hunyinyimin yu guoneilao dongshichang [Social stratification, Vietnamese partners' migration, and Taiwan labour market]. *Taiwan Social Research Quarterly*, 41, 99–127.

Wang, S. Y., Shieh, Y. W., Wen, S. M. L., Whang, N. Y., Huang, J. L., Chen, Y. J., *et al.* (2006). Woguo xinyimin zinuu xuexi chengjiu xiankuang zhi yanjiu [A study of the learning performance of immigrant children in Taiwan]. *Jiayu ziliao yu yanjiu shuang yuekan* [Education Data and Research], 68, 137–170.

Xia, X. J. (1997). Selfing and othering in the "Foreign Bride" phenomenon: A study of class, gender and ethnicity in the transnational marriage between Taiwanese men and Indonesian women. Unpublished dissertation. University of Florida.

Xia, X. J. (2002). *Liuli xunan: Zibenguo jihuaxiade waiji xinniang xianxiang* [Searching for the shore: The "foreign bride" phenomenon under the internationalization of capital.] Taipei: Tangshan.

Yan, G.-H. (2006). *Jialai Taiwan: xinixing yiminde hunyin gushi* [Married into Taiwan: Marriage stories of the new immigrants.] Taipei: New News Culture.

Zhou, M., & Bankston III, C. L. (1998). *Growing up American: The adaptation of Vietnamese adolescents in the United States*. New York: Russell Sage Foundation.

Zhou, X. T. (2004). Waijima yu zinv kecheng tongban tongxue [Foreign mothers and their children can become classmates]. *Zhongguo Shibao* [Chinatimes], December 11, Section A11.

Zhu, S. J., & Meng, X. J. (2004). Zhou Can-de shiyan, renquan tuanti yu chengchu [Zhou Can-de's clinker; human rights activists call for his punishment]. *Lianhe Bao* [United Daily News], July 14, Section B8.

8 The influence of cultural and linguistic backgrounds on the social and academic adjustment of students at an ethnic minority university in China

Mei Wu, Jerry Tuchscherer, and Forrest W. Parkay

Background

This research explores the extent to which cultural and linguistic background influences minority students' social and academic adjustment at the university level. Specifically, the research examined *personal and collective self-esteem, collegiate psychological sense of community,* and *social and academic adjustment* of four types of students, grouped according to self-reported ethnic and Chinese language ability and knowledge of their language and culture.

Though the concepts of self-esteem and self-identity were developed in the West, they have been applied to populations worldwide, including Chinese students. For example, Watkins and Dong (1994) and Watkins, Dong, and Xia (1997) confirmed the appropriateness for Chinese students to use a translation of Marsh's (1988) Self-Description Questionnaire. Similarly, Brown, Cai, Oakes, and Deng (2009) and Ho (2003) used Rosenberg's Self-Esteem Scale (1965) and found it applicable to Chinese populations. Other researchers have examined the self-identities of Chinese students, for example, Lee (2001a, 2001b, 2000), Wan and Wang (2004), and Trueba and Zou (1994).

Minority language diversity

According to the Chinese Constitution, all ethnic groups in China have the freedom to use and to develop their spoken and written languages. The Chinese government contends that its policies help minorities "create, improve, or reform their written language" and "promote the use of spoken and written languages" (*National Minorities Policy and Its Practice in China*, 2004, p. 6). In the 1950s, China organized specialists to investigate the spoken and written languages of ethnic minorities and established special organizations involved in work connected with the spoken and written languages of ethnic minorities. According to the national report, *National Minorities Policy and Its Practice in China* (2004, p. 99):

> All the 55 national minorities, except the Hui and Manchu, who use the Chinese language, have their own languages. Among them, 21 use 27

languages, and more than ten ethnic groups, including the Zhuang, Bouyei, Miao, Naxi, Lisu, Hani, Wa, Dong, Jingpo (Zaiya language family) and Tu, use 13 languages which have been created or improved with the help of the government.

However, according to Stites (1999), estimates of the number of mother tongues spoken in China range from 80 to more than 100, and yet there are only 55 officially recognized minority nationalities. As Stites (1999) pointed out, there was not one-to-one correspondence between language and national identity in China, and the extent and nature of language and dialectical diversity in minority areas of China have not been fully explored.

Language diversity and educational attainment are reflected in various illiteracy rates among minority communities. For example, Zhou (2000) categorized Chinese minority communities into three types according to the consequences of Chinese language policy. In Type 1 communities, those with writing systems in broad usage before 1949 and with regular bilingual education since then, the language policy can generally be viewed "positively," since those communities have illiteracy levels in their native languages that are higher or close to the majority Han communities (except Tibetan communities). In Type 2 communities, those with writing systems in limited usage before 1949 and without regular bilingual education since then, the language policy can be viewed "negatively," since those communities have illiteracy rates in their native languages that are two or three times higher than the Han. In Type 3 communities, those without functional writing systems before 1949 and with limited or no bilingual education since then, the language policy may be viewed "positively" for 27 minorities and "negatively" for the other 15 minorities (Zhou, 2000, p. 145). With reference to the three types of language communities Zhou (2000), it is likely that Type 1 communities have a higher probability of fostering bilingual students, while the same is not true for Type 2 and 3 communities.

Minority higher education

By the end of 1998, the Chinese government had independently founded 12 ethnic universities and institutes, 59 ethnic teachers training schools, 158 ethnic secondary vocational schools, 3,536 ethnic middle schools, and 20,906 ethnic primary schools. More than 80 institutions of higher learning in China held preparatory classes for minority students to help them acquire basic knowledge to continue their studies at higher specialized schools (*National Minorities Policy and Its Practices in China*, 2004, p. 5).

These 12 ethnic universities and institutes are called "universities for nationalities" and "institutes for nationalities." As Huang (2000, p. 205) suggests:

A "university for nationalities" and "higher education for minorities" are two different concepts ... The former has contributed much more to Chinese higher education for minorities than any other ordinary university does, and that almost all the problems of Chinese higher education for minorities are concentrated in it [university for nationalities.

The academic quality and facilities of these universities are generally recognized as poor. They impress people with their "backwardness, conservativeness, low efficiency, and inability to attract talent" (Huang, 2000, p. 1).

The current study

Within this context of diverse challenges for ethnic minority education and limited access to quality higher education for China's ethnic minorities, this study examined the relationships between students' cultural and linguistic backgrounds and their social and academic adjustment while studying at a leading university for nationalities. The study also examined students' self-concepts—i.e., personal self-esteem and collective self-esteem, and collegiate psychological sense of community.

Drawing from Zhou's (2000) typology of language communities in China, we examined the social and academic adjustment of students from four different cultural and linguistic backgrounds: minority students fluent in their ethnic language and the national language (Type 1 Students); minority students fluent in the national but not ethnic language, though it is still widely spoken by other members of their group (Type 2); minority students fluent only in the national language (Type 3); and students of the Han ethnic group fluent in their ethnic (national) language (Type 4).

Since language is tied to culture (Freire, 1985), it seems reasonable to link students' language abilities to their cultural backgrounds. *Cultural background* in this study refers to cultural "distance" from the majority Han culture at the individual level. Therefore, those who rely heavily on their ethnic language and have limited Mandarin ability may be considered strongly "embedded" in their ethnic culture. Those with a higher degree of bilingualism know their own culture and, to varying degrees, the Han culture. Minorities who speak Mandarin but not their ethnic language, although their language still exits, may know more Han culture than their own culture. And, finally, those who speak only Mandarin since their own language disappeared in "competition" with Mandarin, have adapted to Han culture in addition to their original culture, such as the Hui and Man.

The study did not include minority students who cannot speak Mandarin. Those students are seldom enrolled in the university, since the major entrance examination is in Mandarin Chinese, and it is the academic language of the university. While a few of these students are enrolled under national preferential policies, which permit minority students to enter the university by taking the entrance examination in their native language, this study could not gather data from them since the questionnaire for this study was written in Chinese. As a comparison group, however, Han majority students were included in the study.

The following specific research questions provided the primary focus for this study:

1   Are there differences among the four types of students with different linguistic backgrounds in terms of personal self-esteem, collective self-esteem, collegiate psychological sense of community, and social and academic adjustment? If there are differences, what are they?
2   What are the interrelationships among personal self-esteem, collective self-esteem, collegiate psychological sense of community, and social and academic adjustment?
3   What are the relationships between minority students' linguistic ability and their personal self-esteem, collective self-esteem, collegiate psychological sense of community, and social and academic adjustment?

Conceptual framework

Figure 8.1 presents a conceptual framework for the study. Figure 8.1 suggests that a student's overall university experience, i.e., social and academic adjustment, is influenced by cultural and linguistic background as well as self-concept and psychological sense of community. Self-concept consists of two dimensions: personal self-esteem, an overall self-appraisal of one's worth and feelings about oneself (Lemme, 2006); and collective self-esteem, an overall appraisal of one's social identity, which is referred to as "collective identity" in American terminology. According to Tajfel and Turner's (1979, 1986) social identity theory, self-concept consists of two distinct aspects: personal identity and social identity. Personal identity includes specific attributes such as competence, talent, and sociability. Social identity is defined as "that part of an individual's self-concept which derives from his knowledge of his membership in a social group (or groups) together with the value and emotional significance attached to that membership" (Luhtanen & Crocker, 1992). Drawing from social identity theory, Luhtanen and Crocker (1992) developed the Collective Self-esteem Scale to evaluate one's social identity. On the other hand, Rosenberg's (1965) Self-esteem Scale is used to evaluate one's personal identity (Luhtanen & Crocker, 1992).

Collegiate psychological sense of community is a feeling that members have of belonging, a feeling that members matter to one another and to the group, and a shared faith that members' needs will be met through their commitment to be together in a college community (Lounsbury & DeNeui, 1996; McMillan & Chavis, 1986). Lounsbury and DeNeui (1996) developed the theory of Collegiate Psychological Sense of Community to apply the concept to the college campus. In addition, colleges have long been regarded as having a sense of community and have been widely studied as communities (Cruz, 1987; Easthope, 1975; Spitzberg, 1992).

Considered as an overall university experience, *social and academic adjustment* was defined as a behavioral process by which students maintain equilibrium between their various social and academic needs and obstacles encountered in

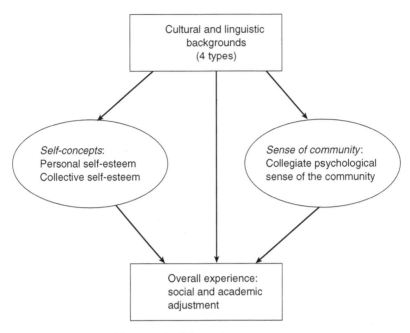

Figure 8.1 Conceptual framework of the study.

their environment. A sequence of adjustment begins when a need is felt and ends when it is satisfied. The Social and Academic Adjustment Scale used in this study was developed by Woosley (2003) and measures overall adjustment at a university.

Instruments

Respondents completed a two-part survey. Part I called for demographic and background information. Part II consisted of data gathered for the following four constructs: (1) personal self-esteem, measured by Rosenberg's (1965) Self-esteem Scale; (2) collective self-esteem, measured by Luhtanen and Crocker's (1992) Collective Self-Esteem Scale; (3) collegiate psychological sense of community, measured by Lounsbury and DeNeui's (1996) Collegiate Psychological Sense of Community (PSC) Scale; and (4) social and academic adjustment, measured by Woosley's (2003) Social and Academic Adjustment Questionnaire. The following sections describe Parts I and II of the survey.

Demographic and background information

Part I consisted of 20 items that included the following: personal information (ethnic group, age, gender, hometown, and religion), academic information (major and degree, year in college, academic cohort rank before and after entering the university, National College Entrance Examinational Score, and College English Test Level 4 and Level 6 scores), language ability (bilingual or monolingual and fluency level), and parents' education level. In the language ability section, participants were asked to respond to the question "Does your ethnic group have its own ethnic language other than Mandarin Chinese?" Those who answered "no," non-Han students, were grouped as Type 3, those who speak Mandarin only, since their ethnic language is no longer spoken or they think they do not have one. Those who answered "yes," continued to identify their "level of ability in their ethnic language" according to the following: (1) "no ability;" (2) "basic;" (3) "fair;" (4) "good;" or (5) "very good." Those who selected (3) "fair," (4) "good," or (5) "very good" were grouped as bilingual students, Type 1. Those who selected (1) "no ability" or (2) "basic" were grouped as Type 2, those who cannot speak their ethnic language, but their language is still spoken by other members of the group. Han students were grouped as Type 4. Participants were also asked to rate their ability in Mandarin Chinese according to the five-point scale.

Self-Esteem Scale

Rosenberg's (1965) ten-item Self-Esteem Scale was used in this study. The Scale is a widely used and well-validated measure of global personal self-esteem, with test–retest reliabilities greater than .80 (Rosenberg, 1965). Each item uses a four-point scale, from "strongly agree" to "strongly disagree." Items numbered 2, 5, 6, 8, and 9 were reverse scored. To be consistent with other scales discussed below, the scores were re-coded as 1 = "strongly disagree;" 2 = "disagree;" 3 = "agree;" and 4 = "strongly agree." Higher scores, therefore, indicate higher self-esteem.

Collective Self-Esteem Scale

The Collective Self-Esteem Scale (Luhtanen & Crocker, 1992) consists of 16 items scored on a 7-point scale: 1 = "strongly disagree;" 2 = "disagree;" 3 = "disagree somewhat;" 4 = "neutral;" 5 = "agree somewhat;" 6 = "agree;" and 7 = "strongly agree." The scale consists of four subscales, each with four items: Membership Esteem, Public Collective Self-Esteem, Private Collective Self-Esteem, and Importance to Identity. Luhtanen and Crocker report that "reliability of the subscales and the total CSES was demonstrated by reasonably high Cronbach's alphas and item-total correlations and adequate test-retest coefficients" (1992, p. 315).

Collegiate Psychological Sense of Community (PSC) Scale

The Collegiate Psychological Sense of Community (PSC) Scale presents 14 items that reflect "psychological sense of community" applied to colleges and universities. Respondents rate each item according to a 5-point scale: 1 = "strongly disagree;" 2 = "disagree somewhat;" 3 = "neutral;" 4 = "agree somewhat;" and

5 = "strongly agree." According to its developers (Lounsbury & DeNeui, 1996, p. 390), the scale encompass "feelings of belongingness, togetherness, attachment, investment, commitment to the setting, positive affect, concern for the welfare of the community, and an overall sense of community." The Scale demonstrates reliability results across settings (Lounsbury & DeNeui, 1996, p. 382).

Social and Academic Adjustment Questionnaire

The Social and Academic Adjustment Questionnaire consists of nine items scored on a five-point scale: 1 = "strongly disagree;" 2 = "disagree;" 3 = "undecided;" 4 = "agree;" and 5 = "strongly agree." According to Woosley (2003), the adjustment scales were developed and tested using factor analysis and confirmatory factor analysis with cohort data from multiple years. The alpha reliabilities of the four items on the social adjustment scale and the five items on the academic adjustment scale were .85 and .74, respectively.

The four instruments were developed in the United States. Rosenberg's (1965) Self-Esteem Scale has been used widely throughout the world. The other three have been used widely at universities and colleges. The four instruments were translated from English into Chinese. To improve accuracy, a back translation method was used. Back translation involves the process of translating the target language version back into the source language by a bilingual person (Kim & Lim, 1999). Numerous international studies have provided evidence that back translation is an essential technique for ensuring psychological equivalence between source and target language versions (Brislin, 1970; Brislin, Lonner, & Thorndike, 1973).

The setting

Data were gathered in May, 2007 at China's leading university for nationalities in Beijing. The university recruits minority students throughout the country. The university is the only one in China that has students from each of China's 56 ethnic groups. Among the 15,000 students at the university in 2007, about 70 percent, or 10,500, were minority students. Since its establishment in 1951, a key function of the university is to train cadres from all minority nationalities to promote the political, economic, and cultural development of minority areas. The university is known throughout the country as "the highest learning institute" for China's ethnic minorities. It has received strong support from the government and it is the only minority university included in the "211 Project" and the "985 Project." These two state projects provide extensive financial support to a small group of universities in China to become "world-class" universities.

Data collection and analysis

During a seven-day period, surveys were randomly distributed to students in campus locations such as cafeterias, classrooms, the library, dormitories, classrooms used for individual study, and a weekend flea market on campus. All students who appeared at the various sites and responded affirmatively to the question "Are you a student at the university?" were asked to complete a survey. After agreeing to participate, it took participants about ten to fifteen minutes to complete the survey. Fewer than 10 percent of students declined to respond to the survey. The main reasons those students gave were that they were "in a rush," "busy," or "not interested."

Data were analyzed by using the Statistical Package for the Social Sciences (SPSS) 15. The analysis included the following computations: (1) descriptive statistics and measurement reliability tests; (2) ANOVA to compare the four types of students in terms of the four factors—personal self-esteem, collective self-esteem, collegiate psychological sense of community, and social and academic adjustment; (3) a correlation analysis to discover the relationships among linguistic abilities and the four factors; and (4) linear regression modeling analysis to explore the interrelationships among the four factors.

Valid survey data were gathered from 347 respondents. Respondents represented 29 different ethnic groups (including the Han majority) and 33 provinces and autonomous regions in China. Respondents included 145 males and 202 females, from 16 to 30 years old, with 81 percent between 18 and 22 years old. Table 8.1 presents demographic information for the respondents.

It is worth noting that respondents from the same ethnicity may be distributed among the different types. For example, 12 percent of Type 1 and 14 percent of Type 2 students are Mongolian, which indicated that among the same ethnic group, some can speak their ethnic language and some cannot. In another case, 20 percent of Type 2 and 88 percent of Type 3 spoke their ethnic language while some did not.

The researchers did not "correct" the perception that the Hui, for example, have no ethnic language. Instead, the data were unchanged to reflect "cultural distance" at an individual level. However, such ambiguity was not surprising. For example, Arabic and Persian words considered as "*Huihui Hua*," (Hui speech) (Gladney, 1999), still are still used internally in Islamic religious activities. The Qur'an, as well as Islamic doctrines, practices, and history automatically dominate the Muslim curriculum (Mackerras, 1999). According to Lin (2008), the Holy Qur'an has never been translated into Chinese. For those who practice their religion, the Qur'an has been read and studied in Arabic at the Mosques. The Hui students from Type 2, who know about *Huihui Hua*, may be more embedded in their Muslim community than those from Type 3 who do not think they have an ethnic language.

Findings

Five major findings emerged from the data analysis: (1) the four types of cultural and linguistic backgrounds were appropriate for the purpose of this study; (2) the instruments in the four measurement areas—personal self-esteem, collective

Table 8.1 Demographic information for respondents

		Type 1		Type 2		Type 3		Type 4	
		#	(%)	#	(%)	#	(%)	#	(%)
Number of participants	Male	39	48.1	41	37.6	25	50.0	40	37.4
	Female	42	51.9	68	62.4	25	50.0	67	62.6
	Total	81	100.0	109	100.0	50	100.0	107	100.0
Ethnicity	# of Ethnicities	14		25		5		1	
	Top Five	Kazak	25.9	Hui	20.0	Hui	88.0	Han	100.0
		Uyghur	22.2	Mongolian	13.8	Manchu	6.0		
		Tibetan	14.8	Manchu	10.1	Bai	2.0		
		Mongolian	12.4	Tibetan	7.3	Gelao	2.0		
		Zhuang	6.2	Miao/Yi	6.4	Miao	2.0		
	% of Total		81.5		57.6		100.0		100.0
Religion		Muslim	51.9	Atheist	45.9	Muslim	68.0	Atheist	46.7
		Buddhist	18.5	Muslim	19.3	Atheist	24.0	Buddhist	19.6
		Atheist	17.3	Buddhist	15.6	Others	6.0	Others	14.0
		Others	7.4	Others	10.1	No response	2.0	Christian	14.0
		Christian	2.5	No response	9.2	—		No response	5.6
		No response	2.5	—		—			
	% of Total		100.0		100.0		100.0		100.0
Hometown	# of Prov. & Reg.	13		23		17		27	
	Top Five	Xinjiang	49.4	Yunnan	12.8	Ningxia	16.0	Hebei	9.4
		Qinghai	13.9	Hunan	11.0	Gansu	12.0	Hunan	9.4
		Guangxi	7.4	Inner Mongolia	11.0	Henan	12.0	Liaoning	7.5
		Inner Mongolia	7.4	Liaoning	10.1	Qinghai	12.0	Shandong	5.6
		Guizhou	5.0	Guizhou	7.3	Shandong	8.0	Shanxi	5.6
	% of Total		83.1		52.3		60.0		37.4
Major	#	30		29		23		32	
	Top Five	Ethnic Language	30.9	Dance	15.6	Finance	12.0	Dance	28.0
		Chinese Literature	6.2	Finance	13.8	Economics	10.0	Music	14.0
		Foreign Language	6.2	Law	7.3	Law	8.0	Economic	7.5
		Tibetology	6.2	Music	7.3	Dance	6.0	Finance	5.6
		Dance	4.9	Ethnology	6.4	Music	6.0	Medicine	3.7
	% of Total		54.3		50.5		42.0		58.9

self-esteem, collegiate psychological sense of community, and social and academic adjustment—were found to be statistically reliable; (3) collective self-esteem is significantly different among the four types of students, while there is no significant difference in personal self-esteem, collegiate psychological sense of community, and social and academic adjustment; (4) Mandarin ability is positively correlated to personal self-esteem; and (5) personal self-esteem is positively correlated with collective self-esteem, which significantly influences collegiate psychological sense of community and social and academic adjustment; and collegiate psychological sense of community is strongly correlated with social and academic adjustment. The following sections explain each of the findings in detail.

The four types of cultural and linguistic backgrounds were appropriate for the purpose of this study

Some 190 students, or 55 percent, reported that they had an ethnic language other than Mandarin. About 157 students, or 45 percent, including Han majority students, reported that they had no ethnic language other than Mandarin. Among those who had an ethnic language, 81, or 23 percent of the students, spoke their ethnic language, while 109 students, or 31 percent, could not speak their ethnic language. Among those 190 who had ethnic language, 32 reported that their language had no written form. Fifty minority students reported that they did not have ethnic language. The number of Han students was 107, or 31 percent of the total. Incidentally, the percentage of Han students in the sample is about the same as the percentage of Han students in the university population. Table 8.2 presents the number of students according to the four types.

The study applied ANOVA to examine whether the four types of students were properly categorized. Ethnic language ability analysis involved Type 1 and Type 2 students who have an ethnic language. Results indicated that Type 1 ($M = 4.21$, $SD = 1.05$) had significantly higher ethnic language abilities than Type 2 ($M = 1.30$, $SD = .60$), $F(1,188) = 583.92$, $p < .001$. The average score of Type 1 ($M = 4.21$) was close to 4, the "good" level. However, the average score of Type 2 ($M = 1.30$) was close to 1, "no ability" level.

Table 8.2 Number of students according to the four types

Ethnic language	Yes		No	
	#	*(%)*	#	*(%)*
Type 1	81	23	–	–
Type 2	109	31	–	–
Type 3	–	–	50	14
Type 4	–	–	107	31
Total	190	54	157	45

Table 8.3 Language abilities of the four types of students

Type		Language ability					Sample		Std. dev.
		No ability	Basic	Fair	Good	Very good	Size	Mean	
1	Ethnic	–	–	25	8	48	81	4.21	1.05
	Mandarin	–	2	26	29	24	81	3.93	0.85
2	Ethnic	70	39	–	–	–	109	1.30	0.60
	Mandarin	–	1	25	40	43	109	4.15	0.8
3	Ethnic	–	–	–	–	–	–	–	–
	Mandarin	–	–	8	17	25	50	4.34	0.75
4	Ethnic	–	–	–	–	–	–	–	–
	Mandarin	–	–	19	27	61	107	4.4	0.78

Mandarin ability analyses involved all four types of students. The results indicated that Type 4 ($M = 4.40$, $SD = .78$) and Type 3 ($M = 4.34$, $SD = .75$) had significantly higher Mandarin abilities than Type 1 students ($M = 3.93$, $SD = .85$), $F(3,342) = 6.00$, $p = .001$. Table 8.3 presents the language abilities of the four types of students.

Figure 8.2 shows that the average Mandarin ability scores of four types of students range from 3.93 to 4.40, which is close to the "good" level and above. This finding met the assumption that the Mandarin of participants is "good" at the fluent level. In addition, Type 1 students' ethnic language abilities, on average, are better than their Mandarin abilities. The following sections describe who the four types of students are in detail.

Type 1 students are bilingual. Their ethnic language abilities were generally higher than their Mandarin ability. Their Mandarin ability was found to be significantly lower than Type 3 and Type 4 students. Most Type 1 students (about 80 percent) are from Xinjiang Uyghur Autonomous Region (49 percent), Qinghai Province (14 percent), Guangxi Zhuang Autonomous Region (7 percent), Inner Mongolian Autonomous Region (7 percent) and Guizhou Province (5 percent). Those areas, especially autonomous regions, were predominantly non-Han. About 70 percent of Type 1 students are Muslim (52 percent) and Buddhist (19 percent), and about 17 percent are atheist. More than 80 percent of Type 1 students are from five ethnicities: Kazak (26 percent), Uygur (22 percent), Tibetan (15 percent), Mongolian (12 percent), and Zhuang (6 percent). Those ethnic groups have their own ethnic language in written form. About 93 percent of them speak their ethnic language at home. According to Zhou's study (2000), these ethnic communities, except Tibetan, implemented a bilingual education system, in which Chinese is taught as the second language. More than half of Type 1 students are majoring in ethnic languages (31 percent), ethnology—Tibetology (6 percent), Chinese language (6 percent), foreign languages (6 percent), and arts—dance (5 percent). Their strong ethnic language abilities and knowledge about their culture may have a positive impact on their areas of study.

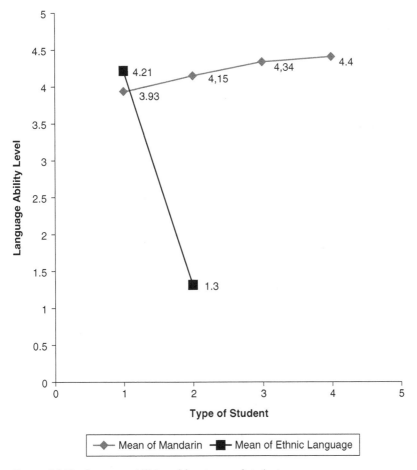

Figure 8.2 The language abilities of four types of students.

Type 2 students could not speak their ethnic language, although their language is still spoken by other members of their group. They were from 25 ethnic groups and 23 provinces and autonomous regions. Those areas are multiethnic provinces and autonomous regions such as Yunnan (13 percent), Hunan (11 percent), Inner Mongolia (11 percent), Liaoning 10 percent), and Guizhou (7 percent). The top six ethnicities were Hui (20 percent), Mongolian (14 percent), Manchu (10 percent), Tibetan (7 percent), Miao (6 percent), and Yi (6 percent). Most Type 2 students are atheist (46 percent). Nineteen percent were Muslim and 16 percent were Buddhist. About 90 percent of them did not speak an ethnic language at home. Since Type 2 students are spread throughout 23 provinces and regions, it seems reasonable that they do not have local bilingual schools and, instead, attend regular schools with other ethnic and Han students.

Type 3 students cannot speak their ethnic language, since their language has been long lost, or, as an individual, they did not think their ethnic group has an ethnic language. These students were from the Ningxia Hui Autonomous Region (16 percent), Gansu (12 percent), Henan (12 percent), Qinghai (12 percent), and Shandong (8 percent). About 88 percent were from the Hui group. The others were Manchu (6 percent), Bai (2 percent), Gelao (2 percent), and Miao (2 percent). About 68 percent of them are Muslim, and about 24 percent are atheist. There were no Buddhists among Type 3 students.

Type 4 students speak Mandarin. They were all majority Han people from 27 provinces and regions. The top five provinces they were from were Hebei (9 percent), Hunan (9 percent), Liaoning (8 percent), Shandong (6 percent), and Shanxi (6 percent). Their Mandarin ability was highest among the four types of students. Most Type 4 students (47 percent) are atheist, and 20 percent are Buddhist. There were no Muslims among Type 4 students.

The instruments in the four measurement areas were found to be statistically reliable

Cronbach's alpha, a reliability coefficient, measures how well a set of items or variables measures a single dimension. In this study, the Cronbach's alphas for the three scales, except the Personal Self-esteem Scale, were higher than .80. By deleting item No. 8, the Personal Self-esteem Scale improved its reliability coefficient from .68 to .75. The analysis suggests that the four measurements— personal self-esteem, collective self- esteem, collegiate psychological sense of the community, and social and academic adjustment—were reliable and theoretically acceptable for this study. Table 8.4 presents the reliability of the instruments.

The deleted item in the Personal Self-esteem Scale stated "I wish I could have more respect for myself." In this study, about 75 percent of respondents "agreed" or "strongly agreed" with this statement. This suggests that, in this environment, most students, regardless of other perceptions about themselves,

Table 8.4 Reliability of the instruments

Variables	N	Min.	Max.	Mean	SD	Cronbach's Alpha	No. of items
Personal Self-esteem	337	1.89	4	2.84	0.36	0.75	9*
Collective Self-esteem	322	2.94	6.75	4.98	0.73	0.81	16
Collegiate psychological Sense of community	321	1.14	4.86	3.24	0.67	0.84	14
Social and academic adjustment	326	1.33	5.00	3.32	0.63	0.82	9

Note: *There are 10 items in the Personal Self-esteem Scale. To improve the measurement reliability of the instrument, Item 8 was deleted.

felt the same. That is, they wanted to have more respect for themselves. This might be a reason why this item reduced the instrument's reliability.

Collective self-esteem

Collective self-esteem is significantly different among the four types of students, while there is no significant difference in personal self-esteem, collegiate psychological sense of community, and social and academic adjustment. An ANOVA, analysis of variance was conducted to compare the four types of students in terms of personal self-esteem, collective self-esteem, collegiate psychological sense of community, and social and academic adjustment. The null hypothesis stated that there is no difference among the four types of students in terms of the four measurements. The omnibus test of ANOVA provided evidence (F (3,318) =5.375, p = .001) of significant differences in mean collective self-esteem among the four types of students in the population. However, there was no evidence showing significant differences in mean scores for personal self-esteem, collegiate psychological sense of community, and social and academic adjustment.

For the collective self-esteem measurement for the four types of students, post-hoc tests suggest that the differences lie between Type 3 and each of Type 1, Type 2, and Type 4 students. Type 3 was 0.53 points higher than Type 1 students (p = .001), 0.38 points higher than Type 2 (p = .014), and 0.33 higher than Type 4 (p = .050). Figure 8.3 illustrates the comparison among the four types of students with respect to collective self-esteem. In conclusion, Type 3 students had significantly higher collective self-esteem than the other three types of students, but there was no significant difference among Type 1, 2, and 3 students.

Mandarin ability is positively correlated to personal self-esteem

The correlation analysis tested the relationship among ethnic language ability, Mandarin ability, and the four measurements among all participants. The evidence (r = .22, $p <$ .001) suggests that Mandarin language ability is significantly correlated with personal self-esteem. The relationship is positive. The strength, however, was statistically weak: only 5 percent of the variance (r^2 = 0.05) in personal self-esteem was affected by Mandarin language ability. Additional evidence (r = -.24, p = .002) suggests that Mandarin ability is negatively correlated with ethnic language ability, which indicates that minority students who have stronger ability in an ethnic language would be weaker in Mandarin.

The same correlation analysis was conducted within each type of student. It was found, interestingly, that Mandarin ability had a significant, positive relationship with personal self-esteem for Type 1 (r = .25, p = .03), Type 2 (r = .26, p = .01) and Type 4 (r = .25, p = .01) but not Type 3 students. Mandarin ability, however, had a significant, negative relationship with collective self-esteem for Type 3 (r = -.32, p = .04). Further study is suggested to explore this finding.

Mandarin ability had no significant relationship with the other three measurements: collective self-esteem, collegiate psychological sense of community, and

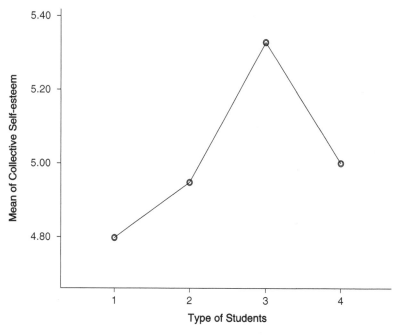

Figure 8.3 Collective self-esteem and the four student types.

social and academic adjustment. Among the four factors, they were all inter-correlated. Table 8.5 presents the correlations among language abilities and four factors.

Personal self-esteem

Personal self-esteem is positively correlated with collective self-esteem, which significantly influences collegiate psychological sense of community *and* social and academic adjustment; and collegiate psychological sense of community is strongly correlated with social and academic adjustment.

The evidence from the correlation analysis (Table 8.5) suggests that four factors are significantly and positively correlated to each other ($rs > 0, ps < 0.05$). The linear regression modeling analysis revealed the causal relationships among linguistic and cultural backgrounds and the four variables as shown in Figure 8.4.

For this study, social and academic adjustment was treated as a response variable, while personal self-esteem, collective self-esteem, and collegiate psychological sense of community were treated as potential explanatory variables. A model was built by adding one variable at a time, while eliminating variables that lost their significance when other variables were added (Agresti & Finlay, 1997). The results revealed that personal self-esteem did not significantly predict

Table 8.5 Correlations among language abilities and the four factors

Correlations		Personal Self-esteem	Collective Self-esteem	Collegiate Psychological Sense of Community	Social and Academic Adjustment	Ethnic Language Ability	Mandarin Language Ability
Personal Self-esteem	Pearson Correlation	1.00	—	—	—	—	—
	Sig. (2-tailed)		—	—	—	—	—
	N	337					
Collective Self-esteem	Pearson Correlation	0.50**	1.00	—	—	—	—
	Sig. (2-tailed)	0.00		—	—	—	—
	N	317	322				
Collegiate Psychological Sense of Community	Pearson Correlation	0.12*	0.32**	1.00	—	—	—
	Sig. (2-tailed)	0.03	0.00		—	—	—
	N	314	304	321			
Social and Academic Adjustment	Pearson Correlation	0.16**	0.30**	0.74**	1.00	—	—
	Sig. (2-tailed)	0.01	0.00	0.00		—	—
	N	319	309	318	326		
Ethnic Language Ability	Pearson Correlation	-0.06	-0.12	0.09	0.14	1.00	—
	Sig. (2-tailed)	0.42	0.13	0.23	0.08		—
	N	171	163	162	164	176	
Mandarin Language Ability	Pearson Correlation	0.22**	0.10	0.02	0.04	-0.24**	1.00
	Sig. (2-tailed)	0.00	0.08	0.77	0.52	0.00	
	N	311	295	296	300	166	320

Notes

*Correlation is significant at the 0.05 level (2-tailed).

** Correlation is significant at the 0.01 level (2-tailed).

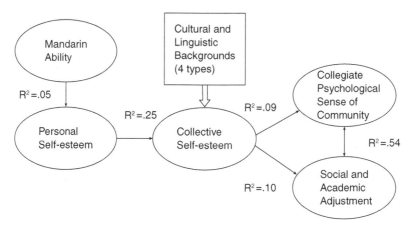

Figure 8.4 Interrelationships among four factors and language abilities.

social and academic adjustment, since, when collective self-esteem was added to the model, the effect of personal self-esteem became insignificant. Its *p*-value increased from .01 to .98.

Since collegiate psychological sense of community was found to be strongly correlated to social and academic adjustment ($r = .74$, $p < .01$) and collective self-esteem had similar or equal weight effects on collegiate psychological sense of community and social and academic adjustment, the interrelationships among the four factors and language abilities is suggested as shown in Figure 8.4.

Conclusion

The study found that Mandarin ability has a positive relationship with personal self-esteem, which suggests that those who speak better Mandarin tend to have higher personal self-esteem. However, personal self-esteem has no direct, significant relationship with social and academic adjustment, which suggests that speaking better Mandarin does not lead to better social and academic adjustment. Therefore, results suggest that students' Mandarin ability has no direct effect on their social and academic adjustment at the university.

The study also found that collective self-esteem is influenced by cultural and linguistic backgrounds, which were defined by students' language ability and their individual cultural "distance" from the Han majority. This finding indicates that Type 3 minority students who speak Mandarin only (since their language has been lost) have the highest collective self-esteem among the four types of students. Those students were mostly from the Hui ethnic group and a few Manchu. Those students who have largely adopted Han culture in addition to their own culture were considered the closest to Han culture among four types of students.

In conclusion, apart from language ability, cultural background is a factor that influences collective self-esteem. Gladney (1999) suggests that the Muslim culture and its educational system, which combined state-sponsored and mosque-sponsored schools, "bind them closer together" than the Han Chinese majority and the other 45 minority nationalities. With reference to Gladney's conclusion, we suggest that the Hui-Chinese Muslims with their unique Muslim culture plus extensive adoption of the majority Han culture as reflected in their high Mandarin ability, have higher levels of collective self-esteem than the three other types of students. In addition, our analysis of collective self-esteem from a religious perspective did not provide any evidence suggesting that Muslims are significantly different from other religious groups.

Although collective self-esteem was significantly correlated to collegiate psychological sense of community and social and academic adjustment, there was no evidence that Type 3 students are different from the other three types of students in these two areas. This might be because the effects of collective self-esteem on the two areas are not strong, only about 9 and 10 percent of the variance in them can be explained by collective self-esteem. Therefore, cultural and linguistic backgrounds of students have little effect on their social and academic adjustment through collective self-esteem.

An important finding from the study was that collegiate psychological sense of community is highly correlated with social and academic adjustment ($r = .74$, $p < .001$). As mentioned, collegiate psychological sense of community refers to members having a shared feeling that they belong, that they matter to one another and to the group, and that their needs will be met through their commitment to be together in a college community. Study results also suggest that a collegiate environment characterized by a sense of belonging, togetherness, and a feeling of respect for one another is very important for students if they are to adjust socially and academically while attending a university for ethnic minorities in China. Therefore, the university should recognize that if it enhances students' sense of belonging to the university (sense of community), it increases the prospects of their academic success.

References

Agresti, A., & Finlay, B. (1997). *Statistical methods for the social sciences*. Englewood Cliffs, NJ: Prentice Hall.

Brislin, R. W. (1970). Back-translation for cross-cultural research. *Journal of Cross-Cultural Psychology*, 1(3), 185–216.

Brislin, R., Lonner, W., & Thorndike, R. (1973). *Cross-cultural research methods*. New York: Wiley.

Brown, J. D., Cai, H., Oakes, M. A., & Deng, C. (2009). Cultural similarities in self-esteem functioning: East is East and West is West, but sometimes the twain do meet. *Journal of Cross-Cultural Psychology*, 40(1), 140–157.

Cruz, F. F. (1987). *John Dewey's theory of community*. New York: Lang.

Easthope, G. (1975). *Community, hierarchy and open education*. Boston: Routledge & Kegan Paul.

Freire, P. (1985). *The politics of education: Culture, power and liberation*. New York: Bergin & Garvey Publishers, Inc.

Gladney, D. (1999). Making Muslims in China: Education, Islamicization, and representation. In G. A. Postiglione (Ed.), *China's national minority education: Culture, schooling, and development* (pp. 55–94). New York: Falmer Press.

Ho, E. S. (2003). Students' self-esteem in an Asian educational system: Contribution of parental involvement and parental investment. *School Community Journal*, 13(1), 65–84.

Huang, J. (2000). Issues in the development of Chinese higher education for minorities. *Higher Education Policy*, 13(2), 203–214.

Kim, A., & Lim, E. Y. (1999). How critical is back translation in cross-cultural adaptation of attitude measurement? *Paper presented at Annual Meeting of the American Educational Research Association*, Montreal, Quebec (ERIC Document Reproduction Service No. ED430014).

Lee, M. J. B. (2000). What minority education in China can teach us about minority education in the US. *Paper presented at the People of Color in Predominantly White Institutions Fifth Annual National Conference, POCPWI*. Lincoln, University of Nebraska-Lincoln.

Lee, M. J. B. (2001a). *Ethnicity, education, and empowerment: How minority students in southwest China construct identities*. Hampshire: Ashgate.

Lee, M. J. B. (2001b). Learning across cultures: How minority students construct identities that foster academic success. *Paper presented at the People of Color in Predominantly White Institutions Sixth Annual National Conference, POCPWI*. Lincoln, University of Nebraska-Lincoln.

Lemme, B. H. (2006). *Development in adulthood* (4 ed.). Boston: Pearson.

Lin, T. (2008). Hui ethnic language. *Hui Ethnic Culture*. Retrieved December 7, 2008, from http://www.yich.org/ayzl/z9/200810/27995.html.

Lounsbury, J. W., & DeNeui, D. (1996). Collegiate psychological sense of community in relation to size of college/university and extroversion. *Journal of Community Psychology*, 24(4), 381–394.

Luhtanen, R., & Crocker, J. (1992). A collective self-esteem scale: Self-evaluation of one's social identity. *Personality and Social Psychology Bulletin*, 18(3), 302–318.

Mackerras, C. (1999). Religion and the education of China's minorities. In G. A. Postiglione (Ed.), *China's national minority education: Culture, schooling, and development* (pp. 23–54). New York: Falmer Press.

Marsh, H. (1988). *The self-description questionnaire 1: SDQ manual and research monograph*. San Antonio, TX: The Psychological Corporation.

McMillan, D. W., & Chavis, D. M. (1986). Sense of community: A definition and theory. *American Journal of Community Psychology*, 14(1), 6–23.

National Minorities Policy and Its Practice in China. December 2004. Retrieved on October 11, 2006, from http://www.china-un.ch/eng/bjzl/t176942.htm.

Rosenberg, M. (1965). *Society and the adolescent self-image*. Princeton, NJ: Princeton University Press.

Spitzberg, I. J. (1992). *Creating community on college campuses*. Albany, New York: State University of New York Press.

Stites, R. (1999). Writing cultural boundaries: National minority language policy, literacy planning, and bilingual education. In G. A. Postiglione (Ed.), *China's national minority education: Culture, schooling, and development* (pp. 95–130). New York: Falmer Press.

Tajfel, H., & Turner, J. C. (1979). An integrative theory of intergroup conflict. In W. G. Austin, & Worchel, S. (Eds.), *The social psychology of intergroup relations*. Monterey, CA: Brooks-Cole.

Tajfel, H., & Turner, J. C. (1986). The social identity theory of inter-group behavior. In S. Worchel, & L. W. Austin (Eds.), *Psychology of intergroup relations*. Chicago: Nelson-Hall.

Trueba, H. T., & Zou, Y. (1994). *Power in education: The case of Miao university students and its significance for American culture.* Washington, DC: The Falmer Press.

Wan, M., & Wang, Y. (2004). Ethnic identity of Tibetan undergraduates (in Chinese). *Acta Psychologica Sinica*, 36(1), 83–88.

Watkins, D., & Dong, Q. (1994). Assessing the self-esteem of Chinese school children. *Educational Psychology*, 14(1), 129–137.

Watkins, D., Dong, Q., & Xia, Y. (1997). Age and gender differences in the self-esteem of Chinese children. *The Journal of Social Psychology*, 137(3), 374–379.

Woosley, S. A. (2003). How important are the first few weeks of college? The long-term effects of initial college experiences. *College Student Journal*, 37(2), 201–207.

Zhou, M. (2000). Language policy and illiteracy in ethnic minority communities in China. *Journal of Multilingual and Multicultural Development*, 21(2), 129–148.

9 Language issues in Chinese higher education

The case of Korean and Mongol minority groups

W. James Jacob and Heejin Park

Introduction

Blessed with the Earth's largest human resource base, the People's Republic of China is home to some 1.3 billion people. While a strong majority of this population is ethnic Han, the government officially recognizes 55 minority groups. Ethnic minority population nationwide exceeds 120 million with more than 100 distinct native languages (Clothey, 2005; de Varennes, 2006; Jacob, 2006; Zhou, 2000, 2001). Recent ethnic demonstrations and clashes with the government in the traditional minority regions of Tibet and Xinjiang highlight some of the tensions that exist in China today (Wong, 2009). The largest ethnic minority groups, in terms of population, are the Zhuang at 16.1 million, Manchu at 10.6 million, and the Hui at 9.8 million (Jacob, 2004). Because China's minority ethnic groups constitute less than 10 percent of the total population, and because they largely reside in rural and hinterland regions of the country (Hawkins, 1978; Kormondy, 2002; Lam, 2007), these minority groups are frequently neglected in terms of education access, especially at the higher education subsector (Zhao, 2007). However, minority populations tend to have higher fertility rates than majority Han Chinese (Yusuf & Byrnes, 1994; Kim, 2003), who are restricted by government laws to no more than one child per couple (Hudson & Den Boer, 2005; Mosher, 2006). According to the National Bureau of Statistics of China (1990, 2000, 2006), the population of Chinese minorities increased approximately 260 percent from 1953 to 1990 while the Han majority increased less than 190 percent so that the proportion of minority nationalities to the country's gross population have also increased from 6.06 percent in 1953 to 8.07 percent in 1990.

In this study, the authors examine the case of Korean (朝鲜族, *Cháoxiăn Zú*) and Mongol (蒙古族, *Měnggŭ Zú*) minority groups, which primarily reside near the northern and eastern borders. Since both Korean and Mongol minorities mainly live along China's borders, they are significant peoples in Chinese foreign policy and military strategy (Dilger, 1984). Moreover, there are roughly twice as many Mongols residing in China today as there are in Mongolia. Along with the Manchu, the Mongols were one of only a few minority groups to reign over Chinese territory in China's long history (Bulag, 2003; Dilger, 1984; Zhao, 2007). Although, it was not until at the end of nineteenth century when Koreans immigrated en masse to China (Min, 1992; Lee, 1990), there have been a myriad of exchanges and historical events between the two countries over several millennia. Border disputes still exist and continue to strain relations between China and the Korean Peninsula (Gomà, 2006).

Like most Chinese minority groups, Korean and Mongol minorities struggle with formal education in China, especially at the higher education level (Kim & Heo, 2001). Language is a recognized predictor for this educational hindrance among minority students and is the primary focus of this chapter. We compare case studies of both Mongol and Korean ethnic groups regarding how language influences their opportunities for access and equity in Chinese higher education. While many studies exist on minority education in China (see Alitto, 1969; Attané & Courbage, 2000; Barnes, 1978; Blum, 2002; Dreyer, 1978; Hannum, 2002), none have examined these two minority groups on a national scale. Nor have any studies been conducted on Mongol and Korean minorities in relation to higher education. This qualitative study helps fill this gap in the comparative and international education literature.

Minorities and education in the People's Republic of China

China is surrounded by 29 countries and shares its border with 16 of them. Along with diverse ethnic groups from these neighboring countries, there are many recognized and unrecognized minorities within Chinese territory. Thus, conflicts and tensions among those diverse ethnic groups have been a constant throughout China's past. Throughout contemporary Chinese history, some minorities have been more successful than others in preserving their language and culture (Lam, 2005; Zhou, 2000). The government has in principle supported the development and use of minority languages since the establishment of the People's Republic in 1949 (Lam, 2005; Li 2007). Although there have been 57 ethnic minority scripts in Chinese since ancient times, only seven nationalities out of those officially recognized have written language systems which are widely used (Li, 2007; Stites, 1999). Those seven nationality languages include Mongolian, Tibetan, Uygur, Kazak, Korean, Liangshan Yi, and Xishuangbanna Old Dai.

In 1955, the Chinese government adopted the Mandarin dialect as the official national language (called *Putonghua*) and reaffirmed that this language should be promoted in the revised 1982 Constitution of China. *Putonghua* is the common spoken language of the modern Han group and became the lingua franca for all ethnic groups in China. Consequently, *Putonghua* has become the first or second language for about half of the people of Chinese minority groups. A considerable number of minorities have given up their native languages as a result of this national policy, language of instruction in schools, and economic demand for *Putonghua* (Zhou, 2000). According to Ma (2007, p. 12), among Chinese minority groups,

One-third function in Chinese as well as in their own language, six of the nationalities have converted mainly or entirely to using Chinese, and a majority of the members of forty of the nationalities can use Chinese as a second language.

The dominant use of *Putonghua* in the Chinese education and economic sectors emphasizes one of the most important rationales for Chinese minority students choosing to learn the national language versus minority languages, yet along with this emphasis come potential socio-cultural drawbacks that threaten to undermine the fabrics of minority languages and culture. Chinese law and approaches to language rights and minorities have not always been antagonistic to the concept of minority peoples and language rights (de Varennes, 2006). Yet, the government is making valid attempts to offset these negative economic pressures for minority languages and has assured support collection and studies on ethnic languages in the future.

Language has significant importance for minorities not only because of its crucial influence on self-identity building and cultural preservation, but also on their social and economic achievement in the society in which they belong. It is language through which one's cultural heritage and traditional assets are preserved from generation to generation. At the same time, proficiency in the national language is necessary for individuals who intend to take essential positions in any society. The dilemma many minority peoples face revolves around a decision of whether they should put emphasis on their own language preservation or on acquiring proficiency in the dominant language. Interviews that Li (2007, p. 25) conducted with ethnic minority government officials discussed this dilemmatic situation that Chinese minority face: "On the one hand the officials complained about the decline of local ethnic culture, while on the other hand teaching their children Putonghua or dialects of Putonghua rather than their ethnic group's language as a mother tongue." The global influence of English has only exacerbated the situation for minorities in China. For example, a Mongolian anthropologist, Bulag (2003) reports that some Mongol minority people "advocate learning English" instead of "favoring retention of the Mongolian language bilingually along with Chinese" (p. 755). The main reason for this rationale for choosing to learn *Putonghua* and/or English over one's indigenous tongue lies on the belief that proficiency of a dominant global language is linked more closely to better education and employment opportunities, especially if the children leave the region to seek a life elsewhere.

Government statistics on higher education enrollment indicate that minority student enrollment since 1949 has steadily increased in Chinese higher education institutions. There were only 1,285 minority students in 1949/1950, which represented less than 1 percent of the total Chinese higher education student enrollment. At the end of the millennium, minority student enrollment increased to around 250,000 (Mackerras, 2003, p. 127). Table 9.1 portrays Chinese higher education enrollments of minority students from 1949 to 2007. The percentage of minority students in Chinese higher education is lower compared with the total population.

Table 9.1 Proportion of ethnic minority student enrollments at Chinese universities

Years	Number of students	(%)
1949–1950	1,285	0.9
1955–1956	14,159	3.5
1960–1961	29,921	3.2
1975–1976	36,578	6.5
1980–1981	51,220	4.0
1985–1986	99,468	5.3
1990–1991	141,767	6.7
1994–1995	160,000	5.7
2004–2005	250,000	5.4

Sources: Sautman (1999, pp. 180–181); Ministry of Education (2005).

Also, the number of minority teachers and faculty members has increased throughout this same time period. According to Mackerras (2003), minority teachers at the Chinese primary education subsector increased from 133,200 (3.5 percent of total students in 1965) to 545,100 (9.3 percent of the total in 1999). The number of secondary school teachers from ethnic minority groups increased in similar proportion from 14,635 (3.2 percent) in 1965 to 271,400 (7.1 percent) in 1999. Despite these gains at the primary and secondary education subsectors, the higher education subsector is a different scenario. The proportion of ethnic minority faculty members in teaching or research positions has not increased as much at the higher education subsector. The number and proportion of minority faculty members in Chinese universities have changed from only 623 (1.84 percent) in 1953 to 21,000 (5.3 percent) in 1994 (see Table 9.2).

The figures in Tables 9.1 and 9.2 emphasize some of the disparities that exist between ethnic minority students and faculty members in proportion to the total Chinese student and faculty member populations. This educational disparity has direct implications for ethnic minority achievement in education as well as socio-economic status. Considering the importance of higher education in improving individuals' socio-economic status and enhancing ethnic minority people's development, issues of access and equity at the higher educational subsector has lasting consequences for ethnic minority peoples.

Background on Korean Chinese and higher education

The ethnic Korean nationality is located primarily in the northern and eastern border regions of the country and is one of five minorities that have their own autonomous region (Postiglione, 1998). Comprising only two million people, Korean Chinese constitute a relatively insignificant number of people when compared to the nation's total population. Along with the Tibetan minority group, however, Korean Chinese represent one of two cultural, political, and socio-economic extremes among the 55 ethnic minority groups in China (Zhou, 2000).

Table 9.2 Proportion of ethnic minority faculty members in Chinese higher education
institutions

Year	Number of faculty members	(%)
1953	623	1.8
1957	1,941	2.8
1965	3,311	2.4
1980	7,808	3.2
1985	12,775	3.7
1990	17,533	4.4
1994	21,000	5.3
2000	37,406	4.8
2005	60,517	4.1

Sources: Sautman (1999, pp. 182); Ministry of Education (2000, 2005).

Different from most other ethnic minority groups—who have lived in China for
many centuries—Korean Chinese immigrated to China quite recently. Mass
immigrations of Koreans to China occurred primarily due to the extreme oppression and hardships inflicted by the Japanese invasion of the Korean Peninsula
motherland early in the twentieth century (Cho, 1992).

Most Korean Chinese reside in the northeast region of the country, especially
concentrated in the Yanbian Korean Autonomous Prefecture in Jilin Province.
Although the North and South Korean governments both acknowledge Yanbian
as Chinese territory, some nationalist groups in Seoul assert that the region is a
historical part of Korea and ought to be returned (Gomà, 2006). There have also
been rigorous political disputes between China and the two Koreas regarding the
history of the Koguryo Dynasty (32 BC to 668 AD). During this period Korea
reigned over a large territory encompassing the Yanbian area and North Korea.
To mediate the conflict, the Korean Ministry of Education and Human Resources
Development included lessons on territorial and historical disputes with Japan
and China in the seventh edition of history textbooks, which will be adopted by
high schools in 2012 (Kang, 2007). These prolonged disputes inherited for such a
long period of time, may take more than just a couple of years to solve, however.
Korean Chinese have successfully established a unique lifestyle that in many
ways differs from both the Han majority and Koreans in the Korean Peninsula.
Despite the differences, Korean Chinese relations with their heritage motherland
seem to be maintained and regularly strengthened. According to recent Republic
of Korea Ministry of Justice statistics (2007), 95,691 Korean Chinese recently
acquired permission from the Korean government to work for a three-year period.
Most Korean Chinese working in Korea are domestic or manual laborers, many
of whom do not have proper legal immigrant status. Thus, the official number of
Korean Chinese working and residing in Korea increases when illegal Korean
Chinese workers are included. Marriages between Korean Chinese women and

South Korean men are also increasing. The close, but complicated political and historical relations between China and Korea have more or less affected Korean Chinese education and their attitudes towards ethnic language acquisition and retention.

Dilger (1984) argues that "most minority nationalities lived socially and economically in greater backwardness than even Chinese peasants in the inner provinces" (p. 157), however, he points out that the Manchu and Korean Chinese are exceptions. Moreover, Korean Chinese are frequently regarded as a "model" people among various minority ethnic groups in China in terms of their successful bilingual education and high enrollment rates in higher education institutions (see, for instance, Zhou, 2000). Scholars from several other studies, however, argue that Korean Chinese have encountered a number of educational problems with the rapid transition of China toward a market-oriented economy (You & Kwak, 2004; Heo, Park, Kim, & Lee, 2003). According to Cai (2004, p. 5), for instance, around 40 percent of primary and middle school students are separated from one or both of their parents who went abroad. Those parents mostly travel to the Republic of Korea to earn money by becoming manual or domestic workers. This phenomenon of separation from one's parents for long and recurring periods of time leads to emotional and psychological challenges and often negatively influences student performance in school (Choi & Kim, 2004). Also, a discouraging education trend among Korean Chinese is the ethnic group's declining scores on the National Entrance Examinations to higher education, which has been on the decline since the 1990s and coincides with the onset of the introduction of the market economy in China (You & Kwak, 2004). At the same time, many Korean Chinese benefit from their bilingual proficiency in the increasing job market competition (Cai, 2004). Largely because of their native language background, Korean Chinese higher education graduates often have an advantage over other Chinese, especially when Korean corporations are looking for employees and managers working in Chinese-based Korean corporations. Korean Chinese professionals are also often more versatile with the ability to work in either of the two countries.

Korean Chinese were the first ethnic minority group to establish its own higher education institution—Yanbian University (Choi & Kim, 2004). From their early settlement in China, Koreans have always been concerned with formal education and place it among the highest cultural value and priority among their people (Cho, 1998). Korean Chinese passion for education enables them to become one of the most successful minorities in achievement at every education level (Postiglione, 1992). Their relatively short immigration entry into China is also a crucial fact that helps Korean Chinese preserve their own culture and language compared with other minority groups. Yet, much like other ethnic minority groups, Korean Chinese constantly face the dilemma of learning Korean and *Putonghua* at the same time (Choi & Kim, 2004). Most Korean Chinese speak Korean as their native language, even though the majority also learn and speak *Putonghua*. Koreans' language proficiency tends to also vary depending on the region in which they live. Koreans in predominantly urban regions tend to adopt

Putonghua instead of Korean as their native language and learn Korean as one of the subjects offered in school and examined on the National Entrance Examination. Rural Korean Chinese are more likely to use Korean as their first language. Korean Chinese residing in both suburban and urban areas have a greater tendency to face the linguistic dilemma described above. Korean Chinese who learn Korean as their first language are at a disadvantage when learning *Putonghua* and this often impedes their opportunity to attend higher education. Koreans who choose to learn and use *Putonghua* as their first language, on the other hand, find themselves losing much of their cultural and traditional heritage (Choi & Kim, 2004).

Background on Mongol Chinese and higher education

There are approximately 5.8 million Mongolian people living in China whereas only 2.4 million currently live in the Mongolian People's Republic (another half a million Mongols also live in Russia). The Mongol Chinese ethnic group are not only widely scattered within the borders of China, but also bound with strong ties to their motherland, the Mongolian People's Republic. Accordingly, Bulag (2003, p. 756) defines Mongols in China as "a transnational minority." Mongols enjoy a rich and comparably long history residing in China. Mongols constitute the eighth largest ethnic group among Chinese minorities.

Mongol Chinese reside predominantly around the Chinese northern borders that parallel or are near to Mongolia. There has been mixed results regarding the assimilation of Mongol Chinese language and culture with the majority Han in China's long history. This struggle to preserve their native language and cultural heritage has continued to the present. As more Mongol Chinese lose their language, "they are becoming a depoliticized and de-territorialized 'ethnic group' in an increasingly primordial and multicultural 'Chinese Nation'" (Bulag, 2003, p. 753).

The Chinese government recognizes both *Putonghua* and minority languages as official languages in many cases such as in autonomous regions. However, the Han do not need to learn a minority language along with or instead of *Putonghua* as there are rarely any economic incentives for so doing. As a consequence, the interaction between Mongol minorities and Han has in contemporary times generally been a one-way transfer rather than a mutual exchange (Ma, 2007). While the majority of Mongols adopt Chinese culture and acquire proficiency in *Putonghua*, very few Han Chinese learn Mongolian. This kind of language acquisition imbalance reflects the practical value placed on various languages spoken in Chinese society. However, some critiques of this minority language acquisition imbalance recognize that "teaching Mongolian language instead of Chinese made students to be dependent on Chinese society more than ever" and that they are often "deprived of the vital social ability they needed to succeed" (Bulag, 2003, pp. 754–755). At the same time, Mongol Chinese who learn Chinese as their first language often risk being alienated from their people and losing their religion, traditions and culture.

Even worse, Mongol Chinese children might "internalize the Chinese ideology of contempt toward the Mongolian language," if they learn Chinese as their first language (Bulag, 2003, p. 754). Mongol Chinese parents tend to prefer regular public schools so that their children can study alongside Han Chinese students and learn the Chinese language (Zhao, 2007). Zhao (2007) further argues that even "Mongol intellectuals have sacrificed speaking their mother tongue so as to attain work-related promotions, in the context of increasing domination of Han cultural capital" (p. 27). Ideally, minority people may maintain one's cultural identity as well as achieve proper competence of the dominant group's language in order to be able to overcome the dilemmatic situation that minorities face. Bilingual education could be one of the solutions as Korean minorities' "high achievements" demonstrate. However, as increasing numbers of Mongols live in urban areas instead of staying with a more traditional nomadic lifestyle on horseback, they become more easily mainstreamed into Chinese culture and society. However, it is hard to say that only Mongols failed to preserve their language and culture successfully. A considerable number of other minority peoples, such as the Zhuang, Sala, Miao, Yao, Dongxiang, Tu, Baoan [Bonan], Jiang, Mulao, and Bai, use Chinese for daily communication as well.

A strong motivation for unification of the Mongol people, at least from a linguistic aspect, came in the ideological unification of sections from three countries in the region: Mongolia, China, and the former Soviet Union. Although the divide-and-rule policy of the Soviet Union prvented the scattered Mongols from sharing a common linguistic background that transcends borders, their aspirations—including remembering the splendor of Genghis Khan's history—still remain in the heart of Mongols wherever they are now. In reality, however, it does not seem easy for Mongol Chinese to preserve their native language, culture, and traditional heritage after they have resided in China for such a long time. Most of all, as Mongolian interviewees express their concerns about education and employment opportunities relating to language acquisition, proficiency in *Putonghua* is essential to get a job or gain higher education outside of the autonomous region. As a result, many Mongol Chinese choose to speak Chinese as their first language rather than learning their traditional native language.

The government has enacted several preferential education policies in recent years including "preferential admissions, lowered school fees, boarding schools and remedial programs" (Sautman, 1999, p. 174). For instance, Mongol Chinese can enter universities with lower exam scores in Inner Mongolia under this preferential admissions policy. Minority nationality students also can choose to take entrance examinations in their native language instead of Chinese, regardless of the language they may use in their study afterwards. While tuition fees have increased high enough to become an obstacle for students from low socioeconomic backgrounds, there are several tuition scholarships available to ethnic minority students including Mongol and Korean Chinese. According to a study that Zhao (2007) conducted on Mongol students at three Chinese universities, however, "Mongol students reported difficulties in their adaptation to university life" (p. 31). He discovered that "Mongol students experience bias and discrimination, both on and off campus" after they enter the university and some students confess that "they felt inferior" to the Han majority (p. 34). Thus, Mongol Chinese students not only struggle with language at the higher education level, they must also overcome intertwined social and cultural problems that are inalienable with their campus and daily life.

Qualitative ethnographic study on Chinese minority education

Chinese minority content area experts (CAE) were identified using a snowball sample method and interviewed by the authors. Initial CAEs were identified by an extensive literature review and asked to participate in this study. Additional CAEs were recruited according to the recommendations of interviewed experts. CAEs were interviewed either by phone, in-person, or responded to the study's questionnaire by email correspondence. The study was approved by the authors' university institutional review board and all participants signed consent to participate in this study. Snowball sampling technique is a nonprobability sampling method appropriate when the members of a special population are difficult to locate, such as Chinese minority CAEs, especially those with expertise with Korean and Mongol Chinese minority groups.

Interviews were recorded, transcribed, translated into English if necessary, coded and analyzed using NVivo qualitative software. Interviews lasted between 30 and 60 minutes. While many studies exist on minority education in China, none have examined these two minority groups on a national scale. Nor have any studies been conducted on Mongol and Korean minorities in relation to higher education. This study helps fill this gap in the comparative and international education literature. From April 2008 to April 2010, 32 CAEs were identified and interviewed for this study (see Table 9.3). Among the participating CAEs, 12 were Chinese, four Korean, one Korean-American, four Korean-Chinese, three Mongolian, and the other eight were from countries other than China, Korea, or Mongolia. All interviewees had substantial language capability in two or more of the study's target languages (Chinese, English, Korean, and Mongolian) and most of them were native Chinese, Korean, or Mongolian speakers.

Table 9.3 CAEs by ethnic origin

Ethnic origin	*Number*
Chinese	12
Korean	4
Korean-American	1
Korean-Chinese	4
Mongolian	3
Other	8
Total CAEs interviewed	32

The names of these scholars are not used in this chapter, but interviewees included government officials, professors, doctoral students, and educators with recognized and demonstrated expertise on Chinese minority education. The following research questions were asked during the interviews that are examined in this chapter.

- Do you think that the government should promote using one national language for China?
- What admissions policies exist that support ethnic minority students attending Chinese higher education?
- How well do the Korean and Mongol minority groups preserve their culture and languages in Chinese society?
- What evidence, if any, exists to indicate that English affects minority language preservation in China?

Respondents provided important insights including the way in which many Chinese minority nationality groups struggle to preserve their native languages; minority languages are especially difficult to preserve at the higher education level. While many respondents provided answers to these questions that relate specifically to the two case ethnic groups, implications were drawn that would lead to understandings of Chinese minority nationalities from a broader perspective.

While all respondents recognized the need for China to adopt a national language, some also indicated that there are constraints associated with Korean and Mongol minorities learning one national language. A Korean expert indicated that "Korean minorities may have less time for minority language learning so that it might lead to threatening minority language acquisition and culture preservation." Several interviewees felt that a one-language policy at the primary and secondary education levels often leads to the neglect or loss of minority languages. We call this phenomenon a *linguistic genocide*, where economic incentives and opportunities, and in some cases government education policies, promote the use of a national language often at the unintended detriment of indigenous languages (Jacob & Bradshaw, 2009). In some cases, a business language, like English, adds to this linguistic genocide conundrum. In addition to the enormous influence of Chinese in Chinese higher education, English is increasingly becoming a second language of choice and it is now a requirement of many universities for students to obtain a level of proficiency before they can graduate with a bachelor's degree. A Chinese graduate student said,

> Theoretically, all Chinese share the identity of *Zhonghua minzu* (Chinese: 中華民族; Pinyin: *Zhōnghuá Mínzú*) that embraces every person who lives within the Chinese territory as a member of one big category of Chinese and this concept transcends ethnic, language, or cultural differences among those people

In practice, however, the concept is not as simple as it has been uttered, but it generates matters of occasional conflict within China as well as with neighboring countries (see also Gomà, 2006).

Another respondent said, "Chinese society is comprised of myriads of different ethnic groups each having its own language, traditions, and culture." Chinese ethnic minorities do not necessarily provide unity or "commonness" among such a diverse group of peoples. "To make the *Zhonghua minzu* concept a reality," she continues, "the country needs a common ground to share among the people, which transcends different ethnic groups." The invention of the unique concept of *Zhonghua minzu*, as well as *Putonghua*, is the outcome of the efforts that the Chinese government has employed for ensuring the common identity among the Chinese people.

All CAEs interviewed agreed that it is better for minority nationalities to have fluency in *Putonghua* so that they can enjoy a rich citizenship within the People's Republic of China. Lack of this fluency will prevent them from enjoying job opportunities and a quality of life that they could have otherwise. At the same time, many interviewees recognized that minority nationalities must also have access to learn their own languages and cultures in schools. Interviewees were particularly concerned if the government gave exclusionary support for the national majority language; thus minority language and culture preservation would be significantly threatened as a result. Having fluency in *Putonghua* guarantees some short-term benefits for minority nationalities by enabling them to enjoy equal opportunities for employment and education in China. As several interviewees mentioned, the economic factors and incentives are the most powerful single elements in the decision of language choice. Without having fluency in the dominant language, minority people can hardly find a job in most of the regions in China except for their local autonomous areas. One expert agreed that a positive aspect linked to a one-language policy is that fluency "in the national language may provide equal opportunity for minority people in the job market." While Korean and Mongol minority people obtain better knowledge and skills in *Putonghua*, however, they may at the same time lose their fluency in their own languages. A CAE mentioned trilingual educational programs where minority students learn their minority language, *Putonghua*, and English at the same time. According to the interviewee, the program has been so successful that students have been able to master three languages without major difficulties. One example school is a middle school attached to the Inner Mongolia Normal University with a Chinese–Mongol–English trilingual program that has experienced much success. Chinese, English, and Mongolian do not have to be confrontational; they can serve in different registers and be complementary. Trilingual education is not an option for all Mongol and Korean secondary students. The monitoring of these successful trilingual educational programs need thorough examination and review so that more ethnic minorities can obtain benefits from these kinds of programs. One interviewee said minority students in her home region do not have even one English teacher and do not have a sufficient number of native Chinese teachers in schools. This lack of qualified teachers makes it especially difficult for ethnic minority students to learn Chinese let alone learn a third language like English.

Several interviewees suggested that while emphasis on using Korean and Mongolian languages in schools may not be in the best short-term interests of the Korean and Mongol Chinese, minority language use in education must be viewed from a long-term perspective. You will not have an advantage for fluency in Mongolian or Korean in most Chinese higher education institutions and certainly a mastery of Chinese is of greater advantage when virtually all higher education instruction is conducted in Chinese. Even future employment opportunities are predominantly offered in Chinese. Yet, being fluent in Korean as well as Chinese does offer many Korean Chinese higher education graduates a competitive advantage over other graduates, two interviewees suggested. The expansion of Korean firms in mainland China emphasizes the need to hire managers who can speak both languages. This competitive language advantage is not an option for Mongol Chinese.

Fluency in one's mother tongue is necessary for culture, identity, and heritage preservation many respondents indicated. When native language is lost, so is one's identity, regardless if you are Korean or Mongol Chinese, one professor said. Perhaps an ideal short- and long-term language policy in education would be one where both languages can flourish. Several interviewees said that an ideal educational setting would be one where Korean and Mongol Chinese would be able to have fluency in their mother tongues by practicing their own languages in their respective communities as well as using them in schools, along with Chinese, as the medium of instruction. In this way, they might be successful in preserving their own languages. It is still very difficult, however, for Mongol and Korean Chinese to acquire fluency in both *Putonghua* and their native languages at the same time *if* they do not learn them in schools. Also, it is difficult for minority students to learn both languages at the same time due to: (1) limited time and resources; (2) limited economic incentives; and (3) limited incentives for continuing the use of the language at the higher education level. Furthermore, the government has recognized that minority languages should be used in schools, but only when they have a written language. Not all minority languages in China have written languages. Fortunately, Korean and Mongolian have a written language and, as such, both are supported in schools in their respective autonomous regions.

Many of the interviewees were against the government's policy to promote *Putonghua* as the exclusive national language, but all of them agreed that Korean and Mongol Chinese students should have no barriers to learning *Putonghua* in school for practical reasons. Several interviewees felt that it was the government's responsibility to provide teaching materials and instruction in both *Putonghua* and the minorities' languages according to each student's ethnic minority origin. However, the reality of offering education instruction in so many different languages is not an easy issue for a nation as large as China. Many Mongol and Korean minority people have little exposure to Chinese. For these minority students to reach higher education, they must break out of this exclusionary linguistic shell. In so doing, it often is at the detriment of one's identity, culture, and language, one CAE said. These findings are in alignment with Rebecca Clothey's (2005) study that found that minority students rarely obtain quality education in the dominant language, since teachers who are fluent in

Chinese tend to find better job opportunities instead of securing employment in rural and hinterland regions where many minorities reside. One of our interviewees stated, "The central policy neither encourages nor discourages minority languages to be used in school. However, if the government applies the same policy both on Mandarin and all minority languages, it engenders disparity between minority and majority languages and cultures." This would ultimately lead to discrimination against minority language use, ethnic minority cultures, and identity preservation.

Interestingly, Chinese interviewees more strongly supported the idea that Chinese society needs one national language enabling its people to communicate. Others argued that the one national language policy was helpful, even among ethnic minority groups, for more economic reasons. Non-Chinese CAEs tended to regard the policy in some cases as too exclusionary and vouched for greater emphasis on cultural and linguistic preservation of minority nationalities. Even with these differences, both Chinese and non-Chinese CAEs interviewed recognized the delicate balancing act that Korean and Mongol Chinese face between learning *Putonghua* as a means for a better life and preserving their native language and culture.

Conclusion

Chinese minority education is continuously being pushed to the forefront of political and media discussions. While the government has not had any major conflicts with Mongol and Korean Chinese ethnic groups in recent years—in comparison to those in Xizang and Xinjiang—the issue of which language of instruction should be taught in schools is a particularly salient topic for many of both ethnic groups. Several government initiatives have been targeted to help these and other ethnic minority groups in China. Recently the government has constructed major railroads to link the nethermost parts of the nation. This transportation infrastructure is an example of the government's recognition that economic opportunities need to be made more readily available to minorities, as well as the Han majority, if China is to become a superpower in the twenty-first century. Other government policies favor minority nationalities. For example, while the government is very strict with its one-child policy towards the Han, it puts less pressure on minority groups. In the education sector, the government employs affirmative action policies in diverse aspects such as bonus scores in the university admission procedure and limited financial aid packages for language and cultural preservation. However, most Korean and Mongol Chinese face obstacles in learning core education subjects in their native languages at the primary and secondary levels. This is only exacerbated at the higher education level, as instruction is rarely offered in minority languages. If minority students cannot be taught with enough teaching materials in their own language, how will they perform well in national higher education entrance examinations, even if they take the exam in their own language?

Home to the world's largest education system, China has many excellent higher education institutions that compete with other world-class universities.

Contained within this massive education system, minority nationality groups such as the Koreans and Mongols, struggle with stereotypes imposed on them as well as dilemmas between their own language preservation and acquiring proficiency in *Putonghua*. Even though the government has adopted various policies to support minority students, the proportion of minorities to total number of university students is still not sufficient. In comparison with other ethnic minority groups in China, Mongolian scholar Xu found that "China's most bilingual ethnic groups, including Korean, Bai and Zhuang, have enjoyed economic development levels and education levels higher than the average level for ethnic minority peoples" (Li, 2007, p. 25).

Koreans, often regarded as a model minority group in China, also experience linguistic dilemmas similar to Mongol Chinese. Yet, the two groups have stark distinctions in terms of economic opportunities and ties with their motherland countries. With the rapid economic development of the Republic of Korea and increasing trade exchanges between China and Korea, Korean Chinese are finding greater opportunities in the job market with their bilingual proficiency than do Mongol and other minority Chinese. Thus, for Korean nationality students, bilingual education is both helpful in pragmatic aspects and needed to preserve their ethnic identity. If a language is used on a limited scale within an autonomous prefecture, however, it would be much harder to conduct bilingual education for minority groups. Thus, nobody should blame Mongols who prefer to learn English instead of Mongolian when they have the chance to learn more than one language. Some scholars argue that according to the economic needs of minority people, "perhaps members of minorities should learn English without learning Chinese" (Ma, 2007, p. 13).

Preferential treatment in higher education is significant in enabling many minority students to gain access to higher education. Higher education is especially important for minority nationality students; the higher education experience affords students the opportunity to preserve and develop their heritage as well as building a pathway for them within the majority society. Ultimately, however, tensions between minority and majority ethnic groups can be mitigated only when minority groups may achieve according to a comparable level of living conditions with the majority population. Thus, Chinese minority languages should be at the forefront of educational reform at all levels. Native language fluency among Korean and Mongol Chinese is of particular importance in preserving their identity, culture, and heritage.

References

Alitto, S. B. (1969). The language issue in Communist Chinese education. *Comparative Education Review*, 13(1), 43–59.

Attané, I., & Courbage, Y. (2000). Transitional stages and identity boundaries: The case of ethnic minorities in China. *Population and Environment*, 21(3), 257–280.

Barnes, D. (1978). The language of instruction in Chinese communities. *International Review of Education*, 24(3), 371–374.

Blum, S. D. (2002). Margins and centers: A decade of publishing on China's ethnic minorities. *Journal of Asian Studies*, 61(4), 1287–1310.

Bulag, U. E. (2003). Mongolian ethnicity and linguistic anxiety in China. *American Anthropologist*, 105(4), 753–763.

Cai, M. H. (2004). 연변 조선족 중소학교 교육문제실태 조사연구 [Research on the elementary and secondary education of Korean Chinese in Yanbian]. 교육문제연구 [Journal of Education Research], 20, 93–111.

Cho, J. H. (1992). 중국 건국이전의 연변 조선족교육 [The education of Korean Chinese in Yanbian before the establishment of the People's Republic of China]. 교육행정학연구 [Journal of Educational Administration Studies], 9(2), 23–32.

Cho, Y. D. (1998). 조선족 교육열과 한국인의 교육열의 비교연구 [A comparative analysis on the education fever of Korean Chinese and South Korean]. *Paper presented at the* 제 124 차 학술대회발표자료 *(The Korean Society for the Study of Sociology of Education, the 124th Conference)*.

Choi, S. H., & Kim, C.-H. (2004). 21세기초 조선족 교육의 문제 및 개혁 연구 [Educational problems and reforms of Koreans in China at the beginning of 21st century]. Seoul: KEDI.

Clothey, R. (2005). China's policies for minority nationalities in higher education: Negotiating national values and ethnic identities. *Comparative Education Review*, 49(3), 389–409.

de Varennes, F. (2006). Language rights of minorities and increasing tensions in the People's Republic of China. *Asia-Pacific Journal on Human Rights & the Law*, 7(2), 1–28.

Dilger, B. (1984). The education of minorities. *Comparative Education*, 20(1), 155–164.

Dreyer, J. T. (1978). Language planning for China's ethnic minorities. *Pacific Affairs*, 51(3), 369–383.

Gomà, D. (2006). The Chinese-Korean border issue. *Asian Survey*, 46(6), 867–880.

Hannum, E. (2002). Educational stratification by ethnicity in China: Enrollment and attainment in the early reform years. *Demography*, 39(1), 95–117.

Hawkins, J. N. (1978). National-minority education in the People's Republic of China. *Comparative Education Review*, 22(1), 147–162.

Heo, M. C., Park, G.-H., Kim, H.-H., & Lee, J. (2003). 연변 조선족 교육의 현황과 과제 [Education of Koreans in Yanbian, China]. Seoul: KEDI.

Hudson, V. M., & Den Boer, A. M. (2005). *Bare branches: The security implications of Asia's surplus male population*. Cambridge, MA: MIT Press.

Jacob, W. J. (2004). Marketization, demarketization, remarketization: The influence of the market economy on Chinese higher education. Doctoral dissertation. Los Angeles: University of California, Los Angeles.

Jacob, W. J. (2006). Social justice in Chinese higher education: Regional issues of equity and access. *International Review of Education*, 52(1), 149–169.

Jacob, W. J., & Bradshaw, B. (2009). Native American cultures: Peace traditions. In Young, N. (Ed.), *International encyclopedia of peace*. New York: Oxford University Press.

Kang, S.-W. (2007). Students to learn disputed history. *Korea Times*, June 3.

Kim, D.-S. (2003). 연변 조선족사회의 최근 변화: 사회인구학적 접근 [Recent changes of the ethnic Korean population in Yanbian Autonomous Prefecture: A socio-demographic approach]. 한국인구학 [Korean Journal of Population], 26(2), 111–145.

Kim, K.-I., & Heo, M.-C. (2001). 중국조선족사회의 문화우세와 발전전략 [The superior culture of Koreans in China and their development strategy]. Jilin: 연변인민출판사 [Yanbian People's Publisher].

Kormondy, E. J. (2002). Minority education in Inner Mongolia and Tibet. *International Review of Education*, 48(5), 377–401.

Lam, A. S. L. (2005). *Language education in China: Policy and experience from 1949.* Hong Kong: Hong Kong University Press.

Lam, A. S. L. (2007). The multi-agent model of language choice: national planning and individual volition in China. *Cambridge Journal of Education*, 37(1), 67–87.

Lee, Y. H. (1990). 연변 조선족의 민족교육 [The ethnic education of Korean Chinese in Yanbian]. 중등우리교육 [Our Secondary Education], 8, 38–43.

Li, L. (2007). Language dilemma. *Beijing Review*, 50(22), 24–25.

Ma, R. (2007). Bilingual education for China's ethnic minorities. *Chinese Education and Society*, 40(2), 9–25.

Mackerras, C. (2003). *China's ethnic minorities and globalisation.* London: RoutledgeCurzon.

Min, P. G. (1992). A comparison of the Korean minorities in China and Japan. *International Migration Review*, 26(1), 4–21.

Ministry of Education, China (2000). *Bulletin for the National Educational Development Statistics.* Beijing: Ministry of Education.

Ministry of Education, China (2005). *Bulletin for the National Educational Development Statistics.* Beijing: Ministry of Education.

Ministry of Justice, Republic of Korea. (2007). New policy on visiting workers from abroad. Gwacheon: Ministry of Justice. Available online at: http://www.moj.go.kr.

Mosher, S. W. (2006). China's one-child policy: Twenty-five years later. *Human Life Review*, 32(1), 76–101.

National Bureau of Statistics of China. (1990). *China statistical yearbook.* Beijing: National Bureau of Statistics of China.

National Bureau of Statistics of China. (2000). *China statistical yearbook.* Beijing: National Bureau of Statistics of China.

National Bureau of Statistics of China. (2006). *China statistical yearbook.* Beijing: National Bureau of Statistics of China.

Postiglione, G. A. (1992). China's national minorities and educational change. *Journal of Contemporary Asia*, 22(1), 20–44.

Postiglione, G. A. (1998). State schooling and ethnicity in China: The rise or demise of multiculturalism? *Paper presented at the 14th World Congress of Sociology.*

Sautman, B. (1999). Expanding access to higher education for China's national minorities: Policies of preferential admissions. In G. A. Postiglione (Ed.), *China's national minority education: Culture, schooling, and development* (pp. 173–210). New York: Falmer Press.

Stites, R. (1999). Writing cultural boundaries. In G. A. Postiglione (Ed.), *China's national minority education: Culture, schooling, and development* (pp. 95–130). New York: Falmer Press.

Wong, E. (2009). Ethnic clashes in Western China are said to kill scores. *New York Times*, 6 July.

You, K. S., & Kwak, J. S. (2004). 연변 조선족 교육의 현황과 발전 과제 [Education of Koreans in Yanbian China and its problems]. Seoul: KEDI.

Yusuf, F., & Byrnes, M. (1994). Ethnic mosaic of modern china: An analysis of fertility and mortality data for the twelve largest ethnic minorities. *Asia-Pacific Population Journal*, 9(2), 25–46.

Zhao, Z. (2007). Ethnic Mongol students and cultural recognition. *Chinese Education and Society*, 40(2), 26–37.

Zhou, M. (2000). Language attitudes of two contrasting ethnic minority nationalities in China: the "model" Koreans and the "rebellious" Tibetans. *International Journal of the Sociology of Language*, 146, 1–20.

Zhou, M. (2001). The politics of bilingual education and educational levels in ethnic minority communities in China. *International Journal of Bilingual Education and Bilingualism*, 4(2), 125–149.

Part III

Theoretical, ideological, and legal issues

10 Chinese–English bilingual education in the PRC

Implications for language education for autochthonous ethnic minorities

Guangwei Hu

Introduction

One of the much discussed consequences of globalization is the intensified spread of English as a global language (Crystal, 2003; Rubdy, 2009), especially in what Kachru (1986) refers to as Expanding Circle countries, where English is studied as a foreign language (Guo & Beckett, 2007; McKay & Bokhorst-Heng, 2008). Because of the popular belief that English provides access to knowledge, development, power and well-being, various top-down and bottom-up initiatives have been staged at an increasing pace to expand English instruction and improve the effectiveness of such instruction in the school systems of these countries (Ho & Wong, 2004; Nunan, 2003; Park & Abelmann, 2004). In this regard, the educational system of the People's Republic of China (hereafter PRC) is no exception (Hu, 2002; Lo Bianco, 2009b). With PRC's growing economic integration into and deepening political engagement with the rest of the world, a modernization discourse on the importance of English for the state and its citizenry has become strongly entrenched (Hu, 2008), and there have been accelerating societal and individual demands, real and imagined, of English proficiency in the past three decades (Hu, 2002). These socio-cultural and economic changes have ushered in successive policy initiatives directed at English language teaching at different levels of the Chinese educational system, from the adoption of communicative language teaching as the officially endorsed pedagogy in the early 1990s to the expansion of English provision into primary schooling at the turn of the twenty-first century, and to the more recent promotion of task-based language teaching (Hu, 2005; Zhang & Hu, 2010).

The most recent initiative introduced in the name of educational reform and quality education is the provision of "Chinese–English bilingual education" at the primary and secondary levels (Hu, 2007). This type of language provision differs from what is traditionally regarded as bilingual education in PRC, namely the education of ethnic minorities in their native languages and Chinese, the dominant majority language (see Feng, 2005; Postiglione, Jiao, & Manlaji, 2007; W. J. Zhang, 2002). It also differs from most forms of bilingual provision typically denoted in international contexts (see Baker, 2006; Hu, 2008). The so-called Chinese–English bilingual education consists of using English as a medium of instruction in the teaching of non-language school subjects for Chinese-speaking students from the socio-culturally dominant ethnic group, the Han majority. In practice, the actual extent of English usage in classroom instruction varies greatly. For example, while English is used exclusively or predominantly as the language of instruction in a small number of well-equipped elite schools that have the resources to hire English-speaking expatriate teachers to staff their English-medium classes (Pi, 2004), there are varying mixtures of Chinese (usually the more frequently used language of instruction) and English in bilingual classes offered by the majority of schools (Zheng, Tian, & Li, 2006). In other classrooms, the use of English is restricted largely to routine expressions in classroom management and, sometimes, to translation of a few concepts, formulae, and definitions (Huang, 2005; Lo Bianco, 2009a; Z. F. Zhang, 2003). Despite much controversy, the use of English as a medium of instruction has quickly gathered popularity and momentum, making significant inroads in the school system (Feng, 2005; Hu, 2007).

This chapter is an attempt to evaluate the English-medium instruction (EMI) initiative and derive implications for a language provision for students from autochthonous ethnic minorities in PRC. To this end, it draws on the recent theoretical work by François Grin (2003a, 2003b, 2005, 2007) which advocates a public policy perspective on language policy and related issues. The chapter consists of four parts. The first part outlines Grin's theoretical perspective on language issues, with a focus on the four key principles (i.e., moral justice, practical feasibility, allocative efficiency, and distributive fairness) that he contends must be integrated in policy-making with respect to language issues. The second part makes a critical evaluation of the EMI initiative in light of these important considerations. The third part then discusses, from the same theoretical perspective, a number of implications that the initiative has for language education for primary and secondary students from autochthonous ethnic minorities. Based on the critical evaluation and discussion, the chapter concludes that EMI is a wrongheaded language education policy for both majority and minority groups in PRC. A call is made to explore alternative approaches to a trilingual provision for ethnic minority children that abide by the four principles underpinning Grin's public policy perspective.

A public policy perspective on language issues and its four fundamental principles

Recent work on language planning and language-in-education policy has often adopted a language rights perspective, anchoring policy criticisms or recommendations on a normative basis of moral justice. While recognizing the valuable insights that such a perspective can yield, Grin (2005) rightly points out that this line of scholarship tends to be ignored by policy-makers because it fails to address many issues that they grapple with. Grin contends that a public policy perspective on language issues is likely to provide a more practical and adequate response to those issues. Thus, Grin argues that it is necessary to go beyond normative rights-based arguments and apply, in the formation and evaluation of language policies, other principles that have been found highly useful in inform- ing and guiding public policies in general. Such principles, whose chief justifica- tion lies in their aim to increase societal welfare, include the additional principles of practical feasibility, allocative efficiency, and distributive fairness. Drawing on Grin's (2003a, 2003b, 2005, 2007) recent works, the following paragraphs sketch out these principles.

That a public policy perspective requires a move beyond rights-based norma- tive arguments does not mean moral justice is unimportant from such a perspec- tive. As a matter of fact, it is still one of the principles on which good public policy is based. A language policy can be informed by, and derive its justifica- tions from, moral arguments that treat language rights as human rights. As Kymlicka and Patten (2003) point out, "Human rights represent a widely accepted normative standard, and if a particular regime of language rights could be shown to follow from human rights, this would offer an impressive normative and political foundation for that regime" (p. 10). In language policy debates, a rights-based approach often aims to maintain linguistic diversity and secure mother-tongue-medium education for children from indigenous and minority groups (see Phillipson, 2000; Skutnabb-Kangas, 2000; Skutnabb-Kangas & Phillipson, 1994). In discussing language rights, it is useful to make a distinction between *non-instrumental* and *instrumental* rights. Non-instrumental language rights "aim at ensuring a person's capacity to enjoy a secure linguistic environ- ment in her/his mother tongue and a linguistic group's fair chance of cultural self-reproduction" (Rubio-Marín, 2003, p. 56). An example is ethnic minority children's right for mother-tongue education. Instrumental language rights

> aim at ensuring that language is not an obstacle to the effective enjoyment of rights with a linguistic dimension, to the meaningful participation in public institutions and democratic process, and to the enjoyment of social and eco- nomic opportunities that require linguistic skills.

According to this definition, access to English, the global language of power and access, is an instrumental language right. Non-instrumental language rights are fundamental, necessary rights, whereas instrumental language rights are deriva- tive and of an enrichment-oriented nature (Skutnabb-Kangas, 2007).

Normative rights, though useful considerations in language policy, are not suf- ficient because many crucial questions about a given language policy "cannot be put to rest simply by an invocation of moral values" (Grin, 2005, p. 450). It is for this reason that Grin calls for "a shift of emphasis away from the intrinsically normative discourse of rights to the positive approach of policy analysis and pol- icy evaluation" (2003b, p. 181). A morally justifiable language policy still needs to be analyzed and evaluated in terms of practical feasibility, the second principle that a public policy perspective endorses. This is because a morally defendable policy may be technically infeasible. At the very heart of this feasibility-based policy analysis and evaluation lie the availability and allocation of resources (i.e., both material and non-material) that are needed to implement the policy option in question. A policy option lacks practical feasibility where the required resources for its implementation are unavailable or insufficient.

The third principle subscribed to by a public policy perspective—allocative efficiency—requires an informed and principled cost-benefit analysis conducted at the societal level (Grin, 2003a). Even when a language policy meets the requirement of the two aforementioned principles, it may still be rejected "on the grounds that it constitutes a waste of scarce resources that society had better spend on other pursuits" (Grin, 2005, p. 451). Allocative efficiency analyses can help inform policy-makers by identifying a policy option or a set of policies that yields a maximal difference between benefits and costs or that is most cost-effective (Grin, 2007). Notably, allocative efficiency analysis focuses on "ensuring that a policy generates a gain in *aggregate welfare*" (Grin, 2003a, p. 25) rather than identifying individuals who gain or lose as a result of the implementation of a given policy.

The principle of distributive justice, on the other hand, deals with "the issue of fairness and focuses on the identification of winners and losers, as well as on the estimation of respective gains and losses" (Grin, 2003a, p. 25) if the policy option in question passes the requirements of moral justifiability, practical feasibility and allocative effectiveness, and is up for implementation. Put simply, this principle requires that individuals who gain from a public policy contribute to the cost incurred in the implementation of that policy or compensate those who lose as a result. Distributive justice is safeguarded when the sharing of the costs and transfers resulting from a policy option is given due attention and provided for. Where distributive inequalities are likely to occur, action must be taken either to redress the injustice or to compensate for the imbalance "on the basis of a reliable and transparent identification of the transfers that arise without a compensation mechanism" (Grin, 2006, p. 86).

The public policy perspective on language policy advanced by Grin, together with the four principles outlined above, forms the theoretical frame for developing a balanced and comprehensive view of language policy initiatives. It draws our attention to the different levels at which language policy options should be considered and the need to integrate these considerations in a coherent manner. The following section is an effort to examine the EMI initiative from a public policy perspective and in terms of its four cardinal principles.

Is EMI for Han majority students a good public policy?

Can EMI for ethnic majority students be justified on a normative moral basis? To answer this question, it is necessary to consider the status of English in PRC and the relationship of EMI to mother-tongue-medium instruction. As many commentators (e.g., Gill, 2004; Hu, 2009; Jiang, 2003) have pointed out, knowledge of English is not only a most valorized form of cultural capital (Bourdieu,

1986, 1991) in the PRC but also the gatekeeper of opportunities to procure various forms of capital: economic, cultural, and social. English proficiency is the passport to many economic, social, educational, and professional opportunities and resources (Guo & Beckett, 2007). For example, promotion for professionals depends crucially on passing a national English test (Jiang, 2003). By the same token, both admission into and graduation from undergraduate and graduate programs turn on students' performance on several high-stakes English proficiency tests. Competence in English has come to be viewed as a sign of excellence—a defining characteristic of talents in the twenty-first century (Shen & Feng, 2005) and an essential component of "a perfect character" (Qian, 2003). Thus, lack of access to the language is a liability in the enjoyment of various socio-cultural and economic opportunities that require proficiency in the language. In view of the opportunities that have been linked to English proficiency, it would seem that the EMI initiative is morally defensible on the grounds of an instrumental language right (Rubio-Marín, 2003; Skutnabb-Kangas, 2007).

The apparent normative justifications for EMI, however, become highly questionable if provision for the instrumental language right negatively affects the effective enjoyment of more important language rights such as mother-tongue-medium schooling during one's early years. Similarly, the normative justifications are seriously undermined if it interferes with such fundamental human rights as entitlement to education that provides "access to socially valuable skills and knowledge, which are key for the achievement of social prestige, economic well-being, and professional self-fulfillment" (Rubio-Marín, 2003, p. 69). As available evidence (Hu, 2008; Jin & Zhuang, 2002; Liu, 2002; Ye, 2002) indicates, the use of English as a medium of instruction has indeed interfered with the learning of valuable skills and knowledge in many EMI programs (this issue will be further discussed in reference to the principle of allocative effectiveness). Such interference occurs because if students do not understand the language in which instruction takes place, they cannot learn the instructional content effectively.

The EMI initiative falls short of the principle of practical feasibility, too. Various constraints have undermined, compromised, and frustrated the envisioned goals for EMI (Hu, 2007). For the sake of space, only three major constraints will be briefly discussed here to illustrate the practical infeasibility of EMI for majority language students in PRC. One constraint is that China lacks a socio-linguistic environment to support EMI. Because English is only a foreign language in mainland China, there is little need for the great majority of Chinese to use English for socio-cultural purposes (Yang, 2006; W. J. Zhang, 2002). To make up for the lack of a favorable socio-linguistic environment, advocates of EMI suggest that schools should spare no means to create an English-rich environment (Z. F. Zhang, 2003; Zheng *et al.*, 2006). Obviously, creating and maintaining such English-rich environments can divert the often pinched financial resources of most schools and, consequently, have important socio-cultural implications. A second, and more serious, constraint is students' lack of academic proficiency in English to benefit from English-medium education. Based on a survey of research since the early 1980s, Cummins (2000) concludes that although immigrant students may quickly develop reasonable functional proficiency in the dominant language of their host countries as a result of exposure to it in the environment and at school, "it generally takes a minimum of about five years (and frequently much longer) for them to catch up to native-speakers in academic aspects of the language" (p. 34). Competence in the academic aspects of the instructional language, Cummins argues, is crucial to school success. Furthermore, Cummins presents empirical evidence for the existence of a threshold level of proficiency in a target language "which students must attain in order to maximize the cognitive, academic, and linguistic stimulation they extract from social and academic interactions with their environment" (p. 37). The great majority of pre-collegiate students in PRC, however, lack a minimum level of functional proficiency in English (Gil, 2010; Yang, 2006), not to mention the threshold of academic competence required to learn the challenging content delivered in it. The final major constraint on EMI to be discussed here is an acute shortage of bilingual teachers. Because the Chinese teacher education system did not run bilingual teacher education programs until very recently, most teachers staffing EMI programs have been trained to be either subject teachers or teachers of English as a foreign language (W. J. Zhang, 2002). Thus, they lack systematic training either in subject content or in English, let alone pedagogy of bilingual instruction. Typically, the teachers do not have the oral or academic language competence to teach non-language subjects bilingually (Hu, 2007). Such an incapacitating constraint would surely add greatly to the practical infeasibility of EMI, especially in view of the scale on which such instruction is expected to occur (Shen, 2004; Su, 2003a, 2003c).

With regards to the principle of allocative effectiveness, the EMI initiative fares even less well. The policy initiative has huge resource consequences for the stakeholders. It requires, for example, tremendous government spending on teacher training, teacher employment, instructional facilities, and learning materials development (Su, 2003c). It also requires additional expenditure on the part of schools that are serious about EMI to provide school-based training for their teachers, bonuses or subsidies as incentives to encourage teachers to use English as an instructional language, and equipment and other facilities needed to create an English-rich environment conducive to EMI (Hu, 2007; Lin, 2003). Even advocates of EMI admit that such instruction is expensive (Su, 2003b; Zhang & Liu, 2005). Apart from a small number of elite schools, however, the tremendous investment of scarce resources has not produced the expected returns. A critical review (Hu, 2008) of the literature on EMI indicates that even the much publicized programs have generally fallen far short of the envisioned goal of raising students' English proficiency greatly. In addition to the major constraints discussed above, factors contributing to this ineffectiveness include the limited extent of use of English as an instructional language, the low quality of the bilingual learning materials available, the absence of curriculum standards to guide program development, the lack of a coherent curricular structure to coordinate programs offered at different levels of the educational system, and the lack of an evaluative mechanism to enforce quality control (Hu, 2007; Zhang & Liu, 2005).

It is also important to consider how EMI may affect students' academic achievement. Although no rigorous longitudinal research on the effects of learning school subjects in English has been reported in the literature, there is growing evidence that the use of English as a language of instruction may affect students' academic achievement negatively. One of the few evaluation studies conducted to date admits that EMI may have a detrimental effect on subject learning (Shen, 2004). Many teachers have also reported that they have to reduce or simplify curricular content in order to accommodate EMI because their students lack the academic language competence needed to understand complex topics and engage in higher-order thinking in English (Pi, 2004). There have also been reports that EMI has made the teaching of school subjects costly and ineffective. For example, in one school after half a semester of EMI in mathematics, the teachers had to re-teach major topics in Chinese because the students had performed poorly in assessment (Jin & Zhuang, 2002). The accumulating evidence points to the conclusion that EMI is often carried out at the expense of curricular content.

Last but not least, the EMI initiative also fails conspicuously in reference to the principle of distributive justice. It channels scarce resources to a select few at the expense of, and without compensation for, the majority of students and schools. At the district or higher levels, elite schools take the lion's share of the resources allocated to EMI (Hu, 2007). Thus, the small number of elite schools can take advantage of their much greater volume of various types of capital—greater financial resources, excellent infrastructure, wider social networks, well-trained staff, and high-caliber students—to offer EMI of a quality that the majority of schools with limited capital cannot hope to emulate. At the school level, it is a common practice to select students for English-medium programs based on their performance on English proficiency tests, and the English-medium programs tend to receive more favorable treatment than other programs (Pi, 2004; Zheng *et al.*, 2006). At the personal level, teachers who are able to offer English-medium classes are often given bonuses, subsidies, reduced workloads, sponsored training at home or overseas institutions, and other incentives (Shen & Feng, 2005; P. Zhang, 2002). Students from socio-economically privileged families stand to gain from EMI because their families have the necessary resources to create conditions of success for them (Feng, 2005). Thus, EMI is becoming a service to the elite in PRC (Gill, 2004; P. Zhang, 2002). However, schools and students entitled to the scarce resources that have been diverted away from them are not compensated in other ways for the losses they suffer. As a consequence, the EMI initiative has not only perpetuated the unequal distribution of power and access but is also creating new forms of inequality.

What lessons does the EMI initiative offer to a language provision for ethnic minorities?

What implications, then, can we derive from the EMI initiative to provide language education for students from the autochthonous ethnic minorities in PRC?

What ramifications can be expected for a policy move towards the use of English as a medium of instruction within a trilingual provision for autochthonous minority students?

As pointed out earlier, proficiency in English is capital with strong exchange value in PRC and provides access to many opportunities that are closely linked with individual well-being. Just as access to effective English language provision is an instrumental language right for the dominant majority group in the country, so it is for its community of ethnic minorities (Guo & Beckett, 2007). For this reason, a rights-based argument for a policy move towards some English-medium schooling for ethnic minority students could be similarly grounded in its aim and potential to provide instrumental access to a language of opportunity. These normative justifications, however, would be counterbalanced by the fact that knowledge of English alone will not go far towards helping instrumentally in the enjoyment of various opportunities by the great majority of people in the majority and minority groups alike. This is because lack of access to English is only one of the liabilities in their effective enjoyment of educational, social, and economic opportunities. The masses lack other forms of capital (e.g., economic and social) that both constitute conditions for the procurement of such opportunities and make proficiency in English relevant in the process. Furthermore, as is the case with EMI for ethnic majority students, the normative ground of a policy option aiming to raise minority students' English proficiency through EMI would be considerably undermined if it interferes with their mother-tongue-medium education in various ways, for example, by diverting precious curricular resources (Adamson & Feng, 2009). Such education is part and parcel of a successful linguistic socialization process in one's own language, and it creates conditions of possibility for cultural reproduction for one's ethnic group (Guo & Beckett, 2007; Wan & Zhang, 2007), and develops one's capacity "to live in one's language in every relevant sphere" (Rubio-Marín, 2003, p. 66). By the same token, the normative justifications would be nullified if the use of English as a medium of instruction undermines effective schooling by creating linguistic barriers. "As with many other rights," Rubio-Marín (2003, p. 65) points out, "the right to education rests for its minimal fulfillment on the possibility of comprehensible linguistic interactions." In this regard, "there are hundreds of reports" (Dutcher, 2004, p. 11) which provide evidence that children receiving early education in their first language learn subject matter better than in a second language (see also Williams, 1998). This importance of minority children's first language in schooling is also appreciated by researchers of minority language education in China. For example, in their discussion of the successful "Tibetan plus Chinese" model of bilingual education, Wan and Zhang (2007) recognize that Tibetan is the most effective learning tool for Tibetan children in primary education.

To complicate the issue, the potential impact of EMI on ethnic minority students' learning of the dominant majority language, *Putonghua* (i.e., standard Mandarin Chinese), needs to be factored in when a rights-based argument for EMI is examined. As Rubio-Marín (2003, p. 65) cogently puts it:

[B]ecause language rights are so crucial to functioning in society, to participating in the political processes, and to interacting with state authorities,
there are many ways in which lack of knowledge of the public and dominant
language(s) can diminish people's chances even where this is not linked to
discrimination.

Notably, quite a few empirical studies (e.g., Adamson & Feng, 2009; Lam,
2007; Postiglione *et al.*, 2007; Tsung & Cruickshank, 2009) of language education for autochthonous ethnic minorities in PRC have found mastery of
Putonghua more instrumental than access to English in the protection of their
socio-economic opportunities and well-being. As Xu (2009) points out, "the
process of glocalization demands that [ethnic learners] learn Putonghua well;
otherwise they will be marginalized" (p. 187). For this reason, EMI should not
be offered to ethnic minority students at the expense of their acquisition of
Putonghua. Where there is a tension between EMI and *Putonghua* learning,
it would be in the interest of the majority of ethnic minority students to give
policy priority to the latter.

If EMI for ethnic majority students scores low in terms of practical feasibility,
the use of English as an instructional language for autochthonous minority groups
would fare even worse due to even greater resource constraints. The 55 officially
designated autochthonous ethnic groups in PRC are largely concentrated in the
least developed inland regions of the country, that is, the rural and mountainous
west. As pointed out by Yang (2005, p. 556), "education of any type among most
of the minorities lags far behind the populous east [inhabited predominantly by
the majority group]" and "English as a school subject fares even worse than
other subjects." This dismal state of affairs has arisen in large measure from
severe resource constraints in the following areas:

- Schools have perennially faced the problem of insufficient funding by
  their local governments (Postiglione, 2000; Tsung & Cruikshank, 2009;
  Yang, 2005).
- There is a severe shortage of qualified teachers in general and English teachers in particular (Jiang, Liu, Quan, & Ma, 2007; Yang, 2005).
- Many schools simply do not have the necessary resources to offer English as
  a school subject (Adamson & Feng, 2009; Tsung & Cruickshank, 2009), not
  to mention resources needed for the much more expensive EMI.
- Where English is taught, there is strong competition for curricular resources
  from Chinese and minority language education (Yang, 2005).
- There are hardly any English textbooks that are specially written for ethnic
  minority students (Feng, 2005).
- Most ethnic minority students have virtually no contact with English outside
  the classroom; and there is little prospect of them securing jobs that require
  even a minimum use of English (Yang, 2005).
- Apart from those aspiring to a university education, ethnic minority students
  generally are not motivated to learn English (Jiang *et al.*, 2007), and their

English proficiency is markedly lower than that of their counterparts from the dominant majority group (Yang, 2005).

All these constitute major resource constraints on the further expansion and improvement of English language provision (Tsung & Cruickshank, 2009). If EMI for ethnic majority students has largely failed to achieve its envisioned goal of additive bilingualism in spite of the much greater resources available, there is little reason to expect English-medium instruction to fare any better or even take off in ethnic minority schools where resources are more limited.

If the dismal results of EMI for ethnic majority students are anything to go by, a policy move towards EMI for ethnic minority students would most likely waste whatever scarce resources are invested in its implementation. Given this likely scenario, such a policy move would not pass the fundamental requirement of allocative effectiveness. While the policy move may be welcomed by some language policy commentators as a useful gesture towards redressing issues of social inequity resulting from unequal access to English between ethnic majority and minority students, it is imperative to recognize that it would be unlikely to increase aggregate welfare for the community of ethnic minorities in the foreseeable future. For ethnic minority students who live in the remote rural inland hardly affected by globalization, English proficiency does not have much practical value (Yang, 2005). They are unlikely to be directly involved in globalized exchanges and do not have any realistic chance of using English. For those students, EMI would be, in the words of Bruthiaux (2002, p. 292), "an outlandish irrelevance," and to allocate scarce public resources to it would most likely turn out to be a misguided, highly questionable investment. As Mufwene (2010, p. 59) explains in reference to the geographical expansion of English in Asia and other parts of the world.

> Language learning is an investment in time and energy, and in some cases a financial one too. Although more and more students are learning English in high school, they are not all equally invested in it, and many are those who forget it as quickly after graduation as they do most of the other subjects they learned that bear marginally on their lives.

In contrast to EMI, policy options that are directed at ensuring the quality of compulsory education and fostering functional literacy in both minority and dominant languages have a better chance and greater potential to improve the socio-economic well-being of the great majority of the ethnic minority community and contribute to local development (Bruthiaux, 2002). Therefore, they are much more likely to be cost-effective policy options (Grin, 2005).

In view of the distributive unfairness resulting from EMI for ethnic majority students, there is every reason to expect that a policy move towards EMI for ethnic minority students would give rise to issues of distributive injustice as well. Given the many resource constraints outlined above, the lion's share of the scarce resources available for education and language provision in the minority community would be likely to flow to a small number of privileged schools and their EMI programs. These schools typically serve "the relatively affluent urban middle class who stand to benefit most from English language education because they are already closer to the opportunities offered by increased trade and communication" (Bruthiaux, 2002, p. 293). Such resource allocation strategies would create an utterly unfair situation where the better-off are subsidized by the worse-off. In a country whose numerous schools in the vast rural areas of the minority-concentrated west are inadequately equipped for basic education and where many ethnic minority children in the underdeveloped areas do not even finish a nine-year compulsory education (Yang, 2005), there is little to justify the elites' privileged access to EMI (Hu, 2007).

Conclusion

To sum up, the analysis presented above suggests that EMI is a wrongheaded language-in-education policy option for both majority and minority groups in PRC. Although a rights-based case can be made for it by appealing to the notion of instrumental language right, the normative justifications can be seriously undermined by other more fundamental considerations. The policy initiative does not stand up to the principle of practical feasibility due to the dire shortages of resources that are needed to implement it uncompromisingly. There is also considerable evidence suggesting that it constitutes a misallocation of precious resources that could otherwise be spent on more encompassing and worthwhile policy options. Last but not least, the policy initiative is destined to be implicated in the creation and perpetuation of distributive injustice, serving only the elite segment of the Chinese society.

It should be pointed out that this critical stance towards a policy move towards EMI for minority groups should not be interpreted as objecting to English provision for minority language students who aspire to a university education or whose well-being can be improved by an adequate knowledge of English in one way or another. What this critical stance is opposed to is the adoption of EMI as a method of English provision for ethnic minority students who need and want to learn the language. Given the current status of English in China as "a gateway to education, employment and economic and social prestige" (Guo & Beckett, 2007, p.118), lack of access to English provision will create a huge obstacle to these ethnic minority students' effective enjoyment of educational, social and economic opportunities that require English skills. In view of the cognitive and cultural benefits of mother-tongue education, the importance of *Putonghua* for functioning in the wider Chinese society, and the many instrumental rights associated with English proficiency, an important means of safeguarding the vitality and well-being of ethnic minorities is to provide trilingual education to whoever needs it. To this end, there is a clear need to explore alternative approaches to trilingual education for autochthonous ethnic minorities in China (Feng, 2007; Guo & Beckett, 2007; Lo Bianco, Orton, & Gao, 2009). In this regard, much can be learned from those successful bilingual and trilingual programs that have been implemented in ethnic minority communities (see Cobbey, 2007; Finifrock, 2010). In selecting and promoting a particular approach to trilingual provision as a policy option, however, it is imperative that the approach meet the paramount criteria of moral justice, practical feasibility, allocative efficiency, and distributive fairness.

References

Adamson, B., & Feng, A. W. (2009). A comparison of trilingual education policies for ethnic minorities in China. *Compare*, 39, 321–333.

Baker, C. (2006). *Foundations of bilingual education and bilingualism* (4th ed.). Clevedon: Multilingual Matters.

Bourdieu, P. (1986). The forms of capital. In J. G. Richardson (Ed.) *Handbook of theory and research for the sociology of education* (pp. 241–258). New York: Greenwood Press.

Bourdieu, P. (1991). *Language and symbolic power* (trans. G. Raymond & M. Adamson). Cambridge, MA: Harvard University Press.

Bruthiaux, P. (2002). Hold your courses: Language education, language choice, and economic development. *TESOL Quarterly*, 36, 275–296.

Cobbey, H. (2007). Challenges and prospects of minority bilingual education in China: An analysis of four projects. In A. W. Feng (Ed.), *Bilingual education in China: Practices, policies and concepts* (pp.182–199). Clevedon: Multilingual Matters.

Crystal, D. (2003). *English as a global language* (2nd ed.). Cambridge: Cambridge University Press.

Cummins, J. (2000). *Language, power and pedagogy: Bilingual children in the crossfire.* Clevedon: Multilingual Matters.

Dutcher, N. (2004). *Expanding educational opportunity in linguistically diverse societies.* Washington, DC: Center for Applied Linguistics.

Feng, A. W. (2005). Bilingualism for the minor or the major? An evaluative analysis of parallel conceptions in China. *International Journal of Bilingual Education and Bilingualism*, 8, 529–551.

Feng, A. W. (Ed.). (2007). *Bilingual education in China: Practices, policies and concepts.* Clevedon: Multilingual Matters.

Finifrock, J. E. (2010). English as a third language in rural China: Lessons from the Zaidang Kam-Mandarin bilingual education project. *Diaspora, Indigenous, and Minority Education*, 4, 33–46.

Gil, J. (2010). The double danger of English as a global language. *English Today*, 26(1), 51–56.

Gill, C. (2004). China offers an English future for some. Retrieved April 6, 2006, from http://education.guardian.co.uk/tefl/story/0,5500,1332331,00.html.

Grin, F. (2003a). Language planning and economics. *Current Issues in Language Planning*, 4, 1–66.

Grin, F. (2003b). Diversity as a paradigm, analytical device, and policy goal. In W. Kymlicka, & A. Patten (Eds.), *Language rights and political theory* (pp. 169–188). Oxford: Oxford University Press.

Grin, F. (2005). Linguistic human rights as a source of policy guidelines: A critical assessment. *Journal of Sociolinguistics*, 9, 448–460.

Grin, F. (2006). Economic considerations in language policy. In T. Ricento (Ed.), *An introduction to language policy: Theory and method* (pp. 77–94). Oxford: Blackwell.

Grin, F. (2007). Economics and language policy. In M. Hellinger, & A. Pauwels (Eds.), *Handbook of language and communication: Diversity and change* (pp. 271–297). Berlin: Mouton de Gruyter.

Guo, Y., & Beckett, G. H. (2007). The hegemony of English as a global language: Reclaiming local knowledge and culture in China. *Convergence*, 40(1/2), 117–131.

Ho, W. K., & Wong, R. Y. L. (Eds.) (2004). *English language teaching in East Asia today: Changing policies and practices*. Singapore: Marshall Cavendish Academic.

Hu, G. W. (2002). English language teaching in the People's Republic of China. In R. E. Silver, G. W. Hu, & M. Iino (Eds.), *English language education in China, Japan and Singapore* (pp. 1–77). Singapore: National Institute of Education.

Hu, G. W. (2005). Professional development of secondary EFL teachers: Lessons from China. *Teachers College Record*, 107, 654–705.

Hu, G. W. (2007). The juggernaut of Chinese–English bilingual education. In A. W. Feng (Ed.), *Bilingual education in China: Practices, policies and concepts* (pp. 94–126). Clevedon: Multilingual Matters.

Hu, G. W. (2008). The misleading academic discourse on Chinese–English bilingual education in China. *Review of Educational Research*, 78, 195–231.

Hu, G. W. (2009). The craze for English-medium education in China: Driving forces and looming consequences. *English Today*, 25(4), 47–54.

Huang, Y. H. (2005). Zhongxiaoxue shuangyu jiaoxue celüe chutan [An exploration of strategies for bilingual instruction at the primary and secondary levels]. *Jiaoyu Shijian yu Yanjiu*, 2, 23–26.

Jiang, Q. X., Liu, Q. G., Guan, X. H., & Ma, C. Q. (2007). EFL education in ethnic minority areas in northwest China: An investigational study in Gansu Province. In A. W. Feng (Ed.), *Bilingual education in China: Practices, policies and concepts* (pp. 240–255). Clevedon: Multilingual Matters.

Jiang, Y. J. (2003). English as a Chinese language. *English Today*, 19(2), 3–8.

Jin, K., & Zhuang, Y. X. (2002). Shuangyu jiaoxue zheng liaoyuan [Bilingual education is spreading like a prairie fire]. *Jiefang Ribao*, March 4, p. 6.

Kachru, B. B. (1986). *The alchemy of English*. Oxford: Pergamon Press.

Kymlicka, W., & Patten, A. (2003). Language rights and political theory. *Annual Review of Applied Linguistics*, 23, 3–21.

Lam, A. S. L. (2007). Bilingual or multilingual education in China: Policy and learner experience. In A. W. Feng (Ed.), *Bilingual education in China: Practices, policies and concepts* (pp. 13–33). Clevedon: Multilingual Matters.

Lin, J. (2003). Shuangyu jiaoxue: Jianle zhima diaole xigua? [Bilingual education: Penny wise and pound foolish?]. *Zhongguo Qingnianbao*, October 8, p. 4.

Liu, H. R. (2002). Shuangyu jiaoxue wuru qitu? [Bilingual education: Going astray?]. *Jingji Daobao*, September 4, p. 4.

Lo Bianco, J. (2009a). Introduction. In J. Lo Bianco, J. Orton, & Y. H. Gao (Eds.), *China and English: Globalisation and the dilemmas of identity* (pp. 1–20). Bristol: Multilingual Matters.

Lo Bianco, J. (2009b). English at home in China: How far does the bond extend? In J. Lo Bianco, J. Orton, & Y. H. Gao (Eds.), *China and English: Globalisation and the dilemmas of identity* (pp. 192–210). Bristol: Multilingual Matters.

Lo Bianco, J., Orton, J., & Gao, Y. H. (Eds.). (2009). *China and English: Globalisation and the dilemmas of identity*. Bristol: Multilingual Matters.

McKay, S. L., & Bokhorst-Heng, W. D. (2008). *International English in its sociolinguistic contexts: Towards a socially sensitive EIL pedagogy*. New York: Routledge.

Mufwene, S. S. (2010). Globalization and the spread of English: What does it mean to be Anglophone? *English Today*, 26(1), 57–59.

Nunan, D. (2003). The impact of English as a global language on educational policies and practices in the Asia-Pacific region. *TESOL Quarterly*, 37, 589–613.

Park, S. J., & Abelmann, N. (2004). Class and cosmopolitan striving: Mothers' management of English education in South Korea. *Anthropological Quarterly*, 77, 645–672.

Phillipson, R. (Ed.). (2000). *Rights to language: Equity, power, and education.* Mahwah, NJ: Lawrence Erlbaum.

Pi, W. B. (2004). Zhongxue shuangyu jiaoxue de shijian yu sikao [Bilingual education in secondary schools and reflections]. Unpublished master's thesis, East China Normal University, Shanghai, China.

Postiglione, G. (2000). National minority regions: Studying school discontinuation. In J. Liu, H. A. Ross, & D. P. Kelly (Eds.), *The ethnographic eye: Interpretative studies of education in China* (pp. 51–71). New York: Falmer Press.

Postiglione, G., Jiao, B., & Manlaji, L. (2007). Language in Tibetan education: The case of the neidiban. In A. W. Feng (Ed.), *Bilingual education in China: Practices, policies and concepts* (pp. 49–71). Clevedon: Multilingual Matters.

Qian, Y. W. (2003). Fenceng duoyuan di shenhua shuangyu jiaoxue shiyan [Promote experimentation with bilingual education at multiple levels and in plural ways]. *Shanghai Jiaoyu Keyan,* 7, 53–57.

Rubdy, R. (2009). Reclaiming the local in teaching EIL. *Language and Intercultural Communication,* 9, 156–174.

Rubio-Marín, R. (2003). Language rights: Exploring the competing rationales. In W. Kymlicka, & A. Patten (Eds.), *Language rights and political theory* (pp. 52–79). Oxford: Oxford University Press.

Shen, P., & Feng, Y. P. (2005). Tuijin shuangyu jiaoxue de tansuo yu shijian [Exploring and implementing bilingual instruction]. *Zhongguo Daxue Jiaoxue,* 2, 24–25/31.

Shen, Z. Y. (2004). Yiyi zai shijian mubiao zai chengxiao [Significance and objectives of bilingual education]. *Zhongguo Jiaoyubao,* May 13, p. 2.

Skutnabb-Kangas, T. (2000). Linguistic genocide in education – or worldwide diversity and human rights? Mahwah, NJ: Lawrence Erlbaum.

Skutnabb-Kangas, T. (2007). Language planning and language rights. In M. Hellinger, & A. Pauwels (Eds.), *Handbook of language and communication: Diversity and change* (pp. 365–397). Berlin: Mouton de Gruyter.

Skutnabb-Kangas, T., & Phillipson, R. (Eds.). (1994). *Linguistic human rights: Overcoming linguistic discrimination.* Berlin: Mouton de Gruyter.

Su, J. (2003a). Shanghai wenbu tuijin shuangyu jiaoxue shiyan [Bilingual education in Shanghai is making steady progress]. *Wenhuibao,* January 7, p. 5.

Su, J. (2003b). Shuangyu jiaoxue ying bianshijian biantigao [Improve bilingual education through experimentation]. *Wenhuibao,* April 21, p. 9.

Su, J. (2003c). Shanghai tuozhan shuangyu jiaoxue shiyan [Shanghai expands experimentation with bilingual education]. *Wenhuibao,* October 21, p. 5.

Tsung, L. T. H., & Cruickshank, K. (2009). Mother tongue and bilingual minority education in China. *International Journal of Bilingual Education and Bilingualism,* 12, 549–563.

Wan, M. G., & Zhang, S. X. (2007). Research and practice of Tibetan-Chinese bilingual education. In A. W. Feng (Ed.), *Bilingual education in China: Practices, policies and concepts* (pp.127–144). Clevedon: Multilingual Matters.

Williams, E. (1998). *Investigating bilingual literacy: Evidence from Malawi and Zambia.* London: Department for International Development.

Xu, H. C. (2009). Ethnic minorities, bilingual education and glocalization. In J. Lo Bianco, J.Orton, & Y. H.Gao (Eds.), *China and English: Globalisation and the dilemmas of identity* (pp. 181–191). Bristol: Multilingual Matters.

Yang, J. (2005). English as a third language among China's ethnic minorities. *International Journal of Bilingual Education and Bilingualism,* 8, 552–567.

Yang, J. (2006). Learners and users of English in China. *English Today,* 22(2), 3–10.

Ye, B. Z. (2002). Bierang shuangyu jiaoxue zoushang xielu [Stop bilingual instruction from going astray]. *Zhongguo Jiaoyu Zixunbao,* April 17, p. B3.

Zhang, L. B., & Liu, X. H. (2005). Shuangyu jiaoxue: Gongshi, fenqi ji wuqu [Bilingual education: Consensuses, controversies, and misconceptions]. *Xiandai Jiaoyu Kexue*, 6, 73–76.

Zhang, P. (2002). Shuangyu jiaoxue: Redian wenti de lengsikao [Bilingual education: Problems and considerations]. *Dongbei Shida Xuebao*, 3, 121–127.

Zhang, W. J. (2002). Shuangyu jiaoxue de xingzhi tiaojian ji xiangguan wenti [The nature and conditions of bilingual education and some related problems]. *Yuyan Jiaoxue yu Yanjiu*, 4, 20–26.

Zhang, Y. F., & Hu, G. W. (2010). Between intended and enacted curricula: Three teachers and a mandated curricular reform in mainland China. In K. Menken, & O. García (Eds.), *Negotiating language policies in schools: Educators as policymakers* (pp. 123–142). New York: Routledge.

Zhang, Z. F. (2003). Shuangyu jiaoxue de yuanze moshi ji celüe [Principles, models, and strategies of bilingual education]. *Zhongxiaoxue Jiaoxue Yanjiu*, 2, 15–16.

Zheng, S. L., Tian, Z. H., & Li, Y. J. (2006). Goujian xiaoxue shuangyu jiaoxue kecheng tixi de yanjiu yu shijian [Researching and developing a curricular framework for bilingual education at the primary level]. *Jiaoyu Lilun yu Shijian*, 26(2), 62–64.

11 From neo-liberal ideology to critical sustainability theory for language policy studies in the PRC

Seonaigh MacPherson

Introduction

The United Nations' (1987) Brundtland Report, *Our Common Future*, redefined 'sustainable development' as an international standard in development policy and policy studies. Since then, researchers across the social and biological sciences have amassed studies positively correlating biological, linguistic, and cultural diversity, loss, extinction, survival, and sustainability (Harmon, 1996; Harmon & Loh, 2009a, 2009b; Maffi, 2001; Nettle & Romaine, 2000). These findings offer incontrovertible evidence of a rapid, correlated decline in biological and social (i.e., cultural and linguistic) dimensions of diversity and sustainability. Furthermore, the extinction rates of human languages and cultures have been found to surpass those of biological species (Sutherland, 2003) with an estimated 3,000 of the current 6,700 languages deemed to be in danger of imminent extinction (UNESCO, 2009).

If governments and educators are serious about addressing the multiple challenges posed to biological, linguistic, and cultural sustainability, which global climate change will only further exacerbate, then *sustainability* needs to be a meaningful and explicit component of all policies, but especially those dealing with language and language education. Yet, the tendency for ideology rather than theory to inform language and language education policy studies and debates, especially in the PRC, has made it difficult to introduce serious scholarly and policy debates on education's impact on sustainability. Furthermore, the troubling divide between research, practice and policies in linguistics and language education has left the concept of *sustainability* inadequately defined and operationalized within language policy studies. These problems have impeded the ability of language education and policy research to inform the sustainability struggles of Indigenous and minority communities and the education systems that impact them. Consequently, in this chapter, I apply the robust view of *sustainable development* presented in the Brundtland Report as grounds to critique two dominant contemporary theories in socio-linguistics—critical linguistics and eco-linguistics. Through this dialectical critique, I recommend a hybrid critical sustainability theory more suitable for language and education policy studies, with particular implications for the PRC.

Language policy studies

Traditionally, language policy studies focused narrowly on official languages and language education, but, more recently, these studies have expanded to consider the multiple policy arenas that impact linguistic and cultural diversity, maintenance, and decision-making by governments, media, education, families, and individuals (Heller, 2006; Schieffelin, Woolard, & Kroskrity, 1998). Indeed, Kopeliovich's (2010) study of a Russian-Hebrew bilingual family in Israel considered decision-making in families as policies with corresponding practices that reflected distinctive "language policies" and "language management" styles. Just as language policies pervade linguistic contexts and domains, so do ideologies, a fact readily recognizable in the pervasive fears driving Asian parents and families to expose children to English education at increasingly young ages, thereby motivating some South Korean parents, for example, to send children overseas to English-speaking countries at very young ages to endure familial separation for the sake of the perceived linguistic advantages (Cho & Shin, 2008).

The neo-liberal ideology in language policies

As agents of states serving in highly politicized and hierarchical bureaucratic environments, policy-makers tend to be dominated and informed by ideology rather than theory. These ideologies are often veiled and obscured by rhetoric linking the policies, however crudely, to current popular scientific or scientifically derived theories such as *sustainability*, *modernity*, or *globalization*. Today, in China and other states, the dominant ideology driving language policy decisions and discourse involves the appropriation of "modernization" and "globalization," which are reinterpreted well beyond their critical, social scientific roots to refer to the unquestioned virtues of a cohesive nation-state competing in a global marketplace. This neo-liberal ideology re-directs development policies in two directions through two, interrelated assumptions: Domestic policies are transacted on the assumption of the ends of secularization and economic integration in which the "citizenry" is reduced to a "workforce," while international policies are transacted on the basis of the assumption of the merits of the "global integration" of the nation-state within a pan-human or biotic global community that is reduced to a "competitive marketplace." Furthermore, Tsuda (1994) demonstrated how this neo-liberal ideology of globalization was driving a third assumption with implications for language policies and linguistic diversity globally, which he referred to as the "diffusion-of-English paradigm."

From ideology to critical-ecological theory

If the value of diversity is reduced to its instrumental economic value, then many languages, cultures, and biological species may well be eliminated through myopic policies aimed at realizing crude economic indicators of growth. However troubling the narrow neo-liberal interpretation of globalization may be, the impact of globalization as an integrative and transformative process beyond the control of any one state or ideology remains uncertain. Two competing dimensions and theories of globalization offer important agendas in support of a genuinely sustainable development agenda: On the one hand, critical theories, including critical neo-Marxist, Frankfurt School or post-modern variants, promote globalization as a potentially liberating process in which fundamental freedoms and values are extended to all human beings. On the other hand, ecological globalization considers humans and other species within biological communities, which connect in nested levels up to and including the biosphere. These ecosystems are the contexts for all forms of exchanges, including economic and knowledge-based exchanges.

Drawing on Tsuda's (1994) efforts to link critical and ecological perspectives in "the ecology-of-language," Phillipson and Skutnagg-Kangas (1995) use this hybrid critical-ecological theoretical lens to critique the impact of the globalization of English on Indigenous language loss. As promising as this scholarship has been, it fails to adequately unpack the conceptual conflicts and points of disjuncture between critical and sustainability theories. Instead, the language ecology perspective merely combines critical discourse on the hegemonic imperialism of English as a global language (Phillipson, 2008) with eco-linguistics (Skutnabb-Kangas, 2000), as if the two discourses were pasted into one with a visible seam. Accordingly, this pre-existing language ecology approach has tended to idealize and overlook key contradictions that impede its ability to withstand the scrutiny of critics. Nevertheless, Phillipson and Skutnagg-Kangas (1995) recognized the need for further refinement of this theory to challenge ideologies, stating, "the contours of language policy as a scientifically explicit and theoretically based concern need to be delineated more thoroughly and clearly" (p. 432).

Language policy contexts and cases

Before turning to identify a critical sustainability theory capable of serving the policy context of China, it is helpful to situate the PRC alongside Europe and North America to appreciate how the neo-liberal ideology of modernity, globalization, and the diffusion of English permeate different language cultures. In the process, the prospects and repercussions of a critical sustainability theoretical turn become more discernible.

The People's Republic of China (PRC)

Policies and policy studies in the PRC tend to reflect these neo-liberal ideological assumptions of economic globalization. This ideological rhetoric reduces the world to a marketplace and well-being to a narrow interpretation of equality of opportunity (i.e., the opportunity to get rich) and material freedom. This reductionist neo-liberal economic agenda was evident by 2003, for example, when the PRC Ambassador to the UK, Zha Peixin, described globalization as "the objective trend of economic development in the world today, featured by free flow and optimized allocation of capital, technology, information and service in the global context" (2003, para. 2). Outlining the PRC's policy agenda, Peixin (2003) described the primary principle to be "to achieve one objective: to maintain a steady and rapid economic growth" (para. 18) which was to be accomplished by "two crucial links: to continue to advance the strategic restructuring of China's economy and continue to open up to the outside world" (para. 19).

This narrow neo-liberal capitalist agenda, now as evident in post-socialist China as in the USA, reflects an ideological commitment to the ability of market forces to negotiate values and exchanges on a global scale. This increased reliance on markets and economic value systems to arbitrate development over other forms of value is antagonist to the sustainability interests of most of the indigenous languages, cultures, religions, and species most endangered and vulnerable to deteriorating populations and extinction. The people who continue to speak these languages and carry the cultures face considerable pressures to shift to regional, official (national), or global languages to access economic opportunities and secure their material survival. Even among languages not endangered, with speakers in excess of 50,000, such as Tibetan and Uygur, the view persists that the indigenous language has little economic value (Beckett & MacPherson, 2005; MacPherson & Ghoso, 2008).

In the PRC, the official language is standard Mandarin or *Putonghua*; however, even among the Han majority, many speak other languages or dialects of Mandarin, including languages misrepresented as dialects for ideological reasons (Erbaugh, 1995). In turn, the 55 recognized "minorities," which include both Indigenous peoples like the Tibetans, Uygurs, and Mongolians and immigrants like the Koreans, continue to speak an array of languages as mother tongues (Baker & Prys Jones, 1998). Language and power have interacted in post-Mao China to generate what Dwyer (1998) described as a highly contained hierarchy of languages in five orders, from the official language through to standard regional languages to primary, secondary, and unrecognized (unscripted) minority languages. These ideological hierarchies have reduced in theory and policies the actual linguistic diversity of large indigenous groups in the PRC, like the Tibetans and Uygurs, by standardizing their diverse languages into a singular, standardized version.

Although bilingual education is available to some minority students in China, these programs tend to reflect subtractive bilingual policies and programs focused on the first three years of primary schooling as children are introduced to Mandarin (Baker & Prys Jones, 1998). Although there are minority language track schools at the secondary and post-secondary level, these institutions face limited or declining enrolment because of space and financial limitations (Upton, 1999) and because of a reduced public commitment to Indigenous language education (Bilik, 1998). Instead, there is an increasing use of boarding schools that relocate cohorts of Tibetan and Uygur students in distant Han communities and schools in central China, thereby dislocating students culturally and geographically. These practices are justified, paradoxically, to fulfil the nine-year compulsory education policy for minorities (Grose, 2010; Wang & Zhou, 2003).

The European Union

Market hierarchies that reinforce language hierarchies are all but "natural;" they are artificially generated and supported through policies, historical inequities, and trade relations. Even in the relatively heterogeneous linguistic and cultural context of the European Union, the artificial nature of language hierarchies and their impact on multilingual practices are apparent. Despite designating 11 official languages, the European Union has since witnessed the formation of distinctive hierarchies within and between these official languages and the excluded languages. For example, although Catalan has over six million speakers, more than the Danish and Finnish languages, it is excluded (Phillipson & Skutnabb-Kangas, 1995). Describing these emerging linguistic hierarchies in the 1990s, Phillipson and Skutnabb-Kangas (1995, p. 433) observed their roots in commercial pressures:

> Bargaining in the linguistic marketplace is also likely to be asymmetrical: The case for dominant languages is put constantly and reinforced in myriad ways, most of them covert hegemonic processes, whereas alternatives to the current linguistic hierarchies are seldom considered and tend to be regarded as counterintuitive and in conflict with a commonsensical, "natural" order of things.

North America

In Canada and the USA, despite language policy differences, similarities exist in the de facto use of English (or French in some cases) as an official language to integrate and, ultimately, assimilate the continuing flow of newcomers. Both states resist formal recognition of the richly multilingual citizenry in policy and state discourse. In contrast, Mexico recognizes 62 of the over 300 estimated Indigenous languages; however, the potential of official recognition is not translated into educational policies, which remain dominated by the same subtractive bilingual education policies and practices that characterize US bilingual education (Flores Farfán, 2002). In the USA, although English does not have an "official" status at the federal level, it is commonly referred to as a *national* language based on naturalization and related laws. In education, the predominant policy is monolingual English language instruction, which has been reinforced in recent years by explicit English-only policies in some states (Cassels-Johnson, 2010). Most bilingual education occurs in subtractive bilingual programs aimed at scaffolding minority learners from their mother tongue (e.g., Spanish) into English.

Although officially *multicultural*, Canada is *not* officially *multilingual*; instead, the *Official Bilingualism Act* of 1969 established official bilingualism, which defined Canada's official French–English bilingual status and established protections for each language in minority contexts. Nevertheless, there remain serious limitations to the official language status of French in practice (Cardinal, 2005). The government of the predominantly French-speaking province of Quebec has attempted to compensate by providing special status for French inside Quebec, where once-bilingual French–English schools have become French only (McGlynn, Lamarre, Laperrière, & Montgomery, 2009). Nevertheless, students continue to derive from the two linguistic communities and their actual educational outcomes are still French–English bilingualism despite the shift to the French language in the delivery of the formal curriculum. In contrast, reflecting the dominance of English in Canada, few students emerge bilingual from English-only schools in English regions of Canada.

For Canadians with non-official native languages, whether as newcomers or Indigenous peoples, the challenges are even greater. They enjoy few language rights in practice despite constituting an increasing proportion of the Canadian population (Statistics Canada, 2009). Official bilingualism impacted language education insofar as the predominant form of bilingual education that emerged were weak forms of English-French bilingual education and French immersion, which has tended to serve elites or families that aspire to upward mobility. In Ontario, bilingual programs in public education are restricted to French–English, whereas in the prairies, there are limited cases of late exit bilingual programs serving other minority linguistic communities like the Ukrainians and Chinese (Schmidt, 2010). Across North America, the failure to provide bilingual education to diverse communities of newcomers persists despite large-scale quantitative studies proving higher achievement for students within long-term bilingual education programs (Thomas & Collier, 2001). Although this equity argument for bilingual education is compelling, the sustainability perspective suggests the intrinsic, not merely extrinsic, value and legitimization of additive bilingual policies and programs.

Sustainability

Sustainability is a robust concept used to address the impact of development on the social and environmental determinants of well-being across generations; however, too often it is misinterpreted as the replenishing of natural resources. Even more alarmingly, the term is reduced in earlier economic (1960s) and contemporary ideological contexts to maintaining *rates of growth* across time (Silverman, 2009). The UN (1987) document *Our Common Future* (The Brundtland Report) formally defined *sustainable development* within public policy and policy studies. According to this document, the key object(s) being sustained were neither resources nor rates of growth but the basic requirements or *needs* for a minimal quality of life across generations. In other words, *sustainable development* was development that enabled human beings of this generation to meet their needs without infringing on the ability of future generations to do likewise. No longer limited to material needs but also to the broad spectrum of social, physical, and psychological needs; no longer limited to the needs of this generation but also to those of future generations; and no longer dissociating human from non-human "generations," this redefined term offered a catalytic concept with which to interrogate economic and educational development policies and practices. Regrettably, it has yet to be understood or applied broadly in this technical sense of the term.

China's sustainability challenge

Nowhere in the world are the transformations associated with globalization more like a canary in a mineshaft than in China. China is *the* critical case to consider the interconnected linguistic, economic, educational, and ecological layers of the impact of globalization and development. Home to over 22 percent (1.5 billion) of the world's human population, China has experienced unrelenting and unprecedented growth rates over the past two decades (Worldwatch Institute, 2006). In 2006, for example, China's economy grew by 8.8 percent, in contrast to the USA at 2.7 percent (Assadourian, 2008). This discrepancy only increased during the 2008–2009 recession, as China continued to register economic growth rates between 7 percent to 7.5 percent, while most other economies, including Canada and the USA, reported negative growth rates (< 0 percent). Yet, China's dramatic growth is directly linked to alarmingly high rates of environmental accidents; in 2006, every second day the Chinese government recorded an environmental accident it considered "serious" (Assadourian, 2008).

The first Green GDP Report released by the Government of China attempted to quantify the high environmental costs of China's economic growth in reporting that environmental pollution cost the Chinese 511.8 Yuan (US$ 63 billion) in economic losses in 2004 alone (Liu, 2006). Releasing the report, the Deputy Director of the State Environmental Protection Administration (SEPA), Pan Yue, noted, "as much as one-fifth of China's GDP growth is attained though 'overdraft' of resources and the environment." Accordingly, what are not reflected in these estimates are the loss of life, suffering, and unknown costs to future generations. As Liu (2006, para. 4) described:

> China is undergoing a serious environmental crisis. One-third of its land area is contaminated by acid rain; more than 300 million rural residents have no access to safe drinking water; over 400 million urban dwellers breathe heavily polluted air (15 million of whom suffer from related respiratory diseases); and the country is home to five of the ten most polluted cities in the world.

These economic and ecological transformations have had complex social reverberations. Economic growth impacted large urban centers, especially those in the east and central regions, disproportionately from rural and more remote regions. Dramatic disparities between the economic opportunities promised in cities in contrast to those in the countryside triggered dramatic levels of rural-to-urban migration; however, most of these rural migrants entered the unskilled labor market with low wages and few protections or benefits. Facing significantly higher costs of living, they struggled as an underclass in burgeoning urban economies. So, with the added burden of alarming increases in urban pollution levels and environmental problems, some have chosen to return to their rural roots (Assadourian, 2008).

Beyond its impact on urban and inter-regional migration, economic development in China poses a challenge to the diverse languages and cultures of the peoples living with the PRC. This constellation of economic, ecological, social, linguistic, and cultural transformations threaten the interconnected biolinguistic and cultural diversity and sustainability of this vast region of Earth. Furthermore, given China's size and its rate of economic development, which outpaces by several percentage points its nearest competitors (Assadourian, 2008), sustainability issues in China are of interest to the people and policy-makers of the world, not just of China.

Harmony and the redefining of human needs

At the core of *sustainable development* as a policy construct is the recognition that human beings must place limits, constraints, or conditions on development for it to culminate in a distributed form of well-being affecting increasing groups and generations of human and greater-than-human life. Human languages and cultures so pervade human ecological niches and the environment to have effectively transformed most, if not all, ecological systems on the planet Earth (Ehrlich, 2000; MacPherson, 2003; Nettle & Romaine, 2000), including, notably, the biosphere itself. Therefore, languages and cultures need to be treated on a spectrum of dimensions of ecological diversity.

The neo-liberal ideology is premised, if at all, on an unsubstantiated assumption that human self-interest and greed can realize a form of natural justice through market forces. Instead, the natural end of such greed is feeding frenzies that mitigate against recognizing our shared interests in the well-being of the commons: our shared environment, planetary space, and future. The concept of *harmony* that has played a significant role in legitimating policies, even neo-liberal policies, in the PRC might be reclaimed by PRC language policy and sustainability scholars and scholarship to strengthen this appreciation of the need for a harmony that extends beyond China's borders, history, and the lives of the people and their varied ethnic communities. All are embedded instead in a greater call for harmony with the Earth itself and the underlying ecosystems on which all current and future generations of life depend.

Towards a critical sustainability theory

Critical sociolinguistics and eco-linguistics (language ecology) are two dominant theories in the field of language policy studies. Both theories provide potent critiques of the deleterious impact of neo-liberal/neo-conservative global policy agendas on diversity and sustainability. Together, these critiques identify four ideological assumptions that threaten global bio-linguistic and cultural diversity and sustainability: (1) assumptions of the inevitable need for, and dominance of, English (Hu, 2005; Pennycook, 1994; Phillipson, 2008); (2) the differential value accorded languages and cultures based on numbers of speakers, statehood, and commitments to the tenets of modernization (Phillipson & Skutnabb-Kangas, 1995); (3) the illegitimate appropriation of liberalism and modernity (Habermas, 1995, 1996; Nussbaum, 1997, 2000; Sen, 1999; Smith, 2008); and (4) the commodification of species, languages and cultures and the associated reduction of value to market value and of the world to a marketplace (MacPherson, 2011). Unlike liberalism, which derives from a coherent *theory* of freedom rooted in neo-Stoic and Western Enlightenment thought, neo-liberalism is an *ideology* serving a narrow capitalist agenda. Although slippage between theory and ideology is inevitable in politics, as Huang (1998) suggests, "What we can avoid, however, is falling into the trap of doing ideologically driven scholarship" (p. 188).

Critical theory

It is a paradox that the critical tradition, which derives from neo-Marxist theories, should continue to be so resisted, if not outright rejected, by policy-makers and scholars of policy studies in the PRC. Instead, these policy gatekeepers in the PRC appear to have embraced the same neo-liberal ideology of globalization, characterizing the world and its inhabitants as a marketplace, as right-wing capitalist proponents in North America and Europe. Unfortunately, in contrast to these Western contexts, China shows less evidence of counter-discourses providing critiques and alternative justifications for globalization as a potential opportunity to extend freedoms, equity, and human rights to those otherwise marginalized or dispossessed by neo-colonial or local elites. Instead, China's language education policies and discourses tend to harbor problematic neo-liberal assumptions that, simply stated, revolve around the notion that language policy should serve the dual purposes of enhancing individual opportunity and national integration, which are then extolled as the purported grounds for "ethnic harmony" without unpacking obstacles such as the stranglehold of Han elites and the lack of autonomy of key ethnic and Indigenous communities (MacPherson & Beckett, 2008).

Critical theory offers language policy-makers a body of research and conceptual tools to address these obstacles to equity and participation, including an understanding of language and communication as potentially democratizing and liberatory enterprises (Habermas, 1970) based on self-reflexivity and critique (Foucault, 1996; Pennycook, 1999) that are impacted by identity dynamics (Pierce, 1995), agency-structure dynamics (Flowerdew & Miller, 2008), politics (Pennycook, 2001), social and discursive inequities (Fairclough, 1995; Kubota, 2004), and, hence, resistance (Canagarajah, 1999). In addition, critical theory offers a key body of scholarship identifying the potential threat posed by the globalization of English (Pennycook, 1994; Tollefson, 1995) to global linguistic diversity.

Yet, critical theory remains limited in its ability to serve as a theory to inform policy to realize sustainability outcomes. In this respect, we might understand it as an unfinished, or evolving, project. Underlying otherwise valid critiques by critical theorists are problematic assumptions rooted in neo-Marxism and structuralism that make critical theory complicit in assumptions that are highly discriminatory against most non-modern cultures and linguistic groups. These include, but are not limited to, materialism; a discursive reliance on economic metaphors; an excessive focus on agency–structure dichotomies; and an orientation on individuals rather than communities. I will elaborate on each of these problems in sequence.

Materialism

The lingering biases of Marxist materialism remain in both the theory and application of critical theory. Even the pre-eminent French neo-Marxist critical theorist, Pierre Bourdieu (1991), who has had a considerable impact on the critical tradition in language studies, identified the need for significant "breaks" with classical Marxism in order to develop a coherent theory of "social space," which included "a break with the tendency to emphasize substances—here, real groups whose number, limits, members, etc. one claims to be able to define—, ... [a] break with economics, ... [and] a break with objectivism" (p. 229). Against these orientations of classical Marxist materialism, Bourdieu posits a "social space" founded on "multidimensional" relations and interactions. Yet, despite acknowledging the limitations of materialism, Bourdieu perpetrates the same errors by reducing all social interactions to economic exchanges: "[T]he structure of the social field is defined at each moment by the structure of the distribution of capital and the profits characteristic of the different particular fields."

Following this line of reasoning, Bourdieu (1991) reduces all cultural, religious, and linguistic knowledge and interactions to *cultural capital*, materialist in analogy if not reality, exchanged in hierarchies determined by symbolic violence, ownership and power that mirror histories of actual violence, ownership and power. In this way, for Bourdieu, culture, religion, and language are *symbolic* exchanges mirroring underlying material exchanges. Setting aside the question of whether this theory is accurate, it is antagonistic to the worldviews of those most vulnerable to assimilative policies and practices: Indigenous peoples with strong spiritual and religious orientations within their lived "cultures" (MacPherson & Beckett, 2008). This commitment to spiritual values, worldviews, and lived-realities has enabled sustainable Indigenous communities, such as those in the Himalayas, to persist and realize quality lifestyles in marginal ecosystems without depending on modern strategies of high consumption or conservative traditional strategies of high reproduction (Norberg-Hodge, 1991). Furthermore, some Indigenous peoples have developed local and distinctive critical traditions established on the basis of these spiritual worldviews (MacPherson, 2005; Milligan, 2009).

Economic metaphors

The use of these materialist metaphors suggests that all interactions involve actual or symbolic marketplaces and exchanges in which individuals negotiate their self-interested needs by investing time and energy in a social context with expectations of dividends on their investments. These economic metaphors only further de-value languages whose continued use is not economically motivated but rather undertaken to respect and to forge historical, spiritual, familial, and community relations. The identity theory of Norton (1997; Pierce, 1995) that focuses on *investment* in language learning and the *ownership* of English derives directly from this economic metaphor. Although no doubt intended to accentuate agency in the face of structural inequities, this metaphor connotes a controlled, rational decision-making process that is as untrue in economic exchanges as it is in culture. In the case of language and culture, what is the currency of investment and return—time, education? If so, neither is much within the control of modern middle-class people, let alone impoverished Indigenous peoples and their communities.

Agency–structure dichotomies

As well intentioned as interpretations of critical theory have been in applied linguistics and language policy studies in their attempt to shift emphasis from structures to agents, these distinctions reflect antiquated views of the relationships between individuals and environments. From particle physics (Zylinger, 2008) through to environmental studies and the biology of cognition (Maturana & Varela, 1988; Varela, Thompson, & Rosch, 1991), science has come close to proving post-modern (and Buddhist) theories that existence is characterized by deep interdependence and interconnections that render self–other, self–environment, and agency–structure dichotomies invalid. Although environmental perspectives need not erase the possibility of free choice, to be sure, it does suggest the need for a theory of identity that deconstructs agent–structure and individual–community–environment dichotomies. After all, at what point do the "investment" decisions of "agents" experience a definitive break with the conditioning of their desires by ecological relations and social structures?

Individuals or communities?

In the same way, critical theory has an implicit modernist bias towards representing the world as organized into individuals and groups of individuals rather than into interconnected communities. Embedded in the concept of *community* are the words *commune*, a verb connoting a process of union beyond the self, and *communion*, a term with decidedly religious overtones that suggests union with the commons or the world. A sustainability approach requires that communities are understood to exist across time, space, and species. For example, the technical meaning of "sustainable development" requires that future generations of communities be considered on equal grounds with existing generations. To frame decisions with such accountability in mind, future generations must be operationalized as communities rather than individuals. Likewise, ecological perspectives emphasize communities because their scientific and theoretical lenses reinforce the insight that no individuals exist independently from the communities on which their sustenance and livelihoods depend. Any social and identity theory that is not ultimately grounded in our biotic inter-dependence is incapable of serving the full needs of a sustainability policy theory.

Eco-linguistics and language ecology theories

In contrast to critical theory, eco-linguistics and language ecology theories are paradigms directly derived from ecology and applied to sustainability policy studies in language and language education, where they have been popularized by Hornberger (1997; Hornberger & Johnson, 2007) and Skutnabb-Kangas (2000). This theoretical orientation derives from linguistic anthropology research that chronicles the deep entanglement between linguistic, cultural, and biological diversity (Maffi, 2001; Nettle & Romaine, 2000). Using interdisciplinary approaches, this body of bio-linguistic and bio-cultural diversity research offers near-irrefutable evidence that human social and broader biotic communities are interdependent and impossible to untangle, with correlated rates of diversity and extinction (Sutherland, 2003). These theories of eco-linguistics and language ecology account for biological and diversity value against economic value with obvious implications for policies affecting Indigenous languages and peoples. These researchers focus on those communities with fewer than 50,000 or even 10,000 speakers, whose circumstances are analogous to the plight of endangered species. These correlation studies offer quantitative tracking data and methods important for policy decision-making and rationalization.

Potential advantages to this narrow focus notwithstanding, there are serious shortfalls to the eco-linguistic and language ecology perspectives. One limitation is their tendency to overlook subtle forces of discrimination and power inequities that obstruct local attempts to address the challenges on the ground. Identifying this weakness in the language ecology approach, May (2005) argued "the loss of a minority language almost always forms part of a wider process of social, cultural, and political displacement" that needs to be considered within any effective theoretical lens (p. 2060). Although the focus on linguistic and cultural rights is relevant for policy studies and works well in Europe and North America, it depends on a significant acceptance of rights discourses, which tends not to be the case in the PRC. Furthermore, the primary research based on this paradigm focuses on numbers of speakers as indicators of both threat and potential value, thereby accentuating extremely small linguistic and cultural communities, which are the most difficult to support through policy. Educational and policy interventions and supports tend to be most effective for slightly larger Indigenous languages and communities, such as the Uygurs, Tibetans, and Cree people (Canada), whose languages show signs of imminent decline yet are, theoretically, excluded from high-risk "threatened" or "vulnerable" labels. Clearly, the designation 'minority' or endangered is contextual and depends on socio-political considerations.

In conclusion, critical theory and eco-linguistics/language ecology theories fall short of providing comprehensive theories to frame and direct language policy research and language policies to realize the full potential of the sustainability outcomes of development envisioned in the Brundtland Report, *Our Common Future*. While critical theory fails to account for the deep entanglement between agents and environments, eco-linguistics fails to offer ecological explanations for fundamental human social aspirations such as liberation from oppression and domination. Accordingly, each is inadequate as a theoretical anchor to develop a robust interpretation of sustainability capable of bridging biological and social sustainability factors.

Critical sustainability theory

More promising to the project of developing an effective language and cultural sustainability policy framework is a hybrid critical-sustainability theory in which the best of critical and eco-linguistic approaches are invoked and combined. First, this hybrid theory requires a critical lens to critique how social hierarchies based on dominance and oppression are rooted in deep cultural assumptions concerning the relations between humans, and human and non-human realms, without collapsing the analysis into extended economic metaphors of utilitarian exchanges. Second, this hybrid approach requires a strong ecological lens in which intersecting communities from the biotic through to the "ethnic," economic, national and global are recognized as having value and claim over the language practices of an individual, a family, a region, and an education system. As Hornberger (1997) suggests, this ecological orientation offers a strong endorsement for bottom-up language policy formation and planning. By combining sociolinguistic and ecological discourses, this hybrid theory becomes uniquely suited to reinvigorate and integrate two key 'traditional' cultural perspectives and policy orientations in China: Marxism (critical theory) and Tao-Confucianism (ecological relations theories).

Conclusion

This analysis began by identifying the dangers of continuing to rely on neo-liberal ideologies of globalization to inform minority language and language education policies and policy studies. Instead, the study sought to identify a coherent theory that can render policy frameworks and designs more accountable to the high standards of equity outlined in the official United Nations' definition of sustainable development while offering a systematic conceptual framework to organize and relate scientific research to sustainability policy considerations. On critiquing the two dominant pre-existing theories promoting sustainability in language policy studies—critical and language ecology theories—neither theory on its own was found to be adequate for these tasks.

Having identified key points of conflict between these theories and between both theories and the full ends of sustainability, I argued for the need to retain those aspects of each theory that serve language sustainability policy and research ends and to discard those that do not. The resulting critical sustainability theory offers a way to ground a more authentic use of the term 'ethnic harmony' within the broader objectives of 'ecological harmony,' thereby promising to re-orient policy considerations and development on the objectives of peaceful co-existence on the planet Earth beyond a particular ethnic group, nation-state or species. This renewed critical sustainability theory has the capacity to realize the explicit content and implied intention of "sustainable development" as outlined in the United Nations' vision as articulated in *Our Common Future*.

References

Assadourian, E. (2008). Economy and strain on environment both grow. *Vital Signs 2007-2008*, (pp. 54–55). Washington, DC: Worldwatch Institute.

Baker, C., & Prys Jones, S. (1998). *The encyclopedia of bilingualism and bilingual education*. Clevedon: Multilingual Matters.

Beckett, G., & MacPherson, S. (2005). Researching the impact of English on minority and Indigenous languages in non-"Western" contexts. *TESOL Quarterly*, 38(2), 299–308.

Bilik, N. (1998). Language education, intellectuals and symbolic representation: Being an urban Mongolian in a new configuration of social evolution, *Nationalism and Ethnic Politics*, 4(1), 47–67.

Bourdieu, P. (1991). *Language and symbolic power (Trans. G. Raymond and M. Adamson)*. Cambridge, MA: Harvard University Press.

Canagarajah, S. (1999). *Resisting linguistic imperialism in English teaching*. Oxford: Oxford University Press.

Cardinal, L. (2005). The ideological limits of linguistic diversity in Canada. *Journal of Multilingual and Multicultural Development*, 26(6), 481–495.

Cassels-Johnson, D. (2010). The relationship between Applied Linguistics research and language policy for bilingual education. *Applied Linguistics*, 31(1), 72–93.

Cho, E. K., & Shin, S. (2008). Survival, adjustment, and acculturation of newly immigrated families with school-age children: Cases of four Korean families, *Diaspora, Indigenous, and Minority Education*, 3(1), 4–24.

Dwyer, A. (1998). The texture of tongues: Languages and power in China. *Nationalism and Ethnic Politics*, 4(1), 68–85.

Ehrlich, P. (2000). *Human natures: Genes, cultures, and the human prospect*. Washington, DC, Covelo, CA: Island Press/Shearwater Books.

Erbaugh, M. S. (1995). Southern Chinese dialects as a medium for reconciliation within greater Greater China. *Language in Society*, 24(1), 79–94.

Fairclough, N. (1995). *Critical discourse analysis: The critical study of language*. Harlow: Pearson Education.

Flores Farfán,, J. A. (2002). Language revitalization, maintenance and development in Mexico: The case of the Mexicano (Nahuatl) language. *Paper presented at World Congress on Language Policies*, Barcelona. Retrieved from: http://www.linguapax. org/congres/taller/taller2/Flores.html.

Flowerdew, J., & Miller, L. (2008). Structure and agency in second language learning: Evidence from three life histories. *Critical Inquiry in Language Studies*, 5(4), 201–224.

Foucault, M. (1996). What is critique? In J. Schmidt (Ed.), *What is enlightenment? Eighteenth-century answers and twentieth-century questions* (pp. 382–398). Berkeley: University of California Press.

Grose, T. (2010). Guest Editor's Introduction: The Tibet and Xinjiang Neidi classes. *Chinese Education and Society*, 5(3), 3–9.

Habermas, J. (1970). *Toward a rational society: Student protest, science, and politics*. Boston: Beacon Press.

Habermas, J. (1995). *The philosophical discourse of modernity: Twelve lectures (Trans. F.G. Lawrence)*. Cambridge, MA: MIT Press.

Habermas, J. (1996). The unity of reason in the diversity of its voices. In J. Schmidt (Ed.), *What is enlightenment? Eighteenth-century answers and twentieth-century questions* (pp. 399–425). Berkeley: University of California Press.

Harmon, D. (1996). Losing species, losing languages: Connections between biological and linguistic diversity. *Southwest Journal of Linguistics*, 15, 89–108.

Harmon, D., & Loh, J. (2009a). Index of biocultural diversity. *Terralingua*. Retrieved from: http://www.terralingua.org/projects/ibcd/background.html.

Harmon, D., & Loh, J. (2009b). Index of linguistic diversity. *Terralingua*. Retrieved from: http://www.terralingua.org/projects/iLd/ild.htm.

Heller, M. (2006). *Linguistic minorities and modernity*. London: Continuum.

Hornberger, N. (1997). *Language planning from the bottom up: Indigenous literacies in the Americas*. Berlin: Mouton de Gruyter.

Hornberger, N., & Johnson, D. (2007). Slicing the onion ethnographically: Layers and spaces in multilingual language education policy and practice. *TESOL Quarterly*, 41(3), 309–332.

Hu, G. (2005). English language education in China: Policies, progress, and problems. *Language Policy*, 4, 5–24.

Huang, P. J. J. (1998). Theory and the study of Chinese history: Four traps and a question. *Modern China*, 24(2), 183–208.

Kopeliovich, S. (2010). Family language policy: A case study of a Russian-Hebrew bilingual family: Towards a theoretical framework. *Diaspora, Indigenous, and Minority Education*, 4(3), 162–178.

Kubota, R. (2004). Critical multiculturalism and second language education. In B. Norton, & K. Toohey, (Eds.), *Critical pedagogies and language learning* (pp. 30–52). New York: Cambridge University Press.

Liu, J. (2006). *China releases green GDP index: Tests new development path*. Washington, DC: Worldwatch Institute. Accessed September 12, 2009 at: http://www.worldwatch.org/node/4626.

MacPherson, S. (2003). TESOL for biolinguistic sustainability: The ecology of English as a lingua mundi. *TESL Canada Journal*, 20(2), 1–22.

MacPherson, S. (2005). Negotiating language contact and identity change in a bilingual Tibetan/English program. *TESOL Quarterly*, 39(4), 585–607.

MacPherson, S. (2011). *Education and sustainability: Learning across the diaspora, Indigenous, and minority divide*. New York: Routledge.

MacPherson, S., & Beckett, G. H. (2008). The hidden curriculum of assimilation in modern Chinese education: Fuelling Indigenous Tibetan and Uygur cessation movements. In Z. Bekerman, & E. Kopelowitz, (Eds.), *Cultural education = Cultural sustainability: Minority, diaspora, Indigenous and ethno-religious groups in multi-cultural societies* (pp. 103–122). Mahwah, NJ: LEA.

MacPherson, S.A., & Ghoso, D. B. (2008). Multilingual practices in emerging diasporas: A Tibetan case study. *Diaspora, Indigenous & Minority Education: An International Journal*, 2(3), 188–216.

Maffi, L. (2001). *On biocultural diversity: Linking language, knowledge, and the environment.* Washington, DC: Smithsonian Institution Press.

Maturana, H., & Varela, F. (1988). *The tree of knowledge: The biological roots of human understanding.* Boston: Shambhala Press.

May, S. (2005). Language policy and minority language rights. In E. Hinkel (Ed.), *Handbook of research in second language teaching and learning* (pp. 1055–1073). Mahwah, NJ: Lawrence Erlbaum Associates.

McGlynn, C., Lamarre, P., Laperrière, A., & Montgomery, A. (2009). Journeys of interaction: Shared schooling in Quebec and Northern Ireland. *Diaspora, Indigenous, and Minority Education, 3*(4), 209–225.

Milligan, J. A. (2009). Prophetic pragmatism? Post-conflict education development in Aceh and Mindanao. *Diaspora, Indigenous, and Minority Education, 3*(4), 245–259.

Nettle, D., & Romaine, S. (2000). *Vanishing voices: The extinction of the world's languages.* New York: Oxford University Press.

Norberg-Hodge, H. (1991). *Ancient futures: Learning from Ladakh.* San Francisco, CA: Sierra Club Books.

Norton, B. (1997). Language, identity, and the ownership of English. *TESOL Quarterly, 31*(3), pp. 409–429.

Nussbaum, M. (1997). *Cultivating humanity: A classical defense of reform in liberal education.* Cambridge, MA: Harvard University Press.

Nussbaum, M. (2000). *Women and human development: The capabilities approach.* Cambridge: Cambridge University Press.

Pennycook, A. (1994). *The cultural politics of English as an international language.* Harlow: Addison Wesley Longman Ltd.

Pennycook, A. (1999). Introduction: Critical approaches to TESOL. *TESOL Quarterly, 33*(3), 329–348.

Pennycook, A. (2001). *Critical applied linguistics: A critical introduction.* Mahwah, NJ: Lawrence Erlbaum Associates.

Phillipson, R. (2008). The linguistic imperialism of neoliberal empire. *Critical Inquiry in Language Studies, 5*(1), 1–43.

Phillipson, R., & Skutnabb-Kangas, T. (1995). English only worldwide or language ecology. *TESOL Quarterly, 30*(3), 429–452.

Peixin, Z. (2003). China and globalization (2003/10/10). Speech by H.E. Ambassador Zha Peixin at Chinese Economic Association Annual Conference (14 April, 2003). Embassy of the People's Republic of China in the United Kingdom of the Great Britain and Northern Ireland. Retrieved at:http://www.chinese-embassy.org.uk/eng/dsjh/t27161.htm.

Pierce, B. N. (1995). Social identity, investment, and language learning. *TESOL Quarterly, 29*(1), 9–31.

Schieffelin, B. B., Woolard, K. A., & Kroskrity, P. V. (Eds.) (1998). *Language ideologies: Practice and theory. Oxford Studies in Anthropological Linguistics.* Oxford: Oxford University Press.

Schmidt, C. (2010). Multilingualism in Canadian schools: Current issues and perspectives. In U. Neumann, & J. Schneider, (Eds.), *Schule mit Migrationshintergrund: wie vielfalt an Schulen vom Problem zur Resource werden kann* [Schools with migration background: How diversity at schools can change from problem to resource]. Münster: Waxmann.

Sen, A. (1999). *Development as freedom.* New York: Anchor Books.

Silverman, H. (2009). Sustainability: The S-word. *People & places: Ideas that connect us.* Accessed Sept. 06, 2010: http://www.peopleandplace.net/perspectives/2009/4/15/sustainability_the_s-word.

Skutnabb-Kangas, T. (2000). Linguistic genocide in education—or worldwide diversity and human rights? Mahwah, NJ: Lawrence Erlbaum Associates.

Smith, D. G. (2008). From Leo Strauss to collapse theory: Considering the neoconservative attack on modernity and the work of education. *Critical Studies in Education*, 49(1), 33–48.

Statistics Canada. (2009). Mother tongue of recent immigrants, 1981 to 2006. Retrieved from: http://www.census2006.ca/census-recensement/2006/as-sa/97-557/figures/c3-eng.cfm.

Sutherland, W. J. (2003). Parallel extinction risk and global distribution of languages and species. *Nature*, 423, 276–279.

Thomas, W., & Collier, V. (2001). *A national study of school effectiveness for language minority students' long-term academic achievement*. A report for the Centre for Research on Education, Diversity & Excellence. Available at: http://www.crede.ucsc.edu/research/llaa/1.1_final.html.

Tollefson, J. W. (Ed.). (1995). *Power and inequality in language education*. Cambridge: Cambridge University Press.

Tsuda, Y. (1994). The diffusion of English: Its impact on culture and communication. *Communication Review*, 16, 32–34.

UNESCO. (2009). UNESCO Atlas of the world's languages in danger. Endangered languages. Retrieved at: http://www.unesco.org/culture/ich/index.php?pg=00139.

United Nations World Commission on Environment and Development. (1987). *Our Common Future (The Brundtland Report)*. New York: UN.

Upton, J. (1999). The development of modern school-based Tibetan language education in the PRC. In G. Postiglione (Ed.), *China's national minority education: Culture, schooling and development* (pp. 281–340). New York: Falmer Press.

Varela, F., Thompson, E., & Rosch, E. (1991). *The embodied mind: Cognitive science and human experience*. Cambridge, MA: MIT Press.

Wang, C., & Zhou, Q. (2003). Minority education in China: From state's preferential policy to dislocated Tibetan schools. *Educational Studies*, 29(1), 85–104.

Worldwatch Institute. (2006). *State of the World 2006: China and India hold fate of the world in balance*. Washington, DC: Worldwatch Institute. Accessed September 12, 2009 at: http://www.worldwatch.org/node/3893.

Zylinger, A. (2008). Interview with Anton Zeilinger. Institute of Physics. Retrieved at: http://www.iop.org/activity/awards/Internationalpercent20Award/newton08/page_3198.html.

12 Minority language rights and education in China

The relevance of human rights law and substantive equality

Kelley Loper

Introduction

Many multicultural societies struggle to achieve a workable dynamic that encourages cultural and linguistic diversity as well as social integration while avoiding the imposition of a majority culture on minority communities against their will. A key challenge involves formulating laws and policies which allow for full participation, prevent the assimilation of groups which are characterized by difference, and move toward the accommodation and celebration of that difference. In reality, an appropriate balance is often difficult to realize. As Dunbar notes, while "an integrationist policy toward minorities is not necessarily inconsistent with cultural and linguistic plurality ... the borderline between integrationist and assimilationist policies is a murky one at best" (2001, p. 104).

A number of contributors to this volume have explored these tensions with respect to minority language education in China, an area of policy which also involves careful mediation of competing interests and objectives. On the one hand, minority communities have an interest in learning and using their own languages as part of exercising a right to identity. On the other, learning the state's "official," majority language may be necessary to facilitate participation and access to opportunities in higher education and employment. Language policy has the power to marginalize and the lack of knowledge of the dominant language may limit opportunities.

This chapter considers the potential contribution of international human rights law to the process of delineating appropriate boundaries and crafting effective solutions. In particular, it examines standards applicable to China which create binding duties on the Chinese state as a matter of international law to ensure substantive equality in the area of education. Although questions remain about the extent to which China complies with these obligations in practice, its ratification of the instruments and active participation in the reporting procedures indicate at least formal acceptance of the system (for a discussion of China's interaction with the human rights system, see, e.g., Kent, 1999; Woodman, 2005). The chapter will not investigate broader questions about the enforceability of international human rights standards, but assumes that the framework of rights can form the basis for discussion, negotiation and advocacy as states such as China develop policy and legal responses to the challenges posed by linguistic diversity. It concludes that international human rights instruments elaborate principles which can offer guidance for states and minority groups when faced with difficult choices and conflicting claims. At the same time, political obstacles such as China's state-building priorities and its emphasis on economic reform interfere with the incorporation of these treaties at the domestic level and limit their impact. Although rights such as freedom of expression, assembly and association are also relevant (as discussed, e.g., by de Varennes, 1996, pp. 33–53 and Dunbar, 2001, pp. 104–107), the chapter focuses on the right to equality in particular. It recognizes, however, that rights cannot be interpreted in isolation and that equality must be comprehended in connection with other rights which together elaborate a more robust protection framework.

Human rights and minority claims

The above issues form part of a broader debate about whether human rights law, which initially arose in the mid-twentieth century as the foundation for the protection of individual rights, is adequate to address group-based cultural and linguistic claims and secure positive rights to identity. When contemplating the potential contribution of human rights law to the project of balancing the imperatives of diversity and multiculturalism, some have commented on its flexibility and capacity to transform itself. For example, Ghai notes that the "framework of rights has been used with considerable success in mediating competing ethnic and cultural claims. As the cultural problems of more and more states take on a common form, a new version of human rights is emerging" (2000, p. 1099). When examining the international regime for the protection of minority language rights, de Varennes similarly argues that "human rights can help to provide a flexible, realistic mechanism which can adapt to a variety of situations" (1996, p. 2). Fredman (2008, p. 9) observes that the realization of rights requires more than curbing the abuse of state power—or imposing duties of "restraint"—but also necessitates positive state action:

> Human rights are based on a much richer view of freedom, which pays attention to the extent to which individuals are in a position actually to enjoy that freedom … While the State needs to be restrained from abusing its power, only the State can supply what is needed for an individual to fully enjoy her human rights.

Others have expressed less confidence in the capacity of law to address diversity. Macklem notes that although sources of international human rights law "provide minorities with several avenues for challenging the exercise of state power," these treaties "have come to be understood in terms that display a deep ambivalence about the international legal significance of minority status" (2008, p. 534). In the education context, when writing about students with disabilities in

Canada, MacKay (2010, p. 466) notes that some stakeholders have regarded law-yers and judges more often "as sources of fog shrouding the education process" (p. 466) rather than "beacons of light to guide educators through the complex fog of public education" (p. 466). Despite this perception that the law contri-butes to a *lack* of clarity, he argues that: "the concept of equality, [reflected in the law and] properly understood and applied with adequate resources, can be the lighthouse that guides us to more inclusive, effective and even safer public schools" (MacKay, 2010, p. 466).

The next two sections examine this concept of equality and how it has been expressed as a legal right in international human rights treaties and developed through interpretation toward a more robust principle which requires positive duties and attention to the accommodation of multiplicity. Equality, when under-stood according to a substantive model, elaborates guiding principles which can inform the task of balancing linguistic diversity and integration in minority language education policy.

Concepts of equality

The effectiveness of a legal right to equality in contributing to a positive accep-tance of difference depends to a large extent on the concept of equality conveyed by the law. Theories of formal and substantive equality promote varying objec-tives which can lead to divergent outcomes and may have conflicting implications for the law's potential to successfully contend with diversity. Substantive equality goes beyond a formal notion that "likes should be treated alike" and requires a careful analysis of context and an assessment of the actual situation of disadvan-tage faced by particular groups and individuals within those groups. When indi-viduals and groups are competing from unequal starting positions due to past discrimination, lack of language education, etc., then strict equal treatment—in a formal sense—could in fact amount to discrimination. Substantive equality on the other hand "tries to identify patterns of oppression and subordination" (Baines and Rubio-Marín, 2005, p. 14) and then correct them.

Fredman proposes a framework of substantive equality which is directed toward achieving four primary aims which have implications for addressing the challenges of linguistic diversity. First, equality should promote "respect for the equal dignity and worth of all, thereby redressing stigma, stereotyping, humilia-tion, and violence because of membership of an out-group." Second, it should entail an "accommodation and positive affirmation and celebration of identity within community." Third, it should break "the cycle of disadvantage associated with out-groups." Finally, it should facilitate "full participation in society" (2008, p. 179, 2002). She adds that "[p]articipation is a multi-layered concept" and that "equality law should specifically compensate for the absence of politi-cal power of minority groups" (Fredman, 2008, p. 180).

Achieving these objectives—and thus conforming to a substantive equality principle—may require positive duties, special measures, and other forms of adaptation. Dunbar divides rights related to minority languages into two categories: (1) a "regime of linguistic tolerance" (i.e., formal non-discrimination—characterized by restraint or refraining from interference); and (2) a "regime of linguistic promotion" (requiring positive action such as providing education through the medium of minority languages) (2001, pp. 91–92). This classification illustrates the dichotomy between obligations of restraint and formal equality, on the one hand, and obligations on states to take positive action to achieve substantive equality, on the other.

If framed with reference to Fredman's equality goals and Dunbar's dichotomy of obligations, a legal right to equality has the potential to serve as a mediating principle for resolving issues in minority language education. To conform to the demands of equality, states must first analyze the existing situation to identify any disadvantage caused by language policies and practice—or a lack of such policies. They must then remove any obstacles and/or institute measures to provide minority language education while at the same time ensuring official language acquisition. The resulting policy choices can then be measured by their ability to achieve and support the goals of equality: greater participation, the redressing of disadvantage, the celebration of identity, and respect for human dignity.

The international human rights framework

Equality forms a basic, foundational principle underpinning the international human rights regime (Human Rights Committee, 1989, paras. 1–3). As Thornberry notes, "the underlying emphases in [the canon of human rights] are on equality as a governing principle in society and law" (2005, p. 240). The Universal Declaration of Human Rights, adopted by the United Nations General Assembly in 1948, proclaims that "all human beings are born free and equal in dignity and rights" (Article 1) and the right to equality is expressly and prominently included in most of the core human rights treaties. These provisions create obligations on states to employ measures which achieve both formal and substantive equality. The human rights framework therefore requires that states ensure equality in education by refraining from interference with the exercise of individual liberty, including the freedom to use a minority language, as well as by taking positive action when needed to realize equality in effect. States must also guarantee that other rights, such as the right to education, be implemented without discrimination of any kind. Together these provisions create an overlapping arrangement of rights and obligations which should inform the development of policies involving minority language education.

China is party to several of the core international human rights treaties including the International Covenant on Economic, Social and Cultural Rights (ICESCR); the Convention on the Rights of the Child (CRC) and the International Convention on the Elimination of all Forms of Racial Discrimination (ICERD) which are particularly relevant to minority language rights in education. It has also signed, though not yet ratified, the International Covenant on Civil and Political Rights (ICCPR) which is therefore not yet strictly binding on the PRC. The ICCPR has applied to the Hong Kong and Macau SARs, however, both before and since their return to Chinese sovereignty in 1997 and 1999. In addition, by signing the Covenant, China has agreed to refrain from acts which would defeat the object and the purpose of the treaty (1969 Vienna Convention on the Law of Treaties, Article 18). China is also bound by the 1960 UNESCO Convention against Discrimination in Education which elaborates a framework for equality in education. It arguably provides a weaker basis for claiming minority language rights, however, than the later instruments which constitute the core human rights canon. For example, while Article 5 states that it is "essential to recognize the right of members of national minorities to carry on their own educational activities, including the maintenance of schools," it also clarifies that the use or the teaching of a minority language depends on the educational policy of each state. In addition, this right must not be exercised in a manner which "prevents the members of minority groups from understanding the culture and language of the community as a whole and from participating in its activities, or which prejudices national sovereignty" (Article 5).

The UN human rights treaty bodies, the committees tasked with monitoring the implementation of states' obligations under the human rights conventions, have issued General Comments and other interpretive materials which provide guidance for states to better comprehend the content of the rights enumerated in these instruments. Although the right to equality and non-discrimination has traditionally been construed in its formal sense, increasingly these committees have paid greater attention to the need for positive action within a richer model of substantive equality. While debate continues about whether a right to education or a right to equality requires states to provide education in minority languages at public expense (Marks & Clapham, 2005, p. 140), this discussion suggests that the answer depends on context and that policy can be guided by the theoretical framework of substantive equality discussed above and reflected in the human rights instruments examined below.

The International Covenant on Civil and Political Rights (ICCPR)

Although the ICCPR is an instrument which was initially conceived within an individual rights—as opposed to a group rights—paradigm, it nevertheless provides some protection for minority communities to develop their own languages. The right of members of minority groups to enjoy their culture, the right to equality, and participation rights are of particular significance.

Article 27 of the Covenant affirms that state parties must not deny the right of persons belonging to ethnic, religious or linguistic minorities, in community with other members of their groups, to enjoy their culture, to profess and practice their own religion, or to use their own language. On a plain reading of the text, this article is constructed as a duty of restraint (i.e., an obligation on the state to refrain from interfering with the exercise of the right) rather than as a positive duty to promote minority languages. Although drafted in a tentative manner (members of minority communities "shall not be denied" the right to enjoy their culture), it has implications for language rights in education since a right to *use* a language depends on the ability to *learn* the language (OSCE, 1999 citing the Foundation for Inter-Ethnic Relations, 1996, as cited in Dunbar, 2001, p. 109). Similarly, Thornberry argues that Article 27 "goes beyond a guarantee of non-discrimination towards a more positive notion of conservation of linguistic identity. Thus ... failure to allow minority languages to be taught in schools ... when a minority desires this" would breach Article 27 (Thornberry, 1991, p. 197).

When setting out states' general obligations, the ICCPR provides that states must respect and ensure to all individuals subject to its jurisdiction the rights granted by the Covenant without distinction of any kind such as race, color, sex, language, religion, political or other opinion, national or social origin, property, birth or other status (Article 2(1)). In addition, Article 26 guarantees an autonomous right to equality and non-discrimination which applies beyond the parameters of the rights in the Covenant and so would also necessitate the realization of a right to equality in the education context. The Human Rights Committee (HRC), the expert monitoring body which oversees implementation of the ICCPR, has explained that these provisions contain a right to substantive equality. It recognizes that the meaning of discrimination includes distinctions, exclusions, restrictions or preferences which have the effect as well as the purpose of impairing the enjoyment of human rights (HRC, 1989, paras. 6 and 7). This has been interpreted to include policies which apply equally to all, but which disproportionately and negatively affect a particular group (sometimes referred to as "indirect discrimination"). The principle of equality may also require states to take affirmative action "to diminish or eliminate conditions which cause or help to perpetuate discrimination prohibited by the Covenant." Therefore "where the general conditions of a certain part of the population prevent or impair their enjoyment of human rights, the State should take specific action to correct those conditions" (HRC, 1989, para. 10).

The HRC has also observed that language is important in relation to the full enjoyment and exercise of other rights, including political rights. For example, in its General Comment on the right to participate in the conduct of public affairs the Committee affirms that states must remove barriers in order to ensure the enjoyment of participation rights under the ICCPR and that "[p]ositive measures should be taken to overcome specific difficulties such as illiteracy, language barriers, poverty, or impediments to freedom of movement which prevent persons entitled to vote from exercising their rights effectively" (HRC, 1996, para. 12).

The International Covenant on Economic, Social, and Cultural Rights (ICESCR)

The ICESCR also includes a right to equality as well as a general right of everyone to education which "shall enable all persons to participate effectively in a free society [and] promote understanding, tolerance and friendship among all nations and all racial, ethnic or religious groups" (ICESCR, Article 13). Like Article 2(1) of the ICCPR, Article 2(2) obligates state parties to guarantee that the rights enunciated in the Covenant—including the right to education—be exercised without discrimination of any kind on the same range of grounds, including race and language. Despite the lack of an equivalent to Article 27 of the ICCPR or other references to minority rights, the Committee on Economic, Social and Cultural Rights (CESCR) frequently raises questions during the state reporting process concerning minority language education (Åkermark, 1997, p. 193).

The CESCR has recognized that Article 2(2) provides for a right to substantive as well as formal equality observing that "[m]erely addressing formal discrimination will not ensure substantive equality as envisaged and defined by Article 2(2)." In order to eliminate discrimination in practice, states must pay "sufficient attention to groups of individuals which suffer historical or persistent prejudice instead of merely comparing the formal treatment of individuals in similar situations." To achieve this, states must "immediately adopt the necessary measures to prevent, diminish and eliminate the conditions and attitudes which cause or perpetuate substantive or de facto discrimination" (CESCR, 2009, para. 8(b)).

The CESCR has commented that in order to eliminate substantive discrimination, states "may be, and in some cases are, under an obligation to adopt special measures to attenuate or suppress conditions that perpetuate discrimination" (CESCR, 2009, para. 9). These measures are

> legitimate to the extent that they represent reasonable, objective and proportional means to redress de facto discrimination and are discontinued when substantive equality has been sustainably achieved. Such positive measures may exceptionally, however, need to be of a permanent nature, such as interpretation services for linguistic minorities.

In its Concluding Observations on China's state report in 2005, the CESCR expressed concern about reports of discrimination against ethnic minorities, including in the field of education, and information relating to "the use and teaching of minority languages, history, and culture" in the Xinjiang Autonomous Region and the Tibet Autonomous Region (CESCR, 2005, para. 38). It recommended that China "increase public expenditure on education in general" and "take deliberate and targeted measures towards the progressive realization of the right to education" for disadvantaged and marginalized groups (CESCR, 2005, para. 66).

The Convention on the Rights of the Child (CRC)

The Convention on the Rights of the Child (CRC) is the only other core human rights instrument—apart from the ICCPR—which mentions minority groups explicitly. Article 17(d) obligates states to "[e]ncourage the mass media to have particular regard to the linguistic needs of the child who belongs to a minority group or who is indigenous." It also duplicates the language of Article 27 of the ICCPR in relation to children who are members of minority or indigenous groups (Article 30). Article 29(1)(c) further provides that

> States Parties agree that the education of the child shall be directed to ... [t]he development of respect for ... his or her own cultural identity, language and values, for the national values of the country in which the child is living, the country from which he or she may originate, and for civilizations different from his or her own.

Article 28 reaffirms the right to education with respect to children.

Like the ICCPR and the ICESCR, the CRC also contains a non-discrimination provision (Article 2(1)) and the Committee on the Rights of the Child, the Convention's monitoring body, has similarly interpreted it as a right to substantive equality. The Committee explains that the obligation requires states to actively identify "individual children and groups of children the recognition and realization of whose rights may demand special measures". It also notes that "the application of the non-discrimination principle of equal access to rights does not mean identical treatment" and that special measures may be necessary to diminish or eliminate discrimination (Committee on the Rights of the Child, 2003, para. 12).

The Committee advised China that all teaching and learning materials for primary and secondary level education should be made available in ethnic minority languages and have culturally sensitive content (Committee on the Rights of the Child, 2005, para. 77(d)). It also recommended increasing resources allocated to education generally and targeting these to ensure equal access to education for all, including members of ethnic minority communities (Committee on the Rights of the Child, 2005, para. 77(b)).

The International Convention on the Elimination of All Forms of Racial Discrimination (ICERD)

The ICERD obligates states to "condemn racial discrimination and undertake to pursue ... a policy of eliminating racial discrimination in all its forms" (Article 2(1)). Although it does not mention language or minorities explicitly, the Convention prohibits discrimination on a range of relevant grounds including race, descent (which includes, for example, indigenous communities and caste), and ethnic or national origin. There is often a close connection between race and language and many linguistic minorities fall within the categories protected from discrimination by the Convention (Henrard, 2007). Like the other treaties, the Convention requires substantive equality—an interpretation which is apparent from both a reading of the text as well as the materials produced by its monitoring body, the Committee on the Elimination of Racial Discrimination (CERD).

Similar to the other instruments, the definition of discrimination includes the *effect* (not only the purpose) of a distinction, exclusion, restriction or preference (ICERD, Article 1). Language requirements and policies can sometimes have a racially discriminatory impact and could therefore amount to indirect discrimination. The CERD has confirmed that "[t]he principle of equality underpinned by the [ICERD] combines formal equality before the law with equal protection of the law, with substantive or de facto equality in the enjoyment and exercise of human rights as the aim to be achieved by the faithful implementation of its principles" (2009b, para. 6). The right to education without discrimination in Article 5(e)(v) of the Convention should therefore be read with reference to a substantive equality principle. Thus, where language policies reduce accessibility to education or otherwise negatively impact linguistic minorities in effect, even if they appear "neutral" on their face, then they would contravene the Convention.

The Convention's general obligations also require that states take positive measures to address de facto discrimination in certain circumstances to achieve the rights of both individuals and groups. Article 1(4), which forms part of the Convention's elaboration of the definition of racial discrimination, clarifies that:

> Special measures taken for the sole purpose of securing adequate advancement of certain racial or ethnic groups or individuals requiring such protection as may be necessary in order to ensure such groups or individuals equal enjoyment or exercise of human rights and fundamental freedoms *shall not be deemed racial discrimination.*
>
> (Emphasis added)

Article 2 provides that "[w]hen the circumstances so warrant" states must "take, in the social, economic, cultural and other fields, special and concrete measures to ensure the adequate development and protection of certain racial groups or individuals belonging to them, for the purpose of guaranteeing them the full and equal enjoyment of human rights and fundamental freedoms". These measures must not entail, however, "the maintenance of unequal or separate rights for different racial groups after the objectives for which they were taken have been achieved." According to a General Recommendation issued by CERD,

> The concept of special measures is based on the principle that laws, policies and practices adopted and implemented in order to fulfill obligations under the Convention require supplementing, when circumstances warrant, by the adoption of temporary special measures designed to secure to disadvantaged groups the full and equal enjoyment of human rights and fundamental freedoms.
>
> (2009b, para. 11)

The Australian High Court referred to the special measures provisions in the ICERD when considering a claim under the Australian Racial Discrimination

Act (RDA) which challenged the legality of the Land Rights Act, a law granting special rights to an indigenous group over traditional lands (*Gerhardy v. Brown*). The plaintiff, who was not a member of that particular indigenous community, argued that the Act discriminated against him because he could not access the land without permission solely based on a racial category. Because the definition of racial discrimination in Australian domestic law duplicates the definition in the ICERD, the court looked to the Convention for guidance. In doing so, it decided that although the Land Rights Act violated the RDA in a formal sense, it fell within the special measures provisions in Articles 1(4) and 2(2) and was therefore an *exception* to the prohibition against racial discrimination.

In a critique of this case, Sadurski highlights an important distinction between special measures as an "exception" and special measures as an element of the obligation to prohibit discrimination. He argues:

> By considering the "special measures" as an exception to a general prohibi-
> tion of racial discrimination rather than ... a proper inference from the prin-
> ciple of non-discrimination, the Court has assumed that racial distinctions
> are per se discriminatory and invalid, even if they are aimed at the improve-
> ment of the situation of traditionally disadvantaged groups.

This is inappropriate since "the test of discrimination must not abstract from the invidiousness of its aims and/or effects" (Sadurski, 1986–88, p. 7). Similarly, McKean explains that Articles 1(4) and 2(2) of the ICERD incorporate "the notion of special temporary measures, not as an *exception* to the principle [of non-discrimination] but as a necessary *corollary* to it" and argues that this is "the method by which the twin concepts of discrimination and minority protection can be fused into the principle of equality" (McKean, 1983, p. 159). In their analyses of the special measures provisions in the Convention, both Sadurski and McKean are essentially distinguishing between formal and substantive equality models.

When commenting on China's state report in 2009 and its obligation to ensure equality and non-discrimination in education in particular, the CERD took note of China's "policy of bilingual education for ethnic minorities" but expressed concern about reports that in practice "Mandarin is the sole language of instruction in many schools in the autonomous minority provinces." It recommended that China intensify its efforts to ensure implementation of bilingual education at all levels. It also recommended that China ensure that special measures "to promote access to education for children of ethnic minorities" are available in practice (CERD, 2009a, para. 22).

The content of a Right to Education

Although the ICCPR, ICESCR, CRC, and ICERD present a general framework for equality in education which requires attention to special measures and the rights of linguistic communities, the specific content of the right to education has been more difficult to identify. Fredman points out that this is true because "more than any other socio-economic right, education can be provided according to a range of different models with differing emphases on various elements including mother tongue instruction" (2008, p. 220). In fact, a formulaic response is not desirable given this diversity of situations. Fredman advocates for reliance instead on "prima facie principles" when interpreting the right to education and determining whether states have fulfilled their obligations (2008, p. 220). She refers to a set of four criteria proposed by the Committee on Economic, Social and Cultural Rights and Katarina Tomaševski, the former UN Special Rapporteur on the Right to Education, known as the "4-A" scheme. The first, "availability," requires that states ensure the necessary infrastructure, institutions, functional programs, etc. in sufficient quantity. The second, "accessibility," goes one step further by mandating that education also be accessible to all in a non-discriminatory manner. Third, education must meet standards of "acceptability" in terms of culture, language and religion. Finally, it must demonstrate "adaptability" to changing circumstances (Tomaševski, 1999; Fredman, 2008, p. 220; Marks & Clapham, 2005, pp. 138–141). This scheme, especially its flexibility and attention to context and actual disadvantage, reflects and supports the goals of substantive equality discussed above.

Domestic implementation in China

Language and education can serve as important vehicles for ensuring the survival of minority cultures as well as means for promoting the national language to meet state-building objectives. China's minority language education policy and practice demonstrate the difficulties of balancing cultural preservation with the demands of economic development, state-building priorities and access to opportunities available in the majority language (see e.g., Clothey, 2005; Johnson & Chhetri, 2002; Nima, 2008; Zhou, Postiglione, Zhu, & Jiao, 2004; 2000a, 2000b, 2008, 2011). The international human rights treaties discussed above elaborate a principle of equality which, in conjunction with a right to education and other relevant standards, can arguably inform these balancing efforts and support effective approaches toward minority language education. Nevertheless the implementation of these standards in domestic law and practice is often fraught with difficulties.

This section considers the limits of China's domestic legal framework as a means of achieving substantive equality and minority language rights in education. It also notes a number of language policies and practices which could undermine the realization of de facto equality. As Feng argues, "there is a potentially vicious cycle in which social stratification can be exacerbated by inappropriate language policies, which may result in more severe inequality in education, and in turn lead to further social and ethnic divisiveness" (2009, pp. 98–99). To fulfill their international obligations, the Chinese authorities must refrain from implementing language policies which cause disadvantage (duties of restraint) as well as proactively take measures to correct and remedy the effects of past discrimination (positive duties).

The arrangements for regional national autonomy in the PRC, expressed in the Constitution of the People's Republic of China (Constitution), the Law of the People's Republic of China on Regional National Autonomy (LRNA) and various policy documents, serve as the key legal and political tools for addressing issues of diversity, and define the parameters within which language policy can develop. The Constitution and the LRNA both contain protections for minority language rights. Article 4 of the Constitution, reflected in Article 10 of the LRNA, guarantees the freedom for minorities "to use and develop their own spoken and written languages" (Constitution of the People's Republic of China, 1984 and LRNA, 1984). Article 121 grants "the organs of self-government of the national autonomous areas" power to "employ the spoken and written language or language in common use in the locality" (Constitution, 1984). Article 134 elaborates a right to use the spoken and written languages of one's own nationality in court proceedings (Constitution of the People's Republic of China, 1984).

In the context of education, the LRNA allows the organs of self-government in the autonomous areas to decide on "plans for the development of education" in autonomous areas, "the establishment of various kinds of schools at different levels, and their educational system, forms, curricula, the language used in instruction and enrollment procedures" (LRNA, Article 36). In addition, when most students come from minority communities, schools shall, whenever possible, use textbooks in the minority language and use that language as the medium of instruction (Article 36). At the same time, Chinese must be taught whenever possible at the junior and senior grades of primary school. Previously Chinese language was promoted at a later stage of education. This provision was amended in 2001, however, and is indicative of a shift in language policy during the past decade toward a greater emphasis on learning Chinese and the increasing dominance of the majority language (Zhou, 2008, p. 6 and Chapter 2 in this volume).

Although these documents apparently guarantee minority rights, including the use of minority languages in education, full realization of these rights in practice is often limited by competing political imperatives including the authorities' central concerns with state unity and economic development. In China, as in many countries, the use or promotion of a language often has real or perceived political ramifications which may create obstacles to the enjoyment of minority language rights. Political priorities are reflected in the text of the law itself and demonstrated by the realities of state control. The provisions in Chinese law related to minority rights and ethnic autonomy must be read in conjunction with overarching principles including; (1) the unitary nature of the Chinese state; (2) the supremacy of the Chinese Communist Party; (3) the exercise of autonomy powers under unified state leadership; and (4) the need for autonomous areas to "place the interests of the state as a whole above anything else and make positive efforts to fulfill the tasks assigned by the state organs at higher level" (LRNA, Article 7; see discussion of these provisions in Ghai, Woodman & Loper, 2010, pp. 152–153). He Baogang points out that cultural autonomy may be possible for minorities except where it involves activities which threaten the unity of the state (He, 2005).

State control is also evident in the role the Chinese authorities have played in defining minority cultural identity, including language, and interpreting the "authentic" expression of that identity. For example, Schiaffini argues that while there had been a zealous "destruction" of cultural identity in Tibet in the past, especially during the Cultural Revolution, the state has been "reconstructing" this identity with equal measure of zealousness. She notes that after the Cultural Revolution, the Chinese Government, "[b]y publicly proclaiming the rights of ethnic minorities and promoting the official reconstruction of ethnic identities," was actually "legitimizing and reinforcing its own rule over them" (Schiaffini, 2004, p. 85). This theme of the state's construction—or reconstruction—of minority culture is emphasized in a number of official documents. For example, a State Council White Paper on the Protection and Development of Tibetan Culture asserts that after the liberation of Tibet, the Central People's Government "actively helped Tibet protect and recover its traditional culture, and develop its modern cultural, educational and health sectors, opening up a completely new chapter for the development of Tibetan Culture" (Information Office of the State Council of the People's Republic of China, 2008, Foreword).

Language policies developed in response to state-building and economic priorities reflect this emphasis on the state's control of identity construction and often fail to support substantive equality for members of minority communities. Indeed, scholars have documented the link between language strategies and China's objectives of reform and state unification. Research indicates that in many cases these imperatives have given rise to inequalities and exacerbated—or at least failed to alleviate—the marginalization of minority communities. MacPherson (Chapter 11 in this volume) observes that "[t]oday in China and other states the dominant ideology driving language policy decisions ... involves the appropriation of 'modernization' and 'globalization'" and that "[d]omestic policies are transacted on the assumption of the ends of secularization and economic integration and a 'citizenry' reduced to a 'workforce'" (p. 191). In this context, indigenous language is viewed as having little economic value. Zhou (2011) notes that economic development is one factor affecting the implementation of the PRC's language policy at the local level. Economic reforms have fuelled the demand for a "lingua franca to serve communication needs" and *Putonghua* has taken up this role (Zhou, 2011, p. 25). Zhou argues that *Putonghua* has experienced a "revolution" and has developed "from a state-endorsed language to one that is endorsed by the state and empowered by the market" (2011, p. 25). Ma remarks on the trend toward greater bilingual teaching (in minority languages and *Putonghua)* for minority students in Xinjiang and the need for mastery of *Putonghua* to compete in the job market (2009). He also observes that even with the strengthening of *Putonghua* teaching in minority schools, significant differences in performance standards between Han and minority students persist.

Another result of a "reduced public commitment to Indigenous language education"—and potential obstacle to realizing minority language rights in education—is the "increasing use of boarding schools that relocate cohorts of Tibetan and Uyghur students in distant Han communities and schools in Central China, thereby dislocating students culturally and geographically" (MacPherson, 2011, pp. 193–194).

Reforms have also spurred the "unprecedented" development of English language education (Feng, 2009). In some minority regions, English language is promoted and provided to both minority and majority students. In Xinjiang, however, studies indicate that most minority students have not been not offered English instruction (Feng, 2009). Feng suggests that it may be possible for pupils from Tibetan and Uyghur communities to become empowered through learning English as a third language but this is more likely if the system alleviates disadvantage by fully honoring their "home language" and allowing them to take high-stakes examinations in their mother tongue rather than in *Putonghua* (Feng, 2009, p. 96).

Further research on the impact of these policies on minority identity and on the nature of any disadvantage is needed in order to evaluate China's implementation of its legal obligations to ensure substantive equality. As discussed above, fulfilling a right to substantive equality as mandated by the international human rights instruments applicable to China requires attention to the actual situation and the development of special measures tailored to the specific circumstances. Therefore, sound empirical research—beyond a review of legal and policy documents—is needed to understand how language policies may entrench or reinforce social and economic marginalization in practice. Feng calls for "extensive research" in order to "inform policy making and to develop models that are workable for different minority groups in different contexts" and remarks that "the role of researchers is undeniably crucial" (2009, pp. 98, 99).

Conclusion

The approaches to minority language education in China discussed in this volume and elsewhere demonstrate the difficulties involved in balancing the exigencies of diversity, accommodation, integration and participation. Marks and Clapham note that education can function as an instrument of both state control as well as individual empowerment (2005: 133–134). Because substantive equality emphasizes the latter, implementation of a right to equality in education as required by international law should ensure that state-building imperatives do not negate the expression of identity, including the use of a minority language. Further incorporation and adherence to the international legal standards considered above could serve to reconcile competing objectives and mitigate obstacles such as the perceived political nature of culture and attempts by the state to control and determine the attributes of authentic minority identity.

Substantive equality can help inform this process since it acts as a balancing principle which demands attention to actual disadvantage and is measured according to its capacity to ensure dignity, minority identity, and participation. If the scale is tipped too far toward isolation and exclusion, equality can shift it back toward integration. If on the other hand a culture is in danger of assimilation and identity rights are at stake, then substantive equality can serve as the basis for modifications to restore equilibrium. The appropriate formula will depend on the specific situation in question and cannot conform to a standard equation. Substantive equality is particularly helpful since it recognizes the importance of context. It therefore requires vigilance and continual reevaluation of the placement of groups within social hierarchies. It is empirical and practical and recognizes the rights of minorities as a community as well as the rights of individuals within those communities, other communities and individuals in society.

References

Åkermark, A. S. (1997). *Justifications of minority protection in international law*. The Hague: Kluwer Law International.

Baines, B., & Rubio-Marín, R. (2005). *The gender of constitutional jurisprudence*. Cambridge: Cambridge University Press.

Clothey, R. (2005). China's policy for minority nationalities in higher education: negotiating values and ethnic identities. *Comparative Education Review*, 49, 389–409.

Committee on Economic, Social and Cultural Rights (2005). *Concluding observations: China (including Hong Kong and Macau)*, E/C.12/1/Add.107. Available at:http://www.unhchr.ch/tbs/doc.nsf/(Symbol)/E.C.12.1.Add.107.En?Opendocument. Accessed August 25, 2010.

Committee on Economic, Social and Cultural Rights (2009). *General comment No. 20*, E/C.12/GC/20. Available at: http://www2.ohchr.org/english/bodies/cescr/docs/gc/E.C.12.GC.20.doc. Accessed August 25, 2010.

Committee on the Elimination of Racial Discrimination (2009a). *Concluding observations: China (including Hong Kong and Macau Special Administrative Regions)*, CERD/C/CHN/CO/10-13. Available at: http://www.unhcr.org/refworld/docid/4adc35852.html. Accessed August 25, 2010.

Committee on the Elimination of Racial Discrimination (2009b). *General recommendation No. 32*, CERD/C/GC/32. Available at: http://www2.ohchr.org/english/bodies/cerd/docs/GC32.doc. Accessed August 25, 2010.

Committee on the Rights of the Child (2003). *General comment No. 5*, CRC/GC/2003/5. Available at: http://www.unhchr.ch/tbs/doc.nsf/(symbol)/CRC.GC.2003.5.En. Accessed August 25, 2010.

Committee on the Rights of the Child (2005). *Concluding observations: China (including Hong Kong and Macau Special Administrative Regions)*, CRC/C/CHN/CO/2. Available at: http://www.unhchr.ch/tbs/doc.nsf/(Symbol)/CRC.C.CHN.CO.2.En?Opendocument. Accessed August 25, 2010.

Constitution of the People's Republic of China (1984). Available at: http://english.people-daily.com.cn/constitution/constitution.html. Accessed September 6, 2010.

de Varennes, F. (1996). Language, minorities and human rights. The Hague: Martinus Nijhoff.

Dunbar, R. (2001). Minority language rights in international law. *International and Comparative Law Quarterly*, 50, 90–120.

Feng, A. (2009). English in China: convergence and divergence in policy and practice. *AILA Review*, 22, 85–102.

Foundation for Inter-Ethnic Relations (1996). *The Hague recommendations regarding the education rights of national minorities*. The Hague: OSCE.

Fredman, S. (2002). *The future of equality in Great Britain*. Manchester: Working Paper No. 5, Equal Opportunities Commission.

Fredman, S. (2008). *Human rights transformed*. Oxford: Oxford University Press.

Gerhardy v. Brown (1985). 159 Commonwealth Law Reports 70. (High Court of Australia).

Ghai, Y. (2000). Universalism and relativism: human rights as a framework for negotiating interethnic claims. *Cardozo Law Review*, 21, 1095–1140.

Ghai, Y., Woodman, S., & Loper, K. (2010). Is there space for "genuine autonomy" for Tibetan areas in the PRC's system of nationalities regional autonomy? *International Journal on Minority and Group Rights*, 17, 137–186.

He, B. (2005). Minority rights with Chinese characteristics. In W. Kymlicka, & B. He, (Eds.). *Multiculturalism in Asia* (pp. 56–79) Oxford: Oxford University Press.

Henrard, K. (2007). The protection of minorities through the equality provisions in the UN human rights treaty bodies. *International Journal on Minority and Group Rights*, 14, 141–180.

Human Rights Committee (1989). *General comment No. 18*. Available at: http://www.unhchr.ch/tbs/doc.nsf/(Symbol)/3888b0541f8501c9c12563ed004b8d0e?Opendocument. Accessed August 25, 2010.

Human Rights Committee (1996). *General comment No. 25*, CCPR/C/21/Rev.1/Add.7. Available at: http://www.unhchr.ch/tbs/doc.nsf/(Symbol)/d0b7f023e8d6d9898025651e004bc0eb?Opendocument. Accessed August 25, 2010.

Human Rights Committee (2004). *General comment No. 31*, CCPR/C/21/Rev.1/Add.13. Available at: http://daccess-dds-ny.un.org/doc/UNDOC/GEN/G04/419/56/PDF/G0441956.pdf?OpenElement. Accessed August 25, 2010.

Information Office of the State Council of the People's Republic of China (2008). *White Paper on the protection and development of Tibetan Culture*. Beijing. Available at: http://www.china.org.cn/government/whitepaper/node_7054682.htm. Accessed August 25, 2010.

International Convention on the Elimination of All Forms of Racial Discrimination (1966). *United Nations Treaty Series*, 660, 195.

International Convention on the Rights of the Child (1989). *United Nations Treaty Series*, 1577, 3.

International Covenant on Civil and Political Rights (1966). *United Nations Treaty Series*, 999, 171.

International Covenant on Economic, Social and Cultural Rights (1966). *United Nations Treaty Series*, 993, 3.

Johnson, B., & Chhetri, N. (2002). Exclusionary policies and practices in Chinese minority education: the case of Tibetan education. *Current Issues in Comparative Education*, 2, 142–153.

Kent, A. (1999). *China, the United Nations, and human rights: The limits of compliance*. Philadelphia: University of Pennsylvania Press.

Law of the People's Republic of China on Regional National Autonomy (1984). Available at: http://www.china.org.cn/english/government/207138.htm. Accessed September 6, 2010.

Ma, R. (2009). The development of minority education and the practice of bilingual education in Xinjiang Uyghur Autonomous Region. *Frontiers of Education in China*, 4, 188–251.

MacKay, W. (2010). An international call for action and Canada's long and winding road to inclusion: The Canadian experience. *Hong Kong Law Journal*, 40, 449–479.

Macklem, P. (2008). Minority rights in international law. *International Journal of Constitutional Law*, 6, 531–552.

MacPherson, S. (2011). From neo-liberal ideology to critical sustainability theory for language policy studies in the PRC. In G. H. Beckett, & G. Postiglione (Eds.) *China's assimilationist language policy: The impact on indigenous/minority literacy and social harmony*. London: Routledge.

Marks, S., & Clapham, A. (2005). *International human rights lexicon*. Oxford: Oxford University Press.

McKean, W. A. (1983). Equality and discrimination under international law. Oxford: Clarendon Press.

Nima, B. (2008). The choice of languages in Tibetan school education revisited. *Chinese Education and Society*, 41, 50–60.

Organisation for Security and Co-operation in Europe (OSCE) (1999). *Report on the linguistic rights of persons belonging to national minorities in the OSCE area*. The Hague: OSCE.

Postiglione, G., Zhu, Z., & Jiao, B. (2004). From ethnic segregation to impact integration: state schooling and identity construction for rural Tibetans. *Asian Ethnicity*, 5, 195–217.

Sadurski, W. (1986–1988). *Gerhardy v Brown v* the concept of discrimination: reflections on the landmark case that wasn't. *Sydney Law Review*, 11, 5–43.

Schiaffini, P. (2004). The language divide: identity and literary choice in modern Tibet. *Journal of International Affairs*, 57, 81–98.

Thornberry, P. (1991). *International law and the rights of minorities*. Oxford: Clarendon Press.

Thornberry, P. (2005). Confronting racial discrimination: A CERD perspective. *Human Rights Law Review*, 5, 239–269.

Tomaševski, K. (1999). *Preliminary report of the Special Rapporteur on the Right to Education*, E/CN.4/1999/49. Available at: http://daccess-dds-ny.un.org/doc/UNDOC/GEN/G99/101/34/PDF/G9910134.pdf?OpenElement. Accessed August 25, 2010.

UNESCO Convention against Discrimination in Education (1960). *United Nations, Treaty Series*, 429, 93.

Universal Declaration of Human Rights (1948). General Assembly resolution 217A (III), U.N. Doc A/810, 71.

Vienna Convention on the Law of Treaties (1969). *United Nations Treaty Series*, 1155, 331.

Woodman, S. (2005). Human rights as "foreign affairs": China's reporting under human rights treaties. *Hong Kong Law Journal*, 35, 179–204.

Zhou, M. (2000a). Language attitudes of two contrasting ethnic minority nationalities in China: the "model" Koreans and the "rebellious" Tibetans. *International Journal of Soc. Language*, 146, 1–20.

Zhou, M. (2000b). Language policy and illiteracy in ethnic minority communities in China. *Journal of Multilingual and Multicultural Development*, 21, 129–148.

Zhou, M. (2008). Linguistic diversity and language harmony in contemporary China. *Chinese Education and Society*, 41, 3–9.

Zhou, M. (2011). Historical review of the PRC's minority/indigenous language policy and practice: nation-state building and identity construction. In G. H. Beckett, & G. Postiglione (Eds.) *China's assimilationist language policy: Impact on indigenous/minority literacy and social harmony*. London: Routledge.

Index

"4-A" scheme 217

Abba region 85
academic language competence 180, 181
acceptability 217
accessibility 217
adaptability 217
agency–structure dichotomies 198, 200
aggregate welfare 178
allocative efficiency 177, 178, 180, 184
Applied Transcript for Dongxiang Language 78
attitude-related factors: and academic performance 98
audio courses 64
Australia 215–16
availability 217
Ayagemangan Xiang 54–5

back translation 143
Bao-an people 81
Beijing Norma University Press 68
bilingual and biliteracy programs 111
bilingual education 34, 77, 193; attitudes towards 114; *Nei gao ban* impact on 66–8; in North America 194–5; programs 111; promotion 28; protecting minority groups' enthusiasm for 62–3; teaching materials 68–70; teaching modes 39–44; types 107–8; *see also* Chinese–English bilingual education; Dongxiang bilingual education; Kashgar Prefecture bilingual education; Yunnan bilingual education study
bilingual education of particular minorities 40–3
bilingual experimental classes 44–9; how to develop 60–3; imbalance in developing between areas 47–9; in Kashgar Prefecture middle schools 57–60; in Kashgar Prefecture primary schools 55–7; preferential policies to promote 46–7; progression in primary and middle schools 44–6; teacher training for 63–5
bilingual and monoliteracy programs 111
bilingual teachers: shortage of 180
bilingualism with monoliteracy model 78
biosphere 192, 197
black market certifications 65
boarding schools 3, 71, 193–4, 220
Bourdieu, Pierre 199
Bouyei nationality: Zhuang nationality and 23–4
Brundtland Report *see Our Common Future*

CAEs *see* content area experts
Canada: language policy 194–5
CCP *see* Chinese Communist Party
CERD 214–16
CESCR 213, 217
Chinese Communist Party (CCP) 19; politics within 24; regional autonomy vs. control by 20, 218–19; supremacy 218
"Chinese dream" 27
Chinese–English bilingual education 175–86; *see also* English-medium instruction (EMI) initiative
Chinese FMM *see* female marriage migrants
Chinese language 34; *see also Hanyu*; Mandarin; *Putonghua*
Chinese model 25–7; concepts 26
Chinese proficiency: language factors and 97
church schools 115
citizenship: development 118; dimensions of 20

civilizing approach 19
class arrangement 69
classroom observation 90
collective identity 139
collective self-esteem 149, 153; correlation
    with other factors 150–2; Hui-Chinese
    Muslims 153
Collective Self-esteem Scale 139, 141;
    reliability 148
collegiate psychological sense of
    community: correlation with other
    factors 150–2, 153
Collegiate Psychological Sense of
    Community (PSC) scale 139, 140,
    141–2; reliability 148
Committee on Economic, Social and
    Cultural Rights (CESCR) 213, 217
Committee on the Elimination of Racial
    Discrimination (CERD) 214–16
Committee on the Rights of the Child 214
commune 200
communion 200
communism: evolution to 20
communities: individuals or 200–1
Confucian values 19
Constitution of the People's Republic of
    China 13, 218
content area experts (CAEs) 164–8
Convention on the Rights of the Child
    (CRC) 13, 210, 213–14
cost-benefit analysis 178
cram school 132
CRC 13, 210, 213–14
critical-ecological theory 192
critical linguistics 190
critical sustainability theory 12, 190, 202
critical theory 192, 198–9, 202
critique 198
Cronbach's alpha 148
cultural background 138
cultural capital 199
cultural diversity 118
cultural identity 219
cultural-linguistic identity: of Taiwan 122,
    125, 126–7, 132–3
cultural reproduction 182
Cultural Revolution 5, 19, 24
curriculum: deficiencies 117; set-up 69

Dai–Han bilingual program 110, 113
dalumei 126
Dehong Dai and Jingpo Autonomous
    Prefecture 110, 115
Deng Xiaoping 72

descriptive approach 19
"Diffusion-of-English Paradigm" 191
Diqing Tibetan Autonomous prefecture
    110
discrimination 201, 212, 213, 214–16;
    indirect 212, 215; racial 214–16
discursive inequities 198
distributive justice 177, 178, 181, 184–5
dominance 202
Dongxiang Autonomous Country (DAC)
    75; school finance 80; teacher quality
    79–80
Dongxiang bilingual education 77–82;
    challenges 79–81
Dongxiang education access study 87–102;
    conclusion 101–2; discussion 96–9;
    factors influencing academic
    performance 91–3, 96–9; factors
    influencing Chinese proficiency level
    93–4; findings 91–5; how language
    affects academic performance 99–101;
    influence of background factors on
    academic performance 94–5, 96; major
    findings 95–6; research methodology
    87–91
Dongxiang language 75; lack of tone
    differentiation 100–1; transcript system
    78
Dongxiang people 7–9; adult illiteracy
    rate 75, 86; education achievement
    levels 75, 86–7; migration 81; religious
    belief 87
Dongxiang schools 87–90
dropout rate: factors affecting 97, 101–2

eco-linguistics 190, 201–2
ecological globalization 192
ecological relations theories 202
economic integration 191
economic metaphors 200
education: right to 212–13, 214, 215,
    216–17
EMI initiative *see* English-medium
    instruction (EMI) initiative
employment prospects: bilingual education
    and 61–2
English 11, 165, 166, 169, 220; access to
    177, 182, 185; global influence 158,
    175; globalization of 199; ownership of
    200; status in PRC 178–9; *see also*
    Chinese–English bilingual education
English-medium instruction (EMI)
    initiative 11–12, 176, 178–85; evaluation
    as public policy 178–81; lessons to

language provision for ethnic minorities 181–5
environmental accidents 196
environmental crisis 196
equality: concepts of 209–10; as foundational principle 210
ethnic autonomous regions 4
"ethnic harmony" 197, 203
ethnic minority groups: educational attainment 85; fertility rates 156; identification 13–14; illiteracy rates 137; language as issue in education 86; language provision lessons from EMI initiative 181–5; largest 156; with scripts not in common use 85; with spoken language 85; type classification 137; without scripts 85; *see also* minority higher education
Ethnic Region Autonomy Law 6
European Union: language hierarchies 194
Expanding Circle countries 175

farmers: in Yunnan 113
Fei Xiaotong 26
female marriage migrants 121–33; assimilationist view of 123–5; Chinese vs. SEA 124, 127–8, 130–1; and cultural-linguistic identity of Taiwan 126–7; dark side of Chinese FMMs' high self-regard 130–2; sense of entitlement of Chinese FMMs 127–30; societal perceptions of Chinese FMMs 125–6
fertility rates 156
first language literacy 15
FMMs *see* female marriage migrants
Ford Foundation 80
foreign language courses 38–9
formal equality 209, 210, 213, 216

Gansu Province 75
General Comments 211, 212
Genghis Khan 163
globalization 4, 12, 33, 70, 191–2; ecological 192; neo-liberal ideology of 192, 198; theories of 192; unequal developments of capitalism in age of 121
glocalization 183
Gongban teachers 108
"great Han mentality" 114
Great Leap Forward 24
greed 197
Green GDP Report 196

Grin, François 176–8
growth rates 195, 196
guoyu 122–3, 125

Han chauvinism 19
Han elites 197
Han kao Han 38
Han kao Min 38
Han schools 35–6; *Min kao Han* students in 51–2
Han script: reform 22
Hanyu: promotion arguments 15; *see also* Chinese language; Mandarin; *Putonghua*
harmony 197
higher education: enrollment 158–9
Hinayana Buddhists 115
Hotan Prefecture 47–9, 69
household financial status: and academic performance 99
household registration system 25
HSK: for minority teachers 65
Hui-Chinese Muslims 153
HuiHui Hua 143
human rights 177; China's interaction with system 207; domestic implementation in China 217–20; international framework 210–11; and minority claims 208–9; *see also* language rights
Human Rights Committee (HRC) 212

ICCPR 211–12, 213, 214
ICERD 210, 214–16
ICESCR 210, 212–13, 214
identity construction 18, 219
identity dynamics 198
identity representation 26
in-class support 91–4, 96, 99–100
inclusive Chinese nation 26
indigenous languages: economic value 193
individual–community–environment dichotomies 200
individuals: communities or 200–1
Inner Mongolia Normal University 166
institutes for nationalities 137
instrumental language rights 177, 179, 182
International Convention on the Elimination of all Forms of Racial Discrimination (ICERD) 210, 214–16
International Covenant on Civil and Political Rights (ICCPR) 211–12, 213, 214
International Covenant on Economic, Social and Cultural Rights (ICESCR) 210, 212–13, 214

international hypergamy (marriage) 121–2

Jilin Province 160

Kangding area 86
kao 38
Kashgar City 51, 57, 64
Kashgar Prefecture bilingual education: current situation 53–60; problems in practice 60–70
KMT 121, 122, 123, 125, 133
Koguryo Dynasty 160
Korea, Republic of 160, 161, 169
Korean minority groups 10–11, 156–7, 159–62; and higher education 161–2; language usage 161–2; minority education study 164–8; separation of students from parents 161
Korean Peninsula: Japanese invasion 160; relations with China 157, 160–1

language: functions 71
language ecology theories 201–2
language factors: and academic performance 96–7; and Chinese proficiency 97; and dropout rate 97, 101–2
language hegemonies 121–33; collision of two 130–2
language hierarchy 193
language ideology 20–1
language learning: investment in 200; as panacea for problems 124
Language Maintenance Bilingual Education (LMBE) 108, 111
language order 20–1
language policy 5; bottom-up formation and planning 202; contexts and cases 192–5; neo-liberal ideology in 191, 192–5
language policy studies 191; theories in 197–202
language rights 176–7, 217–20; instrumental 177, 179, 182; non-instrumental 177; *see also* human rights
language rights protests 3–4, 15
language transition 84–7
Law of the People's Republic of China on Regional National Autonomy (LRNA) 218
learning: language in 14
liang mian yi bu 80, 114
liberalism 198
Lijiang county 108

linguistic anthropology research 201
linguistic citizenship 20–1
linguistic genocide 165
linguistic promotion 210
linguistic tolerance 210
Linxia Hui Autonomous Prefecture 75
literacy: functional 184; importance in student achievement 76–7
loanwords 23
LRNA 218
Luntai County 43
Luxi county 108, 110

"Mainland girls" 126
Mandarin 34; as national language in Taiwan 121, 122–3; *see also* Chinese language; *Hanyu*; *Putonghua*
Mandarin ability: and self-esteem 149–50
market-oriented economy 25
Marxism 202
materialism 199–200
meal allowance 46
Mexico: language policy 194
Miao: dialects and writing systems 24
migration: rural-to-urban 196–7
Min kao Han 38; development 49–53; support 65–6
Min kao Min 38
minban teachers 99, 108
minority-Han joint schools 36
minority higher education 137–8, 157–9; qualitative ethnographic study 164–8; *see also* university for nationalities study
minority languages: diversity 136–7
minority nationalities 137
minority schools 35–6
minwen 116
modernity 191
modernization 12
Mongol minority groups 10–11, 156–7, 162–4; and higher education 162–4; minority education study 164–8
Mongolian schools: in Xinjiang 43
monolingualism: as ideology 21
moral justice 176–7
Moyu County: Uyghur students in Han schools 51
multiculturalism 4
multilingualism: as ideology 21
Muslim minorities 81, 153

Narisi (Nalesi) school 77, 86
nation-state building 20, 25
National Common Language Law 28

National Commonly-Used Language and Script Law 6
Nationalist Party (Taiwan) *see* KMT
nationality languages 157
Naxi–Han bilingual program 109–10
Nei gao ban 51–3; admission index 67; impact on bilingual education 66–8
neo-liberal ideology 191, 192–5, 198
neo-Marxism 199
new bilingual teaching mode 43–4; progression in primary and middle schools 44–6
Ninglang county 108
non-accredited teachers *see minban* teachers
non-instrumental language rights 177
normative rights 176–7
North America: language policy 194–5

obligations: dichotomy of 210
one-child policy 168
Ontario 195
"Open Up the West Campaign" 25
Opinions on Strengthening Putonghua Teaching in Minority Schools 39
oppression 202
Our Common Future 12, 190, 195, 202, 203
Oxfam Hong Kong 80

Pan Yue 196
patrilineal ideology 121
People's Education Press 57, 68–9
personal identity 139
personal self-esteem: correlation with other factors 150–2; Mandarin ability and 149–50; *see also* Self-esteem Scale
Pinyin 22, 78
planned economy 25
political approach 19–20
power inequities 201
practical feasibility 177–8, 179, 183
"pragmatism mentality" 114
PRC Minority Regional Autonomous Law 26
PRC National Commonly-Used Language and Script Law 26
preschool bilingual classes 53–4
preferential admissions 163, 169
public policy perspective 176–8
Putonghua: importance of learning 71–2, 166, 183; as lingua franca 24–5, 71, 157, 219; promotion 22; usage 34, 157–8; *see also* Chinese language; *Hanyu*; Mandarin

Qinghai 86
Qu nei chu zhang ban 67
Quebec 195
questionnaires 87–93; factor analysis 91–2; reliability 91–3
Qur'an 143

regional autonomy: in Soviet model 21–2; state control vs. 20, 218–19
"regional languages" 33
religion education 114–15
Republic of Korea 160, 161, 169
resistance 199
rural primary schools: supervision 70

Stalin, Joseph 13
State Council Document #32 24, 26, 27
State Environmental Protection Administration (SEPA) 196
Salar people 81
salary subsidies 46, 47
SBPS 109, 111–13, 114, 117
science: teaching in Putonghua 58–9
script-less minorities *see* Dongxiang education access study; Dongxiang people
secularization 191
Self-Description Questionnaire 136
self-esteem 10
Self-esteem Scale 136, 139, 141, 142; reliability 148; *see also* personal self-esteem
self-reflexivity 198
self-respect 9, 84, 102
Serdyuchenko, G. B. 22
Shangri-la Bilingual Primary School (SBPS) 109, 111–13, 114, 117
shuangyu shuangwen 110–11
shuangyuwen 110–11
Shufu County 46, 53, 54–8, 62–5
Sichuan province 85–6, 109, 111
snowball sampling 164
social and academic adjustment 139–40; correlation with other factors 150–2, 153
Social and Academic Adjustment Questionnaire 140, 142
Social and Academic Adjustment Scale 140; reliability 148
social identity 139
social identity theory 139
social inequities 198
"social space" 199
social stratification 217
socialization 85
socio-linguistic environment 179

Southern Xinjiang: as special area 72
Soviet model 21–5; aspects 22–3; assumptions 23
Soviet Union: collapse 25; divide-and-rule policy 163
spiritual worldviews 199–200
standardization of language 22–4, 193
state building models 5
structuralism 199
substantive equality 13, 209–10, 219, 220–1; in human rights treaties 211, 212, 213, 214, 215–16
sustainability 190, 191, 195–6; challenge in China 196–7
sustainable development 190, 195–6, 197, 201
symbolic exchanges 199

Taiwan 121–33; cultural-linguistic identity 122, 125, 126–7, 132–3; integrationist ideology 122, 123, 125; national language policy 122; *see also* female marriage migrants
Tao-Confucianism 202
task-based language teaching 175
teacher-related factors: and academic performance 98–9
teacher shortages 116–17, 180, 183
teacher training: for bilingual experimental classes 63–5
teachers: numbers from ethnic minority groups 159
Teaching Syllabus of Putonghua 39
temple schools 115
textbooks: in Dongxiang 78–9; in English 183; minority scripts in 85; in Xinjiang 35, 68–9; in Yunnan 110, 111, 114, 116, 117
Tibet Autonomous Region 213
Tibetan Culture 219
Tibetan–Han bilingual program 110, 112
Tibetan language: education studies 85–6
"Tibetan plus Chinese" model 182
time factors: and academic performance 98
Tomasŏevski, Katarina 217
traditional bilingual teaching mode 39–40
Transitional Bilingual Education (TBE) 108, 110
transitional bilingual teaching model 86
transnational homogeneous languages 115
trilingual language provision 15–16, 166, 185–6
"trilingual schools" 44
Trilingualism 11
tuition scholarships 163

"two exemptions and one aid" policy 80, 114

UNESCO Convention against Discrimination in Education 211
Universal Declaration of Human Rights 220
universities for nationalities 137–8
university for nationalities study 138–53; conceptual framework 139–40; conclusion 152–3; data collection and analysis 142–3; demographic information for respondents 143, 144; findings 143–52; instruments and reliability 140–2, 148–9; research questions 139; setting 142; student types and language abilities 138, 141, 145–9
Urumqi 65
USA: language policy 194
Uyghur language: courses 72; education studies 85

Western Development strategy 49

Xibe schools: in Xinjiang 43
xibu da kaifei 25
Xinjiang Education Bureau 56
Xinjiang Education Press 35
Xinjiang University 43
Xinjiang Uyghur Autonomous Region 34–73, 213; attending mode of students 38–44; ethnic groups 35; high school entrance exam performance 40–2; higher education enrollment numbers 49–50; *Min kao Han* development 49–53; minority education system 34–8; schools enrollment numbers 37; *see also* bilingual experimental classes

Yanbian Korean Autonomous Prefecture 160
Yanbian University 161
Yi–Han bilingual program 110, 112
Yi language: education studies 85
Yunnan bilingual education study 108–18; bilingual schools development 111–13; bilingual textbooks development 111; conclusion 117–18; data analysis 109; findings 109–11; gaps between policy and practice 113–17; methodology 108–9; teaching quality 116–17
Yunnan Nationality Press 116
Yunnan province 105; bilingual education research 108; bilingual education types in 109–10; inability to function in Putonghua

105–7; income figures 113; language use of ethnic minority groups 105–6

Zepu County 43; Uyghur students in Han schools 51
Zha Peixin 192–3

Zhongdian county 100, 108, 109, 111–13
zhonghua minzu 26, 165–6
zhonghua minzu duoyuan yiti 18, 26
Zhuang language: education studies 85
Zhuang nationality: Bouyei nationality and 23–4

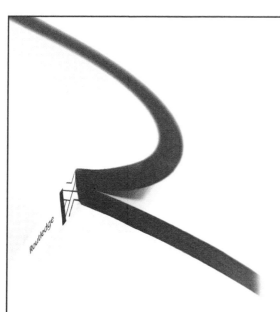

Routledge
Paperbacks Direct

Bringing you the cream of our hardback publishing at paperback prices

This exciting new initiative makes the best of our hardback publishing available in paperback format for authors and individual customers.

Routledge Paperbacks Direct is an ever-evolving programme with new titles being added regularly.

To take a look at the titles available, visit our website.

www.routledgepaperbacksdirect.com

 Routledge
Taylor & Francis Group